Scaffolding Children's Learning:

Vygotsky and Early Childhood Education

Laura E. Berk
and Adam Winsler

National Association for the Education of Young Children
Washington, DC

Cover illustration: Lura Schwarz Smith

Photo credits: Valerie Beardwood Kunze (facing 1); courtesy of James V. Wertsch 4; Subjects & Predicates 8, 19, 47, 85; John Parent Stock 10; Marilyn Nolt 13, 60; Hildegard Adler 25, 98, 105, 120, 143, 148; Anne Marie Mott 28; Jean-Claude Lejeune 31, 82, 152; Francis Wardle 36; Elaine M. Ward 50; Steve Herzog 53, 69; Nancy P. Alexander 57, 90, 134; Faith Bowlus 76; Blair Seitz 80; Karen Kunzelman 88; Lois Main 97; Renaud Thomas 107; Florence Sharp 110; BmPorter/Don Franklin 112, 117, 137; Marietta Lynch 128; Chad J. Walker 144

National Association for the Education of Young Children
1509 16th Street, N.W.
Washington, DC 20036-1426
202-232-8777 or 1-800-424-2460

The National Association for the Education of Young Children (NAEYC) attempts through its publications program to provide a forum for discussion of major issues and ideas in our field. We hope to provoke thought and promote professional growth. The views expressed or implied are not necessarily those of the Association. NAEYC wishes to thank the authors, who donated much time and effort to develop this book as a contribution to our profession.

Library of Congress Catalog Card Number: 95-069457
ISBN Catalog Number: 0-935989-68-4
NAEYC #146

Editor: Carol Copple. *Book design and production:* Danielle Hudson and Jack Zibulsky. *Copyediting and indexing:* Betty Nylund Barr. *Editorial assistance:* Penny S. Atkins and Anika Trahan.

Printed in the United States of America.

Credits:

96799

Contents

About the Authors

Laura E. Berk is a distinguished professor of psychology at Illinois State University. She received her bachelor's degree in psychology from the University of California—Berkeley and her master's and doctoral degrees in educational psychology, with a specialization in early childhood development and education, from the University of Chicago. She has been a visiting scholar at Cornell University, the University of California—Los Angeles, and Stanford University. Laura has published widely on Vygotsky's theory, focusing on the social origins and functional significance of private speech in normally developing children and children with serious learning and behavior problems. Her research has attracted the attention of the general public, leading to contributions to *Psychology Today* and *Scientific American*. Laura's books include *Private Speech: From Social Interaction to Self-Regulation* (coedited with Rafael M. Diaz) and two widely distributed texts, *Child Development* and *Infants, Children, and Adolescents*. She recently completed a term as research editor of NAEYC's journal, *Young Children,* and currently serves as consulting editor of *Early Childhood Research Quarterly.* Laura is a recipient of the DeLissa Fellowship in Early Childhood Development and Family Studies, which will take her to the University of South Australia in 1996.

Adam Winsler is an assistant professor of educational psychology in the College of Education at the University of Alabama. He received his bachelor's degree in psychology from the University of New Mexico and his doctoral degree in education, with a specialization in child and adolescent development, from Stanford University. Adam's areas of interest include children's private speech, self-regulation, early childhood education, attention-deficit hyperactivity disorder, bilingualism, and the social context of cognitive development.

Preface

Interest in social and cultural influences on all aspects of children's development has exploded in the past decade. A major impetus for this trend has been the theoretical perspective of Russian psychologist Lev Semenovich Vygotsky. Vygotsky carried out his highly innovative research during the 1920s and early 1930s, writing prolifically on the relationship of social experiences to children's learning. After the Soviet Union's 20-year ban on his writings was lifted during the mid-1950s, Vygotsky's major works reached the West. They began to be translated into English in the 1960s and 1970s. By the 1980s many American psychologists and educators embraced Vygotsky's ideas with enthusiasm.

In contrast to an individualistic view of the child as an independent discoverer of his or her reality, Vygotsky constructed a fresh perspective that emphasizes the vital connection between the social and the psychological worlds of the child. His theory underscores the importance of adult–child and child–child discourse in cognitive development—as sources of conscious mental life; of distinctly human, higher cognitive processes; and of the capacity to use language to regulate thought and action. In elevating social experience to primary importance, Vygotsky's approach has contributed greatly to our understanding of the impact of culturally specific practices on children's development. In addition, the theory is unique in highlighting not only the role of important people in the child's life but the importance of schooling in leading development forward. Vygotsky emphasized that teaching and benefiting from instruction are basic to human social life; education transforms the mind.

Since teachers, parents, and caregivers—and the contexts they create—are seen as the primary means of fostering children's development, Vygotsky's theory is imbued with pedagogical concerns. His ideas remind us that developmentally appropriate practices open new cognitive vistas for children and that we can easily misunderstand and underestimate children's abilities when we observe and assess them apart from their everyday social environments. In writing this book, our goal was to introduce early childhood educators to Vygotsky's perspective, research on young children that has been stimulated by it, and current educational practices emanating from it. Our discussion is divided into seven chapters.

In Chapter 1 we provide an overview of Vygotsky's life, the social conditions in which his ideas emerged, and factors influencing the spread of his work to the Western world. We also mention Vygotsky's major works and summarize central tenets of his theory.

Chapter 2 offers a detailed description of Vygotsky's perspective on development, including his notions of cognition as socially constructed and shared and language as the critical link between the social and the psychological planes of human functioning. We grant special attention to a central, unifying concept in Vygotsky's writings: the zone of proximal, or potential, development (ZPD). We consider characteristics of ideal adult–child teaching/learning interactions within the ZPD and the vital function of children's private, or self-directed, speech in building a bridge between social experience and inner mental life and in permitting thought to gain mastery over behavior.

Chapter 3 focuses on Vygotsky's view of the development and significance of children's imaginative, or make-believe, play. In Vygotsky's theory, make-believe, like other higher mental functions, has social origins. Once in place, it serves as a vital zone of proximal development in which children's cognitive and social skills advance ahead of their development in other contexts. In make-believe, children enact the rules of social life, subordinate their behavior to those rules, and generate for themselves critical lessons in how to renounce impulsive action in favor of deliberate, self-regulatory activity. Imaginative play, according to Vygotsky, is the preeminent educational activity of the preschool years.

In Chapter 4 we summarize Vygotsky's perspective on children with serious learning and behavior problems. Our discussion underscores Vygotsky's belief that the same basic laws that apply to normal children also govern the development and education of children with deficits and disabilities. Consequently, the optimal development of such children depends on integrating them into the social life of their community and ensuring that their educational experiences lie within their ZPDs. In this chapter we pay special attention to the importance of private speech as a tool that children with learning and behavior problems use over an extended period of development to master their own behavior.

Chapter 5 compares Vygotsky's approach to other major theories of child development of this century, clarifying its profound implications for early childhood education. The distinctiveness of Vygotsky's perspective is highlighted through an analysis of the relationship between learning and development. Vygotsky's theory is unique in regarding learning as leading, or eliciting, developmental change. As a result, it implies a different approach to classroom practice than do other major viewpoints—one that emphasizes an active child collaborating with an active social environment to acquire the ways of thinking and behaving that make up a community's culture.

Chapter 6 addresses contemporary applications of Vygotsky's theory to teaching and learning in early childhood classrooms. We discuss current Vygotsky-based curricular reforms that focus on the quality of teacher–child and child–child interaction during literacy activities, through which children become aware of the symbolic and communicative systems of their culture and start to treat them as objects of attention and reflection. We also consider new "dynamic" techniques for assessing children's readiness to learn, inspired by Vygotsky's concept of the ZPD. Finally, Vygotsky recognized the need for a broad institutional climate that ensures that children will develop at their best. Our discussion concludes with ways that schools can foster collaboration of teachers with teachers, teachers with children, and children with children, thereby creating educational communities that scaffold young children's learning and development.

Chapter 7 considers Vygotsky's theory as a vision for early childhood education—one that resolves the debate over academic versus child-centered programs by advocating responsiveness to children's current capacities in ways that move development forward. Key themes of the Vygotskian approach to early childhood education are summarized.

Acknowledgments

Carol Copple has been a wonderfully supportive editor through all stages of this project, from its inception during editorial meetings at the NAEYC 1993 Annual Conference to its appearance in print. We would also like to express our appreciation to the three anonymous reviewers for their very thorough reading of the preliminary draft, their many helpful suggestions for revision, and their words of praise and encouragement. Each contributed significantly to the quality of the final product. Special thanks to Lisa Otte, graduate student in school psychology at Illinois State University, for her careful and diligent assistance with final editing of the manuscript.

—*Laura E. Berk and Adam Winsler*

The interaction between the adult and the child, for Vygotsky, is like a dance—the child leads and the adult follows, always closely in tune with the child's actions.

Vygotsky: His Life and Works

One of the main tenets of Vygotsky's theory, as we shall see, is that people are products of their social and cultural worlds and that to understand children, we must understand the social, cultural, and societal contexts in which they develop. Consistent with this sociocultural approach to development, our first step on the journey to understanding Vygotsky is to learn about his life and the social conditions in which his ideas emerged. What follows is a brief biographical sketch of Vygotsky. Other, more detailed accounts of Vygotsky's biography are available for interested readers, and these are the sources on which the following account is based (Wertsch 1985b; Blanck 1990; Kozulin 1990; van der Veer & Valsiner 1991; Newman & Holzman 1993).

A brief biography

In 1896, Lev Semenovich Vygotsky was born into a middle-class Jewish family in Orsha, a town in the northern part of Byelorussia. A year later his family moved south to Gomel, a small city of greater cultural vitality near the Ukrainian border and within the Pale of Settlement, where Jews were confined in czarist Russia. Vygotsky was the second of eight children in the family. His father was an executive at a bank. His mother was a licensed teacher, although she devoted most of her time to raising the children. Little is known about Vygotsky's youth except that in his early years he was educated by a private tutor and that he later went to a combination of public and private schools for his secondary education.

As early as middle childhood, the verbal arts—literature, poetry, theater, and philosophy—were Vygotsky's favorite subjects, and they remained strong areas of interest throughout his life. His intellectual prowess began to be recognized as early as adolescence, when friends and family members often called him the "little professor," since he would frequently lead discussions on major topics in philosophy, literature, history, and art. Later in his life, colleagues described Vygotsky as a brilliant man with a vast memory, who was an incredibly fast and avid reader and an unbelievably productive scholar. By the time he entered the disciplines of psychology and education, he brought a wide-ranging background in these fields with him, and he used them in framing his approach to development.

Vygotsky's entrance to university studies and his changing career paths are good examples of how social and cultural conditions shape the individual's activities and therefore the development of the mind. Major universities in Russia at the time allowed only 3% of their student population to be Jewish. To be admitted to a university, therefore, Vygotsky had to be at the very top of his class and pass the entrance examinations with a "gold medal." Vygotsky did, in fact, earn the gold medal, an achievement that seemed to assure him university placement. However, while he was in the process of taking the examinations, the minister of education further restricted university entrance for Jews. To reduce the caliber (in addition to the number) of Jewish students, a new policy was initiated in which the 3% Jewish quota would be filled by selecting students at random rather than on the basis of merit. Vygotsky was crushed, as it seemed that now he had no chance to obtain a university education. But fate was with him (and with us, for that matter), as he was one of the few chosen by lottery for admission!

Vygotsky began his studies at Moscow University in 1914. At that time in Russia, his choice of a field was also limited by the fact that he was Jewish. Although he was interested in history and philosophy, these disciplines led either to academia or to teaching secondary school; however, Jews were not permitted to be employed by state schools. After a brief period of studying medicine (the field his parents wanted him to enter), Vygotsky soon turned to the field of law, in which he remained until he graduated. Law was one of the few professions that allowed Jews to live outside restricted areas. While attending Moscow University, Vygotsky also enrolled at Shaniavsky People's University, an "unofficial" institution formed by a large group of prominent Moscow professors who had been expelled by the government from their former positions for participating in anti-czarist demonstrations in the early 1900s or who left their institutions voluntarily in protest of the expulsions. There, Vygotsky pursued his long-standing interests in literature, philosophy, art, and later, psychology.

Vygotsky graduated simultaneously from both universities in 1917, shortly before the massive revolutions that would dramatically change the direction of his country. Then he returned to Gomel, where he taught literature, history, philosophy, psychology, and pedagogy at a variety of institutions, including Gomel's Teacher's College. It was during this period, between 1917 and 1924, that Vygotsky became more deeply committed to the fields of psychology and education. At the Teacher's College he started a small psychology laboratory. Besides immersing himself in teaching, research, and writing, he spent much time reading. He was literate in eight languages: Russian, German, English, Hebrew, French, Latin, Greek, and Esperanto. This linguistic facility enabled him to read widely in philosophy, psychology, pedagogy, theater, and literature—fields in which major works were emerging at the time across the European continent as well as in the United States.

It was also during this post-revolutionary period that Vygotsky suffered his first major bout with tuberculosis, the disease that would eventually kill him along with thousands of other Russians. After recovering from several attacks, which left him near death and necessitated a short stay in a sanitarium in the early 1920s, Vygotsky seemed to understand that his years were limited, judging from the frantic pace of his activities and his extreme productivity over the last 12 years of his short life.

Several major events took place in Vygotsky's life in the year 1924. First, he married Roza Smekhova, with whom he eventually had two daughters. Second, he delivered an outstanding presentation at an important national conference in psychology. His lecture electrified the audience, which contained several of Vygotsky's future students and colleagues, including K.N. Kornilov, director of the Psychological Institute in Moscow, who was sufficiently impressed to invite Vygotsky to join him and the other prominent Soviet psychologists at the Institute. Consequently, Vygotsky and his wife moved to Moscow. For a while they lived in the basement of the Psychological Institute, which, much to Vygotsky's delight, housed the Institute's library archives. At this point Vygotsky began his professional career as a psychologist, theorist, and researcher.

Because Vygotsky was never formally trained as a psychologist, he was often perceived as an outsider to the field. Since he was very familiar with the works of other major psychologists of his time, such as Piaget (who was born in the same year as Vygotsky) and Freud, Vygotsky's professional role was often one of the objective commentator or critic of contemporary psychology. Vygotsky was, in fact, responsible for disseminating in Russia the works of many important contemporary psychologists, including Koffka, Stern, Köhler, Bühler, Piaget, Gesell, and Freud, as he commonly edited, translated, and/or wrote introductions for the Russian versions of these authors' works. Indeed, this Russian literary scholar-turned-psychologist from a small, provincial town had a lot to say about the field of psychology. It is possible that Vygotsky's creative insights about psychology and child development were partly due to the fresh perspective he brought as an outsider to the field.

An outsider to the fields of psychology and child development, Vygotsky brought a fresh perspective on children's development.

Shortly after his arrival in Moscow, Vygotsky met A.R. Luria (1902–1977) and A.N. Leont'ev (1904–1979), who joined him as students and colleagues and with whom he eventually formed what would become known as the "troika" (trio) of the Vygotskian school of thought. Luria and Leont'ev were primarily responsible for carrying on with Vygotsky's ideas after his death, and both went on to become major figures in Soviet psychology. Luria became world renowned in the field of neuropsychology, and Leont'ev developed a productive and well-known theory of human activity. These and other members of Vygotsky's circle recalled that he had an amazing way of inspiring his students and colleagues and that he was an extremely popular lecturer and clinician. The troika, led by Vygotsky, has often been given sole credit for the origin of sociocultural theory (Wertsch 1985b; Blanck 1990). However, as van der Veer and Valsiner (1991) recently pointed out, accounts of history tend to be simplified, and there is little doubt that other Soviet scholars were involved in the process.

To understand what would become the main thrust of Vygotsky's theory of development, one must appreciate the massive social changes that were occurring at the time. Even though the country was plagued by civil war, world war, famine, and disease, the Soviet Union after the revolution of 1917 was an exciting place to be for young Marxist scholars such as Vygotsky. Energy and enthusiasm were extremely high among

Lev Semenovich Vygotsky with his elder daughter, Gita Vyodskaja, who herself became an educational psychologist. Now retired and living in Moscow, she has provided invaluable information to scholars interested in Vygotsky's life.

the people of Russia as they engaged in the challenging process of designing an entire country, for the first time, on the basis of the Marxist principles of socialism and dialectical materialism. Vygotsky took charge of creating a Marxist theory of psychology and child development, aiming to reconstruct the fields of psychology and education in the Soviet Union in ways consistent with the social and cultural changes taking place around him.

As we have already mentioned, Vygotsky's theory is often referred to as the sociocultural approach, since it is an attempt to understand how social and cultural influences affect children's development. We will use the term *sociocultural* throughout this monograph to refer to his theory. At times, it has also been labeled the *social-historical* and the *cultural-historical* approach, because of Vygotsky's interest in the historical and evolutionary development of the human species in addition to child development. Vygotsky's theory, in fact,

draws on meaningful similarities and differences among four different levels of human development:

• the development of the human species through evolution (phylogenesis),

• the development of humans throughout history,

• the development of the individual through childhood and adulthood (ontogenesis), and

• the development of competence at a single task or activity by a child or adult (microgenesis) (Cole 1990).

For example, consistent with Marxist ideas of how history develops by way of collective social movements and conflicts and how labor and production are key processes in any society, Vygotsky's theory of child development assumes that social interaction and children's participation in authentic cultural activities are necessary for development to occur. Also, similar to how, during evolution, new mental abilities in the human species arose out of the need to communicate and function as a collective, Vygotsky's theory grants a special place to social interaction in ontogenesis as the means of developing all complex, higher mental functions.

What follows is a brief overview of Vygotsky's main ideas. Each will be developed further in subsequent chapters of this book.

• *cross-cultural variation:* Because cultures differ in the activities they emphasize and in the tools they use, higher mental functions in humans vary across cultures.

• *the developmental, or* genetic, *method:* We can understand human behavior only by examining the development or history of behavior. To really know the essence of something, we must see how it was formed developmentally.

• *two lines of development:* There are two distinct planes on which child development takes place: the natural line and the cultural line. The *natural line* refers to biological growth and maturation of physical and mental structures. The *cultural line* refers to learning to use cultural tools and to human consciousness, which emerges from engaging in cultural activity.

• *lower versus higher mental functions:* Similar to the biological and cultural lines of development, human mental activity can be divided into lower and higher mental functions. Lower mental functions are shared with other mammalian species. In contrast, higher mental functions are unique to human beings. They involve the use of language or other cultural tools to guide or mediate cognitive activity. Higher mental functions during development systematically reorganize lower mental functions.

• *general genetic law of cultural development:* Any function in the child's cultural development appears twice, on two planes. First it appears on the *social,* or *interpersonal, plane* and then on the *individual,* or *psychological, plane.* All higher mental functions have social origins that are eventually internalized.

• *language as central:* Language, the primary cultural tool used by humans to mediate their activities, is instrumental in restructuring the mind and in forming higher-order, self-regulated thought processes.

• *education leads development:* Formal education and other cultural forms of socialization are key in leading the child along the developmental pathway to adulthood.

• *zone of proximal development (ZPD):* The zone of proximal development is the hypothetical, dynamic region in which learning and development take place. It is defined by the distance between what a child can accomplish during independent problem solving and what he or she can accomplish with the help of an adult or more competent member of the culture.

Wertsch (1985b) suggests that Vygotsky's work had two major goals. The first goal, as we have already discussed, was to create a Marxist psychology that would both solve problems in the field of psychology and guide people in a newly designed country. The second goal driving Vygotsky's prolific work was the desire to help children with various physical disabilities and psychological problems. As a direct result of years of famine, poverty, war, and massive social change, the Soviet Union in the late 1920s started to see the toll of these turbulent times on children. Record numbers of orphaned, homeless, mentally retarded, physically disabled, and/or delinquent children filled the streets of Moscow. Interestingly, one of the hallmarks of Vygotsky's thinking was the idea that *practice* was the ultimate testing ground of any theory. This idea contrasted with the emphasis of most other psychologists of his time (and today), who were committed to basic research in normal psychology and who were generally uninterested in the clinical applications of psychological theories. Indeed, Vygotsky would go on to have such a large impact in the area of abnormal child psychology that he is often considered to be the father of modern Soviet "defectology," the English transliteration of the Russian term for the field of abnormal child psychology and/or special education (Knox & Stevens 1993). In his final years Vygotsky (together with Luria) became interested in adult psychopathology, as well, especially schizophrenia and issues of neuropsychology and brain functioning.

Vygotsky was an extremely busy man during the last years of his short life. In addition to his position at the Moscow Psychological Institute, where he engaged in the standard academic responsibilities of teaching, publishing, and editing journals, he either founded, directed, or was affiliated with many other psychological or pedagogical organizations, both inside and outside Moscow. These organizations included the Experimental–Defectological Institute, the Academy of Communist Education, the Medical Pedagogical Station of Moscow (in which he organized an abnormal child psychology research laboratory), Moscow State University II, the Ukrainian Psychoneurological Academy (in the distant city of Kharkov), and the Herzen Institute of Education (in Leningrad). Also, to make enough money to free up time for writing and research, Vygotsky edited many books and translated the works of other scholars in a variety of fields.

In 1934, Vygotsky suffered several severe bouts of tuberculosis, and his health deteriorated rapidly. Family members recall that against doctors' recommendations, he worked at a frantic pace in the last few months in an attempt to write as much as he could before his inevitable death. Vygotsky apparently dictated from his death bed the last chapters of what would become one of his most important works: *Thought and Language* ([1934] 1962, [1934] 1986), which was published posthumously. Lev Semenovich Vygotsky died of tuberculosis in June of 1934 at age 37. He was buried in Moscow.

Factors influencing the spread of Vygotsky's ideas

At this point you may be wondering, If Vygotsky is such an important figure for psychology and education, why is his theory only now beginning to take hold in these fields? There are several reasons for the relatively late introduction of Vygotsky's ideas to the United States and the rest of the Western world. The first impediment to the wide dissemination of Vygotsky's theory was simply that his life was tragically short. As a result, he did not have enough time to fully develop his approach or to reexamine and integrate his formulations into a tightly organized, well-structured theory after receiving the usual scholarly criticism. In this sense, it is probably best to think of Vygotsky's work as a series of mini-theories that embody a general theoretical approach but that were ultimately left unfinished. Since then, Vygotsky's ideas have been extended and developed by many scholars in a variety of directions (Leont'ev 1978; Scribner & Cole 1981; Luria 1982; Palincsar & Brown 1984; Wertsch 1985a, 1985b, 1991b; Lave 1988; Pratt et al. 1988; Tharp & Gallimore 1988; Valsiner 1988; Diaz, Neal, & Amaya-Williams 1990; Rogoff 1990; Resnick 1991; Tulviste 1991; Diaz & Berk 1992; Tudge 1992; Berk 1994c).

A second factor in the slow circulation of Vygotsky's theory was the terrible economic and societal conditions of his time. The Soviet Union was experiencing revolution and civil war, World War I, famine, and other difficult circumstances due to the turmoil associated with massive societal change. These conditions, combined with the shortage of basic living materials, including paper, are clearly not conducive to the wide dissemination of scientific writings.

The third and most important factor that slowed the spread of sociocultural thought to the rest of the world was that shortly after Vygotsky's death, his works were banned and kept from public consumption for 20 years by Stalin's administration. In what was becoming a more and more dogmatic and repressive political regime, it was not unusual for a scholar's works to be included in Stalin's purge list of material opposed to the State. As the government, under the dictatorship of Stalin, started to stray further from the original Marxist ideals of socialism, steadfast Marxist scholars such as Vygotsky were seen as a threat. Vygotsky was probably perceived as too cosmopolitan, because of his familiarity and communication with international, "bourgeois" scholars who held different political philosophies. This fall of Vygotsky's ideas into disrepute started shortly before his death. During his last few years, Vygotsky did not enjoy the popularity he had during his earlier days. To stay academically secure, students and followers of Vygotsky branched off into new areas and modified their original approach.

For the 20 years preceding Stalin's death, Vygotsky's works were banned in the Soviet Union, and during the Cold War era, translation into English and dissemination into the United States were still slow.

As is the case with most great thinkers and scholars, therefore, there was a period in Vygotsky's life when his ideas were under critical review. However, as we have seen, the reasons for the decline in popularity of his theory during his lifetime were more politically than scientifically based. It is tragically ironic that the very reasons for Vygotsky's rapid ascent to the forefront of Soviet psychology in the 1920s—namely, his fresh, outsider's perspective on the field; his strong commitment to Marxist philosophy; and his vast knowledge of the work of other, international scholars from a variety of perspectives—were the very reasons that led to his eventual (but historically temporary) downfall.

Shortly after Stalin died in 1953, the ban on Vygotsky's and other scholars' works was lifted, and his papers began to emerge again in the Soviet Union. Translation of Vygotsky's articles into English and their dissemination in the United States, however, were still delayed for at least two reasons. First, systematic scholarly exchange between the Soviet Union and the United States did not occur during the era of the Cold War. Second, awareness and acceptance of Vygotsky's theory by American investigators was impeded by the extreme popularity of Piagetian and behaviorist perspectives on developmental psychology and education during these times.

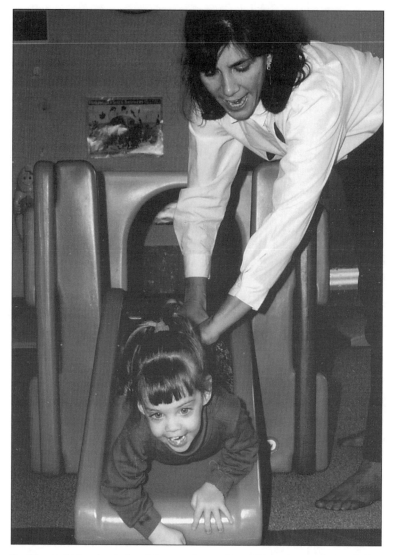

In Vygotsky's view, the primary focus for educators and psychologists should be on the strengths and capabilities of children with developmental problems, rather than on their limitations or deficits.

Vygotsky's major works

Describing Vygotsky's publications is made difficult by the fact that although certain major works were originally published during his lifetime in Russian (Vygotsky 1925, 1926, 1931, 1934; Vygotsky & Luria [1930] 1993) and occasionally in English (Vygotsky 1925, 1929), several papers were either published for the first time or republished much later in Russian (Vygotsky [1925] 1986, [1931] 1960, 1972). Also, English translations of some works started to appear in the 1960s (Vygotsky [1934] 1962, [1925] 1971, [1930–1935] 1978, [1934] 1986). Added to these publications are the compilations of his complete works in six volumes, which recently were published in Russian (Vygotsky 1982a, 1982b, 1983a, 1983b, 1984a, 1984b) and are now beginning to appear in English (Vygotsky [1934] 1987, 1993). There is considerable overlap in the material published in these various forms; however, some articles appear only once in these references. And, as is usually the case with translated works, debate exists among Vygotskian scholars about the quality of various translations. There are important differences in interpretation in the translations of Vygotsky's writings (see van der Veer & Valsiner 1991).

Vygotsky's first major works concerned literary criticism and the psychology of art, as would be expected, given his early interests. One of his earliest essays was a literary analysis of *Hamlet* (Vygotsky [1916] 1986), and his dissertation, which was also published, was entitled *The Psychology of Art* (Vygotsky [1925] 1971). Vygotsky's early commitment to educational psychology is reflected in the topic of his first major book, *Pedagogical Psychology* (Vygotsky 1926), a textbook for future teachers that summarized what was known at the time about psychological principles relevant to education. Included as topics in this book were the functioning of the nervous system; reflexes; Pavlovian classical conditioning; the role of education in society; the importance of classrooms with a heterogeneous mix of pupils; language development; mental testing; and the aesthetic, sexual, and moral development of the child.

Between 1924 and 1931 Vygotsky published a number of important articles concerning special education, or what was then called *defectology*—the psychology of children with mental or physical disabilities (i.e., Vygotsky [1925] 1931). His complete works in this area were recently released in English (Vygotsky 1993), after a compilation of his papers on the topic appeared in Russian in 1983 (Vygotsky 1983b). Vygotsky included the following central themes in these works about children with special learning problems:

• The same basic laws of development and education apply to normal children and children with disabilities. For this reason, both groups of children should be educated together and participate in the same kinds of activities as much as possible.

• The primary focus for educators and psychologists should be on the strengths and capabilities of children with developmental problems, rather than on their limitations or deficits.

• The social and/or cultural deficit created by the inability of a child with a disability to participate normally in collective or collaborative activity is often worse for the child than the original organic deficit.

• The higher-order social or cultural deficit is usually more amenable to treatment than is the original problem.

• A process of psychological and/or physical compensation characterizes children with various disabilities, and this process creates unique personalities and developmental trajectories for such children.

Each of these ideas will be discussed in more detail in Chapter 4.

The fundamentals of Vygotsky's sociocultural theory appeared in *Thought and Language* (Vygotsky [1934] 1962, [1934] 1986) and in a variety of works between 1930 and 1935 that were published for the first time in English as *Mind in Society* (Vygotsky [1930–1935] 1978). Other works that contributed importantly to Vygotsky's theory include his book with Luria, *Studies on the History of Behavior: Ape, Primitive, and Child* (Vygotsky & Luria [1930] 1993), and an important paper entitled *The Development of Higher Mental Functions* (Vygotsky [1931] 1960). In all, Vygotsky published about 180 works. If we include the numerous publications of the same work in different forms, as well as unpublished manuscripts found in family archives, his works number more than 300. (For the most thorough description of Vygotsky's writings to date, see van der Veer & Valsiner 1991).

2

Vygotsky's Approach to Development: The Social Origins of Individual Mental Functioning

Many children from the African American community of Trackton, located in a southeastern city, were uncomfortable and uncommunicative in the classroom. Teachers reported that the children seemed unable to answer even simple questions. Anthropologist Shirley Brice Heath speculated that the key to this communication breakdown might be discovered by observing the language customs of the Trackton community and the teachers themselves. She watched the White teachers interacting with their own young sons and daughters, as well as with the children in their classrooms. In both settings the teachers asked a great many questions, most of which were designed to find out what children knew and to extend their knowledge about the world, as in "What kind of truck is that?", "Where's the puppy in that picture?", and "What's this story about?"

By contrast, very young children living in Trackton were seldom asked questions by parents and other adults in the community. Adults postponed question-asking until they saw children as competent conversationalists and sources of information. When adults did ask young children questions, they tended to ask, not instructional or knowledge-training questions, but "real" questions—questions to which they themselves did not know the answers and to which there was no single "right answer." At home the children developed complex verbal skills, such as storytelling and exchanging quick-witted remarks, that did not serve them well in the classroom. Confused by the questions asked in school, the children often withdrew into silence.

Once teachers began to design classroom activities that took into account children's home language experiences, the formerly passive, reticent children became lively, eager participants. (A more detailed account of this study appears in the box on pp. 16–17).

In most theories of cognition and cognitive development, the social and the cognitive make contact only minimally. Rather than being truly joined and interactive, they are viewed as separate domains of functioning. At best, the social world is a surrounding context for cognitive activity, not an integral part of it (Resnick 1991). Early childhood professionals have a long tradition of regarding what the young child knows and develops as personally rather than socially constructed—a tradition that flows from Piaget's massive contributions to our field. According to the strong Piagetian stance, as children independently explore their physical and social worlds, they build knowledge—a process located within and governed by the individual. If ways of understanding reality are similar across human beings, it is because all of us have the same biological equipment for interpreting experience: the human brain.

The Vygotskian view is unique in that thinking is not bounded by the individual brain or mind. Instead, the "mind extends beyond the skin" (Wertsch 1991a, 90) and is inseparably joined with other minds. According to Vygotsky's ([1930–1935] 1978) sociocultural theory, cognition is a profoundly social phenomenon. Social experience shapes the ways of thinking and interpreting the world available to individuals. And language plays a crucial role in a socially formed mind because it is our primary avenue of communication and mental contact with others, serves as the major means by which social experience is represented psychologically, and is an indispensable tool for thought (Vygotsky [1934] 1987; Leont'ev 1959). Because Vygotsky regarded language as a critical bridge between the sociocultural world and individual mental function-

ing, he viewed the acquisition of language as the most significant milestone in children's cognitive development.

In the following sections we examine these two complementary facets of Vygotsky's perspective more closely: (1) cognition as socially constructed and shared, and (2) language as the critical link between the social and the psychological planes of human functioning.

Socially shared cognition

A basic premise of Vygotsky's theory is that all uniquely human, higher forms of mental activity are derived from social and cultural contexts and are shared by members of those contexts because these metal processes are adaptive. They lead to knowledge and skills that are essential for success within a particular culture. Consequently, sociocultural theory places strong emphasis on the wide variation in cognitive capacities among human beings. Vygotsky underscored this theme in his "general genetic law of cultural development." To understand the development of the individual, he emphasized, it is necessary to understand the social relations of which the individual is a part:

Any function in the child's cultural development appears twice, or on two planes. First it appears on the social plane, and then on the psychological plane. First it appears between people as an interpsychological category, and then within the child as an intrapsychological category. This is equally true with regard to voluntary attention, logical memory, the formation of concepts, and the development of volition. We may consider this position as a law in the full sense of the word . . . . Social relations or relations among people genetically underlie all higher functions and their relationships. ([1960] 1981, 163)

Although the sociocultural perspective stresses cultural variation, neither Vygotsky nor his followers claimed that universals of cognitive development—ones that characterize children everywhere—do not exist. Indeed, a wealth of research indicates that human biological equipment supports many cognitive universals. These are as diverse as the capacity of infants and young children to perceptually integrate pattern elements into organized wholes, imitate the actions of others, grasp the emotional meaning of facial expressions, appreciate the permanence of hidden objects, and acquire language (Baillargeon 1987; Baillargeon & De Vos 1991; Bornstein & Lamb 1992; de Villiers & de Villiers 1992; Meltzoff & Gopnik 1993). In addition to biologically grounded human capacities, sociocultural theory recognizes that some universals are a direct outgrowth of the fact that humans are inherently social and communicative beings. For example, around the world, children become remarkably skilled conversationalists by 2 to 3 years of age. They follow the rules of human verbal interaction by taking turns, making eye contact, responding appropriately to their partner's remarks, and maintaining a topic over

Because Vygotsky regarded language as a critical bridge between the sociocultural world and individual mental functioning, he viewed the acquisition of language as the most significant milestone in children's cognitive development.

time (Garvey 1974, 1990; Podrouzek & Furrow 1988). These advanced conversational abilities probably grow out of early interactive experiences with caregivers and siblings.

Nevertheless, the stress on universal cognitive milestones that has dominated the field of child development for decades has hindered efforts to address the social basis of cognition in a serious way (Wertsch 1991a). Today, developmental psychologists and educators are beginning to embrace the notion that the social and the cognitive are essential aspects of one another. Growing evidence that social influences are ever-present in cognitive skills widely accepted as universal and that social engagement is a powerful force in transforming children's thinking has played a major role in convincing child development specialists that cognition is socially situated.

Social embeddedness of cognitive skills: Social interaction

Consider, for example, the accumulating literature on conservation, the Piagetian milestone that marks the transition from childish, illogical ways of reasoning to an adultlike, logical approach to tasks and problems. Many studies reveal that the forms of questioning adults use in administering conservation tasks are processed through "social lenses" that profoundly affect children's performance (Resnick 1991, 5).

Earlier we noted that in the process of interacting with others, young children quickly learn to appreciate the rules of everyday conversation. They come to expect that an interactive partner's messages will be relevant to what has been said before and will be sincere in delivery of an intended message. Yet when questioned about concepts, such as con-

servation, children may not understand the need to depart from these rules of everyday dialogue. In interviewing children, adults ask about aspects of reality that are rarely topics of interest in everyday interaction, posing the same query two or more times in succession, and challenging the child's initial response to see if it truly represents his or her thinking. Consequently, a well-meaning adult's questions may be misinterpreted, and children may respond incorrectly—not because they do not know the answer but because the conversational rules being used by the adult and the child clash.

One aspect of conservation interviewing is the use of repeated questions. For example, in the well-known conservation-of-liquid problem, we ask the child whether the amount of water is the same or different on two occasions—once before and once after it is poured into a differently shaped container. Does asking children the same question twice affect their answers? Consider your own interpretation of questions presented more than once. When a co-worker says, "How are you?" or "Did you have a nice weekend?" repeatedly, you are likely to change your response the second time, concluding that the first answer given must not have met your partner's expectations. A series of studies conducted by Siegal, Waters, and Dinwiddy (1988) indicates that children bring a similar social perspective to the conservation interviewing situation.

In an initial experiment, half of 180 4- to 6-year-olds were randomly assigned to a standard two-question conservation-of-number condition, half to a one-question condition. The first group was asked to "point to the row that has more buttons" both before and after a row of 20 counters was rearranged by an adult; the second group was asked this question only after the row was transformed. The large majority of children (78%) tested under the one-question condition conserved, whereas only a small minority (28%) tested under the two-question condition did.

In a second investigation, the researchers delved further into the reasons behind this inconsistent pattern of responses. Children watched videotaped segments of puppets being interviewed about conservation in one-question and two-question conditions. After viewing each segment, they were asked if the puppet answered a certain way "just to please the grownup" or "the way the puppet thought was true." When puppets gave nonconserving responses in the two-question condition, most children (69%) said they did so just to please the grownup. In contrast, fewer children (44%) thought that a nonconserving response in the one-question condition masked puppets' true understanding and reflected their search for a socially desirable response. In yet another study supporting the conclusion that many nonconserving responses of 4- to 6-year-olds reflect children's attempts to apply everyday rules of discourse to the conservation interview, the adult who first asked the conservation question was replaced by a second, naive adult who asked the question again after the materials had been transformed. Under these circumstances, considerably more preschoolers conserved (Perner, Leekam, & Wimmer 1986).

In sum, children bring to the interviewing situation assumptions and purposes that grow out of their history of social experiences. Besides trying to understand the cognitive task presented by the adult, they try to make sense of the social relationship in which the task

Teachers need to adjust classroom learning experiences so as to acknowledge and make productive use of the social histories of ethnic-minority children.

is embedded. When adults fail to recognize that children can easily be misled by the nature of their questioning, they are likely to underestimate children's knowledge and skills.

Sometimes adult questioning defies even more pervasive and deeply held expectations about social interaction. For instance, in middle-class homes children are frequently asked instructional questions that adults already know the answers to, such as, "What color is that car?", "What's the shape of that puzzle piece?", or "Do you have just as many pennies in your pile as I have in mine?" But, as box on pages 16 and 17 reveals, these types of questions are rare in other communities that value and promote quite different discourse styles. This example underscores an additional premise of sociocultural theory: Ways of thinking are socially situated not just at the level of dyads and small groups but also at the broader institutional and cultural levels within which face-to-face interaction is embedded (Vygotsky [1930–1935] 1978; Wertsch 1991a). The "instructional questioning" so pervasive among middle-class parents is similar to the type of discourse that takes place in schools, and it prepares children to be successful communicators in classroom and testing situations. Many investigators have observed that the difficulties faced by non–middle-class children in Western schools are partly the result of a mismatch in communication styles between home and classroom (Edwards 1989; Heath 1989; Miller-Jones 1989; Rogoff, Mistry, et al. 1993). Consequently, teachers need to adjust classroom learning experiences so as to acknowledge and make productive use of the social histories of ethnic-minority children. This is an issue to which we will return in Chapter 6 when we discuss classroom discourse from a Vygotskian perspective.

Social embeddedness of cognitive skills: Task and setting conditions

The impact of the larger cultural context on cognition is equally apparent when we consider the nature of the task in relation to children's social experiences. To illustrate, let us return once again to the conservation problems. A large body of evidence reveals that conservation is often greatly delayed in non-Western village and tribal societies. For example, among the Hausa of Nigeria, who live in small agricultural settlements and rarely send their children to school, even the most basic conservation tasks—number, length, and liquid—are not understood until age 11 or later (Fahrmeier 1978). This delay occurs despite the fact that Hausa children's everyday environments are generally stimulating—the experiential criterion set by Piaget for movement to the concrete operational stage.

Questioning at Home and at School:
Early Language Environments of Low-Income
African American Children

Anthropologist Shirley Brice Heath (1983, 1989) studied the language customs of Trackton, a small African American community in a southeastern city, and compared them to White teachers' interactions with their own children at home and with the children they taught at school. The children of Trackton attended integrated public schools, where they were taught by White teachers. Heath noticed that Trackton parents were disturbed by their children's dislike of school and discomfort communicating in the classroom. The teachers commented that many children seemed unable to answer even simple questions.

Heath speculated that observations of language might hold the key to this communication breakdown. She concentrated on question asking, since questions are a particularly important classroom communication tool. Watching the White teachers interact with their own young children, Heath discovered that they constantly used questions. More than 50% of their utterances were interrogatives, most of which were used to train children in knowledge about the world, as in "What kind of truck is that?", "Where's the puppy in that picture?", and "What's this story about?" Teachers' classroom discourse also consisted largely of questions, and the types of questions used by teachers at home were the same as those used in school.

In Trackton, however, very young children were seldom asked questions. Black adults postponed question-asking until children were seen as competent conversationalists and sources of information. When adults did ask children questions, these were of a very

How can we account for such wide disparity in the timing of conservation attainment across cultures? According to Light and Perret-Clermont (1989), for children to master conservation and other concepts, they must take part in everyday activities that promote this way of thinking. Many children in Western nations, for example, have learned to think of fairness in terms of equal distribution of resources—a value emphasized by their culture. They have numerous opportunities to divide materials, such as crayons and Halloween treats, equally among themselves and their peers. As a result, they often see the same quantity arranged in different ways, and they grasp conservation early.

But in cultures where activities that promote these experiences are rare, conservation is unlikely to appear at the age expected in Western cultures.

Similar findings exist for cognitive tasks once thought to be only minimally affected by specific experiences or practice; the Block Design subtest of the Wechsler Intelligence Scale for Children–Revised, a commonly used, "culture-fair" measure of spatial reasoning, is a case in point. In one study, elementary school children's Block Design performance was correlated with the extent to which they had played a popular but expensive commercial game that (like the test items) required them to arrange small cubes to duplicate a design as quickly as pos-

different sort than the ones White teachers posed to their children. Instead of instructional or knowledge-training questions, Black parents asked only "real" questions—ones to which they themselves did not know the answers. Often these were analogy questions (e.g., "What's that like?") or story-starter questions ("Didja hear Miss Sally this morning?") that called for elaborate responses about whole events for which there was no single "right answer." Trackton children developed complex verbal skills at home, such as storytelling and exchanging quick-witted remarks. Unfortunately, these skills worked poorly when they got to school. The children were confused by questions in classrooms and often withdrew into silence.

Once Heath got teachers to incorporate analogy and story-starter questions into classroom activities, Trackton children changed from passive, reticent pupils to lively, eager participants. Using photos of the community, teachers started by asking, "Tell me, what did you do when you were there?" and "What's that like?" Then they taped children's responses and added specific, school-type questions to the tapes. These were placed in learning centers where children could listen to themselves and give responses appropriate in their own community along with ones expected in school. Gradually children were helped to prepare new questions and answers for the tapes. As a result of these experiences, they soon caught on to classroom verbal customs and began to realize that school-type questions need not threaten their ways of talking at home.

When teachers understand the cultural experiences that give rise to the distinct verbal customs of ethnic-minority children, they can incorporate these customs into classroom activities. Then effective bridges can be built between the learning styles fostered by children's cultural communities and the styles of learning that are necessary for school success.

sible (Dirks 1982). Low-income ethnic-minority children, who often grow up in more "people-oriented" than "object-oriented" homes, may lack experiences with certain games and objects that promote particular intellectual skills (Okagaki & Sternberg 1993).

Vygotsky and his followers were keenly aware of schooling and its associated literacy activities as an especially powerful context for shaping cognitive development (Luria 1976). According to Vygotsky, mastery of academic tasks leads to dramatic transformations in children's memory, concept formation, reasoning, and problem solving—an observation confirmed by recent research (Ceci 1990, 1991). These developmental changes make sense in terms of the kind of knowledge acquisition typically demanded of children in classrooms. However, the same strategies are not always effective when children engage in out-of-school practical activities. For example, in a study in which researchers asked 9-year-old children to remember information embedded in a meaningful context (the placement of 40 objects in a play scene), many American children tried to rehearse object names—an inefficient strategy they had learned to apply when required to retain disconnected bits of information in school. In contrast, Guatemalan Mayan children more often kept track of spatial relations. The Mayan children did slightly better than their American counterparts on the meaningful memory problem but more poorly when asked to recall a list of unrelated words (Rogoff & Waddell 1982).

Taken together, the findings just reviewed remind us that all children in all cultures do not face identical tasks. Instead, cultures—and the institutions within them responsible for socialization—*select* different tasks for children's learning. As a result, children's cognition is *contextualized*; it emerges out of and derives meaning from particular activities and social experiences (Perret-Clermont, Perret, & Bell 1991). In sum, according to sociocultural theory, forms of thinking assumed to develop universally in early and middle childhood are much more a product of specific contexts and cultural conditions than was previously believed.

Social engagement as a stimulus for cognitive development

Evidence of the power of social engagement to transform children's thinking is another body of research that has attracted psychologists and educators to Vygotsky's sociocultural perspective. Interest in social interaction as a stimulus for individual cognitive growth dates back to the early work of Piaget ([1923] 1926), who emphasized the role of *conflict,* especially between peers, in promoting cognitive restructuring. According to Piaget, through arguments and disagreements with agemates, children are repeatedly jarred into noticing that others hold viewpoints different from their own. Indeed, Piaget regarded contact with agemates as more valuable than contact with adults for stimulating cognitive change, since children might superficially accept an adult's perspective without critically examining it, out of unquestioning belief in the adult's authority. Thus, Piaget contended that clash of peer opinion, combined with cognitive maturity, leads to a decline in the egocentrism believed to underlie the illogical thinking of children in the preschool years. As a result, children begin to reflect on their own cognitions and adapt to the perspectives of others (Tudge & Rogoff 1987).

Conflict and disagreement do not seem to be as critical in fostering development as the extent to which children resolve differences of opinion and share responsibility.

Piaget's ideas prompted many investigations aimed at inducing operational abilities through social experience. The findings confirmed that more mature performance on Piagetian tasks could, indeed, be trained by having agemates with differing opinions exchange ideas. Also proven effective in promoting logical thought have been a variety of additional social inputs and supports, including instruction from adults that points out contradictions in children's logic, that provides correct explanations, or that helps children remember the component parts of the problem (Beilin 1978).

In the meantime, a separate line of research inspired by Vygotsky's views focused on *collaboration* as a source of cognitive development. According to Vygotsky ([1930 –1935] 1978), through cooperative dialogues with more knowledgeable members of their society during challenging tasks, children learn to think and behave in ways that reflect their community's culture. Vygotsky believed that as more mature partners—both adults and peers—offer guidance to children mastering culturally meaningful activities, the communication with these partners becomes part of children's thinking. Once children internalize the essential features of these dialogues, they can use the strategies embedded in them to guide their own actions and accomplish skills on their own (van der Veer & Valsiner 1991).

Studies emanating from the Vygotskian perspective suggest that what is important is not so much *who* participates in social exchanges—adult–child or child–child—as *how* partners organize their joint activity. Conflict and disagreement do not seem to be as important in fostering development as the extent to which differences of opinion are resolved, responsibility is shared between participants, and discourse reflects cooperation and mutual respect (Forman 1987; Perlmutter et al. 1989; Nastasi, Clements, & Battista 1990; Tudge 1992). And in line with Vygotsky's theory, research indicates that children's problem solving seems to improve most when their partner is an "expert"—a person especially capable at the task—who can provide new ways of approaching the situation not already within the child's repertoire (Azmitia 1988; Radziszewska & Rogoff 1988).

Barbara Rogoff (1990; Rogoff, Mosier, et al. 1993) has termed the type of social experience that seems most effective in stimulating children's cognitive growth *guided participation.* By this she means active involvement by children in culturally structured activities with the guidance, support, and challenge of companions who transmit a diverse array of knowledge and skills. A second, more specific label used to capture the quality of relationship especially conducive to development is *scaffolding.* Introduced by Wood and his collaborators (Wood & Middleton 1975; Wood, Bruner, & Ross 1976; Wood 1989), the scaffolding metaphor connotes a support system for children's efforts that is sensitively tuned to their needs. Adults adjust the communication they provide to children's momentary competence, offering the necessary assistance for mastery while prompting children to take more responsibility for the task as their skill increases. We will discuss the ingredients of this special form of social encouragement for children's learning later in this chapter. At present, let us turn to the central means through which Vygotsky believed that culturally adaptive, higher cognitive processes are socially transmitted: language. In the following section we consider why language is such an important feature of Vygotsky's approach.

The importance of language

A unique feature of Vygotsky's theory is that a social perspective pervades even those circumstances in which children and adults seem to be involved in private cognitive activity—alone in a room reading a book, drawing a picture, solving a puzzle, ruminating on a past event, or daydreaming. All higher mental functions—those that are unique to human beings—are initially created through collaborative activity; only later do they become internal mental processes (Wertsch 1985b, 1991a; Kozulin 1990). In Vygotsky's words, "the social dimension of consciousness is primary in time and in fact. The individual dimension is derivative and secondary" ([1925] 1979, 30).

What enables this transfer of cognition from the social to the individual plane? According to Vygotsky, the answer lies in human beings' use of "tools of the mind," or signs, to *mediate* relations between people. Eventually the signs and sign systems used between people are *internalized.* Once this occurs, the signs mediate the individual's psychological processes. To clarify the role of language in the emergence of uniquely human cognitive activity, let us consider in greater detail two essential features of the sequence of development just described: (1) mediation through signs, and (2) internalization of those signs.

Mediation through signs

Vygotsky emphasized that signs, or symbolic tools, are the critical link between the social and psychological planes of functioning ([1930] 1981). He noted that a wide variety of symbolic tools are generated by human beings: deliberate memory aids, various systems for counting, algebraic symbol systems, works of art, writing, diagrams, and maps. But the "tool of the mind" of pre-eminent importance in Vygotsky's theory is language, the most frequently and widely used human representational system.

To explain how mediation through symbolic tools in general, and language in particular, leads to the development of higher mental processes, Vygotsky drew an analogy between symbolic tools and technical tools ([1930] 1981). A technical tool is a mediator of human influence on the surrounding environment. Consider the hammer, which is a means of gaining control over and transforming physical objects. Language plays a corresponding role on a psychological level, since it is a major means for influencing thinking and behavior—that of another person or one's own (Wertsch 1985b).

The notion that language shapes mental functioning is not unique to Vygotsky's approach. Many contemporary theories emphasize that cognitive development involves increasingly sophisticated forms of representation, each advance permitting the child to engage in more complex cognitive operations (e.g., Piaget 1950; Siegler 1981; Fischer & Pipp 1984; Case 1992; Halford 1993). But Vygotsky's ideas are unique in that he viewed signs as *socially generated,* not as biologically given or individu-ally constructed (Wertsch 1985b, 1991a). The social origins and social nature of signs are evident in two ways. First, language and other representational means are products of the social history of a cultural group, the result of members' collective efforts to create a social way of life. Consequently they are "inherently situated in sociocultural context" (Wertsch 1991a, 91). Second, in discussing language, the most flexible psychological tool, Vygotsky underscored that the central purpose of speech, from its moment of emergence, is "communication, social contact, influencing surrounding individuals" ([1934] 1987, 45). Only later does speech become an individually applied tool for governing one's own thoughts and behaviors.

To illustrate how Vygotsky envisioned movement from the social plane of functioning to the individual plane through "tools of the mind," let us look closely at a familiar interactive sequence between a caregiver and baby. Imagine an infant trying to grasp an object out of reach, an action that begins as an unmediated impulse. When the child whimpers in frustration, the caregiver turns and notices. She quickly comes to the baby's aid, comprehending his action as a call for help and thereby introducing *meaning* into the situation. As a result, the baby's primitive gesture toward an object becomes a socially communicative act, a gesture toward another person (Leont'ev 1981). Soon the infant begins to use the gesture in a deliberately communicative fashion, orienting it toward the caregiver, as in the following interaction between a 14-month-old and his mother:

Jordan: *(Vocalizes repeatedly until his mother turns around)*

Mother: *(Turns around to look at him)*

Jordan: *(Points to one of the objects on the counter)*

Mother: Do you want this? *(Holds up milk container)*

Jordan: *(shakes his head "no"; vocalizes, continues to point)*

Mother: Do you want this? *(Holds up jelly jar)*

Jordan: *(Shakes his head "no"; continues to point; two more offer–rejection pairs)*

Mother: This? *(Picks up sponge)*

Jordan: *(Leans back in highchair, puts arms down, tension leaves body)*

Mother: *(Hands Jordan sponge)*

(Golinkoff 1983, 58–59)

Eventually words are uttered along with the gestures that make up the toddlers' preverbal communicative acts; children and their social partners use them as tools for influencing one another's behavior.

The example just given also highlights Vygotsky's view of the early genesis of higher mental functions. He believed that during the second year of life, the natural and the social lines of development come together and intermingle to form a single line of change. Psychological development is viewed as the transition from lower, naturally emerging processes of perception, memory, attention, and learning to higher mental processes that share their names but function by way of mediation through signs, language, or some other cultural tool. For Vygotsky, higher mental functions are not a direct continuation of corresponding elementary functions that originate in human biology. Instead, they constitute a new type of formation that is molded by social life—specifically, the intervention of gestures, symbols, and especially language, which serve as mediators of action in socially meaningful contexts (see box on p. 23).

Internalization

An essential element in the formation of higher mental functions is the process of internalization of signs exchanged between people. According to Vygotsky, what first appears as an external mediator of social behavior later becomes an internal psychological process:

Any higher mental function necessarily goes through an external stage in its development because it is initially a social function. This is the center of the whole problem of internal and external behavior . . . . When we speak of a process, 'external' means 'social.' Any higher mental function was external because it was social at one point before becoming an internal, truly mental function. (Vygotsky [1960] 1981, 162)

Vygotsky's belief that speech as a "tool of the mind" is an outgrowth of the primary communicative function of language has important implications for the quality of mental processes. It implies that cognition continues to display communicative properties and the mark of the sociocultural settings in which it originated long after it has been internalized and exists on the psychological plane, within the individual. Thus, the central role of language in Vygotsky's theory, first as the vehicle of communication between people and then as the central means of communication with the self, brings us full circle, back to the socially shared and situated nature of cognition that is at the heart of his sociocultural approach to mind.

Although Vygotsky regarded mental functions as internalized social processes, he was careful to note that they are not the result of children simply mimicking features of social interaction. His vision is very different from traditional behaviorist and social learning views, which regard development as a consequence of

Joint Attentional Focus Between Caregivers and Infants: A Stepping Stone to Higher Cognitive Processes

How do young children make the leap from a primitive, natural level of mental organization to higher cognitive processes with the assistance of their caregivers? Research on joint attentional focus between adults and infants provides a concrete illustration.

From birth on, babies scan the environment, track moving objects, initiate interaction by making eye contact, and terminate it by looking away. Around 4 months, they start to gaze in the same direction adults are looking, and adults follow the baby's line of vision as well. When this happens, caregivers often comment on what the infant sees. In this way, the environment is labeled for the baby.

Research shows that this kind of joint attentional focus provides a communicative context that supports advances in language and problem solving during the second year. When adults describe aspects of the environment that capture the baby's attention, children pick up adult meanings rapidly, making faster progress in vocabulary acquisition as toddlers (Tamis-LeMonda & Bornstein 1989; Tomasello 1990; Dunham & Dunham 1992). In addition, high levels of maternal affection, teaching, and

positive interaction in the context of joint attention predict children's ability to solve challenging puzzles at 2 years of age (Frankel & Bates 1990).

Joint attentional focus is an excellent example of how the development of higher cognitive processes is mutually driven by caregiver and child. Infants often determine the targets of joint attention. Indeed, collaborative gazing and adult labeling work best when the objects and events of focus are of high interest to the baby. Because of their investment and curiosity, children are most likely to add words for these experiences to their vocabulary (Nelson 1973). Adults, in turn, surround joint attentional focus with a rich linguistic context, providing "tools of the mind" for toddlers to appropriate into their own repertoire and creating conditions especially suited for spurring cognition forward.

These findings underscore the importance of caregivers' sensitive efforts to maintain infants' attention during interaction and to provide short, clear explanations of what the baby is looking at, long before children are capable of responding with words.

modeling and reinforcement and as directly shaped by or copied from external sources. Instead, Vygotsky regarded children as active agents in development, contributing to the creation of internal mental processes by collaborating with others in meaningful cultural activities.

The *combination* of the child's and the more expert partner's behavior leads to the generation of signs between them. Then children actively and constructively take over those signs. As they are internalized, the signs undergo changes in structure and function. As we will see when we discuss additional features of Vygotsky's theory in the following sections, the structure of speech is modified when it begins to transfer to the internal plane and become self-communicative. In addition, the function of language undergoes revision when it moves from being other-directed to being self-directed. It becomes oriented toward clarifying thoughts and regulating, or gaining voluntary control over, behavior.

Because the term *internalization* (or *interiorization,* as it is sometimes translated) has the unfortunate and misleading connotation of simple transmission of knowledge from adults to children, or direct copying of social information from the external world to the internal world of the child, some Vygotskian scholars have suggested that other words be used that more adequately reflect Vygotsky's original meaning. Barbara Rogoff and others, for example, use the term *appropriation* rather than internalization to capture the idea of children actively choosing from cultural tools they encounter during social collaboration in ways that fit their particular goals (Rogoff 1990; Rogoff, Mistry, et al. 1993). Other investigators continue to use the concept of internalization but emphasize the child's unique contribution to both adult–child interaction and the internalization process (Elbers et al. 1992; Packer 1993; Goudena 1994). For example, Lawrence and Valsiner (1993) argue that it is best to think of Vygotsky's concept of internalization as the child's "constructive transformation" of the social world to restructure his or her own individual mental functioning. Stone (1993) believes that at the heart of internalization is the challenge that new information provided by a communicative partner poses to the child (or listener). To make sense of the information, the listener must "construct a set of

assumptions" about the speaker's meaning. In the process, "the listener is led to create for himself the speaker's perspective on the topic at issue" (1993, 171). According to this view, active engagement on the part of *both* adult and child, resulting in a "meeting of minds," is central to the internalization process.

Investigators continue to grapple with the question of just what children do when they appropriate, or construct, the social context internally. Nevertheless, in each Vygotsky-inspired account of internalization, there is an inherent relationship between external social and internal cognitive activity, but it is a *developmental* relationship, not a mirror-image relationship. As Wertsch (1985b) points out, internalization is not a process of copying external reality onto a pre-existing internal plane; rather, it is the process through which an internal plane of consciousness and self-regulation is formed.

The zone of proximal development

As we indicated earlier, Vygotsky's general genetic law of cultural development states that new capacities in the child are first developed during collaboration with adults or more competent peers and then internalized to become part of the child's psychological world. The region in which this transfer of ability from the shared environment to the individual occurs, according to Vygotsky, is called the *zone of proximal development,* or the ZPD ([1930–1935] 1978). Vygotsky's notion of the ZPD is probably the most well known of his ideas in the United States. It is closely related to his theorizing about the role of instruction and formal education in child development. As we will see in

According to Vygotsky, the role of education is to provide experiences that are in the child's zone of proximal development—activities challenging for the child but achievable with sensitive adult guidance.

greater detail in Chapter 5, Vygotsky viewed education as *leading* development. Through collaboration and interaction with teachers, parents, and other children, the child actively constructs new cognitive abilities.

Vygotsky originally introduced the ZPD in the context of arguing against standard intelligence and achievement testing procedures and against the view of development and education that emerges from the use of such tests (Vygotsky [1930 –1935] 1978). He regarded the traditional tests of intellectual functioning of his time (such as those emerging from the work of Alfred Binet in France) as extremely limited because they only assessed "static" or "fossilized" abilities, leaving out the dynamic and ever-changing quality of human cognition. Vygotsky suggested that what we should be measuring is not what children can do by themselves or already know but rather what they can do with the help of another person and have the potential to learn. Therefore, he defined the ZPD as "the distance between the actual developmental level as determined by independent problem solving and the level of potential development as determined through problem solving under adult guidance or in collaboration with more capable peers" (Vygotsky [1930–1935] 1978, 86).

The ZPD is the dynamic zone of sensitivity in which learning and cognitive development occur. Tasks that children cannot do individually but that they can do with help from others invoke mental functions that are currently in the process of developing, rather than those that have already matured. Consistent with his steadfast developmental approach, Vygotsky chose to focus on children's cognitive processes that are still growing—the processes of today or

tomorrow rather than those of yesterday or those that are already mastered.

According to Vygotsky, the role of education is to provide children with experiences that are in their ZPDs— activities that challenge children but that can be accomplished with sensitive adult guidance. Consequently, adults carry much responsibility for making sure that children's learning is maximized by actively leading them along the developmental pathway. The teacher's role, rather than instructing children in what they are ready for or giving them tasks for which they have already acquired the necessary mental operations, is to keep tasks in children's ZPDs, or slightly above their level of independent functioning. In this way, adults can "rouse to life" the cognitive processes that are just emerging in rudimentary form (Tharp & Gallimore 1988).

Scaffolding

We have already mentioned the metaphor that has emerged in the literature to describe effective teaching/learning interactions within the ZPD: that of a *scaffold* for a building under construction. Now let us consider further the ingredients of this special quality of adult–child collaboration. The child is viewed as a building, actively constructing him- or herself. The social environment is the necessary scaffold, or support system, that allows the child to move forward and continue to build new competencies. The term *scaffolding,* although not originally used by Vygotsky, was introduced by scholars trying to determine the most important components of tutoring (Wood & Middleton 1975; Wood, Bruner, & Ross 1976; Wood 1989). It has since become an extremely popular and useful idea in the fields of psychology and education. As we will soon see, this interaction style has repeatedly been shown to foster general cognitive growth and to increase children's performance on a wide variety of tasks (Wood & Middleton 1975; Wood, Bruner, & Ross 1976; Palincsar & Brown 1984, 1989; Pratt et al. 1988; Diaz, Neal, & Amaya-Williams 1990; Diaz, Neal, & Vachio 1991; Fleer 1992; Pratt et al. 1992).

Here is a brief example of an adult scaffolding a young child's efforts to put a difficult puzzle together:

Jason: I can't get this one in. *(Tries to insert a piece in the wrong place)*

Adult: Which piece might go down here? *(Points to the bottom of the puzzle)*

Jason: His shoes. *(Looks for a piece resembling the clown's shoes but tries the wrong one)*

Adult: Well, what piece looks like this shape? *(Points again to the bottom of the puzzle)*

Jason: The brown one. *(Tries it and it fits; then attempts another piece and looks at the adult)*

Adult: There you have it! Now try turning that piece just a little. *(Gestures to show him)*

Jason: There! *(Puts in several more pieces while commenting to himself, "Now a green piece to match," "Turn it [meaning the puzzle piece]," as the adult watches)*

(Adapted from Berk 1993, 324)

Consistent with this illustration, research shows that effective scaffolding has the following components and goals:

Joint problem solving. The first component of scaffolding is engagement of children in an interesting and culturally meaningful, collaborative problem-solving activity. Participants can be either adult–child or child–child groupings; what is important is that children interact with someone while the two are jointly trying to reach a goal. Related to the notion of socially shared cognition discussed earlier in this chapter is a second complementary idea: that cognition is always situated in activity, that children's learning cannot be separated from the task in which it takes place, and that people learn best when they are working with others while actively engaged in a problem (Brown, Collins, & Duguid 1989; Lave & Wenger 1991).

Intersubjectivity. Intersubjectivity is another important quality of good scaffolding. A concept introduced by Newson and Newson (1975), *intersubjectivity* refers to the process whereby two participants who begin a task with a different understanding arrive at a shared understanding. To achieve true collaboration and to communicate effectively during joint activity, it is essential that the participants work toward the same goal. If one person thinks about a task in a very different way than the other person, then the first person cannot guide the second effectively.

Intersubjectivity creates a common ground for communication as each partner adjusts to the perspective of the other. Adults try to promote it when they translate their own insights in ways that are within the child's grasp. For example, a teacher might point out the links between a new task and ones the child already knows. As the child stretches to understand the interpretation, she is drawn into a more mature approach to the situation (Rogoff 1990). In sum, an essential element of scaffolding is that the participants in social interaction negotiate, or compromise,

Children, like adults, do much of their best learning when they are actively engaged in a problem, especially with other people.

Scaffolding Children's Learning

by constantly striving for a shared view of the situation—one that falls within the child's ZPD.

Warmth and responsiveness. Another important component of scaffolding concerns the emotional tone of the interaction. Children's engagement with a task and willingness to challenge themselves are maximized when collaboration with the adult is pleasant, warm, and responsive and the adult gives verbal praise and attributes competence to the child, as appropriate (e.g., "Now you're getting it!" "Great! You did it!"). A useful analogy for the complex interaction that occurs during scaffolding is an intricate dance between a teacher (the adult) and a pupil (the child), with the child leading and the adult following for instructional purposes. In this dance the adult gives the child clues as to where to go next when the child temporarily loses his or her step. At other times the child actively seeks information and support (e.g., "Where does this piece go?" "I'm not sure what to do next."). The adult remains closely in tune with the child's actions, carefully anticipating the child's next moves and remaining engaged in the activity just enough to provide support as it is needed.

Keeping the child in the ZPD. A major goal of scaffolding, and education in general, is to keep children working on tasks in their ZPDs. This is usually achieved in two ways: (1) by structuring the task and the surrounding environment so that the demands on the child at any given time are at an appropriately challenging level, and (2) constantly adjusting the amount of adult intervention to the child's current needs and abilities.

The first responsibility, that of structuring the task and the environment, can be done both tacitly and explicitly. Adults tacitly structure children's activities by selecting which options are available as choices at any given time. They also set up rules within which children must function. For instance, a child who has devoted little energy to working on particular skills might be asked to spend a certain amount of time each day in activity centers that foster those skills. There are also many explicit ways to reduce the difficulty of highly challenging tasks for children, including verbally or physically breaking down a task into smaller components or rearranging task materials so that the child can see which item is needed next. Alternatively, if a task is too easy, scaffolders can increase the degree of challenge by renegotiating the goal, adding more components, or changing the rules of the activity.

A second way in which good scaffolders keep learners in their ZPDs during collaborative activity is to carefully adjust the amount of help or instruction they give to be commensurate with the child's momentary competence. This is the most common and basic interpretation of scaffolding—providing assistance when children need help and reducing the amount of assistance as children's competence increases. Responsive and contingent interaction provides the child with an appropriate challenge and a supportive environment. Of course, there are many different ways adults can provide assistance to children. Until now, we have discussed only the quantity and timing of support, not its kind. The quality of assistance provided is the next component of good scaffolding.

Promoting self-regulation. Another goal of scaffolding is to foster self-regulation by allowing the child to regulate joint activity as much as possible. This requires the adult to relinquish control and assistance as soon as the child can work independently. It also means that adults should permit children to grapple with questions and problems and should intervene only when the child is truly stuck. When adult intervention has these characteristics, the child stays in what has been called the *zone of executive functioning,* a mode in which he or she is largely responsible for making decisions and determining joint activities—in other words, the child is much like a manager in an "executive" role (Diaz 1990). In sum, as soon as a common goal is established, a combination of active withdrawal by the adult in response to active takeover by the child is crucial for the development of self-regulation.

Granting the child responsibility by stepping back as much as possible implies that the manner in which adults give assistance is important for promoting children's learning and mastery over their own behavior. Consistent with this idea, the adult's degree of directiveness or explicitness during the interaction has implications for the child's self-regulation. When adults continually influence children's behavior through explicit commands and by giving them immediate answers to momentary problems ("Put this here." "It's the green one."), learning and self-regulation are reduced. In contrast, when teachers and parents regulate children's task behavior by asking questions that permit the child to participate in the discovery of solutions, learning and self-regulation are maximized (Diaz, Neal, & Amaya-Williams 1990; Roberts & Barnes 1992; Gonzalez 1994). Adult conceptual questions encourage independent thinking as well as use of higher-order verbal problem-solving strategies. By intro-

ducing language as a mediator of activity, such questions intercede in the simple stimulus–response associations that characterize impulsive responding, thereby allowing children to distance themselves from the immediate environment so they can think (Sigel, McGillicuddy-DeLisi, & Johnson 1980; Diaz, Neal, & Amaya-Williams 1990).

Besides degree of directiveness, adult speech can vary in how much it encourages the child to think about the activity. Sigel and his colleagues (Sigel, McGillicuddy-Delisi, & Johnson 1980; Sigel 1982) define three levels of adult assistance, or *distancing strategies,* that vary in the extent to which they foster awareness of relations not perceptually present in the situation and, therefore, promote effective problem solving:

• *Low-level distancing:* Adult questions or statements that refer to objects or events present in the immediate environment (i.e., labeling or describing, as in "What color is this?" and "This dinosaur has big teeth.")

• *Medium-level distancing:* Adult utterances that elaborate somewhat on the immediate environment by mentioning the relationship between two visibly present dimensions (i.e., comparing, categorizing, or relating, as in "Which one is bigger?" and "This green piece looks different from that one.")

• *High-level distancing*: Adult utterances that encourage children to formulate a hypothesis or elaborate an idea by going beyond what is given in the immediate environment (i.e., planning, inferring, or deducing, as in "What will happen if we put this one here?" and "Why do we need to put this one in next?")

In sum, scaffolding connotes a warm, pleasant collaboration between a teacher and a learner while the two are engaged

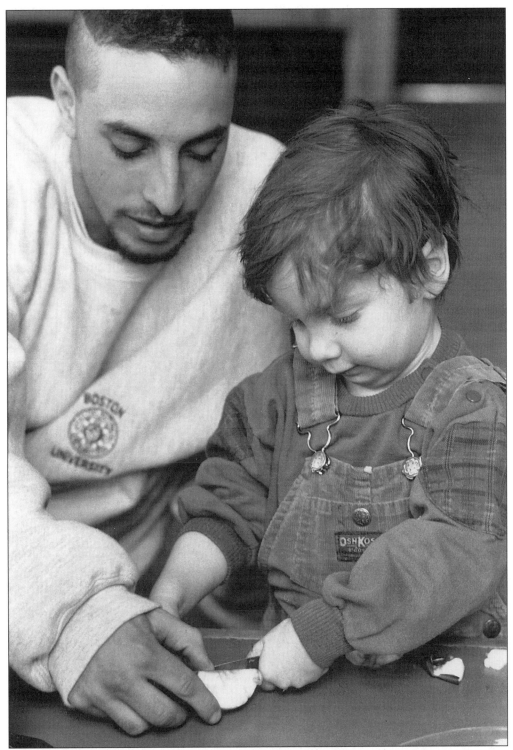

The adult supports children's autonomy by providing sensitive and contingent assistance, facilitating their representational and strategic thinking, and prompting them to take over more responsibility for the task as their skill increases.

in joint problem-solving activity. During this collaboration the adult supports the child's autonomy by providing sensitive and contingent assistance, facilitating children's representational and strategic thinking, and prompting children to take over more responsibility for the task as their skill increases.

Research on scaffolding

Scaffolding techniques, as just defined, consistently predict increased learning and positive outcomes in children. A common method that researchers use to investigate the effect of scaffolding is to (1) observe an adult–child pair working together on a problem-solving task, (2) classify teaching behaviors and child responses that occur during the collaborative session, (3) observe the child completing the same (or a similar) task independently, (4) note the child's task performance and behavior, and (5) examine which components of scaffolding are associated with either positive or negative child behavior and/or performance.

For example, Rafael Diaz and his colleagues videotaped 51 3-year-old children and their mothers as they worked together on classification and story-sequencing tasks. Mothers were instructed to teach the child the tasks "so that next time he/she can do it by him/herself" (Diaz, Neal, & Vachio 1991, 91). In addition to maternal utterances during the joint session, the extent to which mothers and children physically manipulated the task materials was also recorded. After the mother–child session, the child worked on the same task alone, and measures of performance were taken. The researchers found that the more the mothers praised their children for competent performance, the better the children did when they worked by themselves. Also, maternal relinquishing of control was positively associated with children's task engagement.

In a similar study, Roberts and Barnes (1992) found that the best predictor of 4- to 5-year-olds' scores on standardized measures of intelligence was parental distancing strategies and scaffolding. Directive and commanding maternal utterances were negatively related to children's performance, whereas mothers' use of questions and verbalizations that gave children opportunities to think and speak about the task were positively associated with test scores. Also, children whose mothers initiated much physical contact with either the task or their child performed worse on measures of cognitive development. In contrast, children whose mothers stepped back and allowed their child to touch the task materials and intervened physically only when it was absolutely necessary had higher scores. A similar study by McCarthy (1992) showed that children learn and perform best at a spatial construction task when the prior teaching by their mothers included two characteristics: (1) "chunking," or dividing the task into smaller, more manageable pieces, and (2) sensitive withdrawal, or reducing assistance when the child no longer requires it.

In an investigation of older children, Pratt and his collaborators (Pratt et al. 1992) measured parents' use of scaffolding while helping their fifth-graders with math homework. By grouping parental teaching behaviors into nine levels of directiveness in relation to the momentary actions of the child, the researchers measured the degree to which adults contingently shifted their level of intervention to fit the child's "region of sensitivity to instruction" (another name for the ZPD). An adult who stays within this region increases his or her directiveness when the child is having difficulty just enough to provide support (but not so much as to take over the task) and reduces directiveness when the child begins to succeed. Findings revealed that use of this contingent shifting principle predicted gains in children's learning of mathematics.

In this study and in a similar investigation of mothers assisting their preschoolers with challenging construction tasks, effective parental scaffolding was associated with an authoritative parenting style (Pratt et al. 1988). *Authoritative parenting,* a term first introduced by Diana Baumrind (1966), refers to a childrearing style characterized by appropriate structure and expectations combined with warmth and responsiveness—a democratic approach that encourages child independence within limits negotiated between parent and child. Additional research shows that authoritative parents, compared to authoritarian (strict and punitive) and permissive (warm but disengaged) parents, have children who are more cognitively and socially competent and emotionally well adjusted (Baumrind 1967, 1971; Dornbusch et al. 1987; Steinberg, Elmen, & Mounts 1989).

Furthermore, investigations exploring the effects of parental distancing strategies indicate that encouraging children to engage in strategic thinking promotes cognitive development. Parents who emphasize medium- and high-level distancing strategies have children who perform better on a variety of tasks and score higher in cognitive competence than children of parents who use predominantly low-level distancing strategies (Sigel 1982; Roberts & Barnes 1992; Gonzalez 1994).

Teachers and parents can be successfully trained to use the scaffolding techniques we have described. For example, Pacifici and Bearison (1991) observed preschoolers under two conditions: (1) while working with their mothers, and (2) while working with an experimenter who was specially coached in scaffolding. In addition to the usual finding that children learn more when they are with an adult who is carefully scaffolding their problem solving, the researchers found that the trained experimenter used more effective scaffolding procedures and that children scored higher after collaborating with the experimenter than with their parents.

The studies just reported focused on one-on-one adult–child interaction; however, the same basic principles can be applied to small- and large-group instructional settings, as well. Scholars in the Vygotskian tradition have developed pedagogical techniques that use scaffolding and the ZPD as the basis for fostering learning in school settings. These techniques will be discussed in detail in Chapter 6.

A cautionary note about scaffolding

Whereas substantial support exists for the benefits of scaffolding in promoting children's task mastery, several Vygotskian scholars have argued that the typical image of an effective scaffolder—an adult engaged in moment-by-moment adjustment of interaction to the needs of the child—requires elaboration and (in some circumstances) substantial modification. Stone points out that in the past, discussions of scaffolding have overemphasized the instructional component of breaking down the task into subgoals—a description that tends to

What makes effective "scaffolding" varies from culture to culture; its characteristics can only be understood in terms of the values and requirements of the child's society as a whole.

reduce the child to a passive recipient of the adult's didactic efforts. According to Stone, "scaffolding is a much more subtle phenomenon, one that involves a complex set of social and [communicative] dynamics" (1993, 180). The quality of adult support, the interpersonal relationship between adult and child, the meanings expressed, and the value attached to the situation, the task, and its associated behaviors are also important. Future investigations into these aspects are likely to clarify the dimensions of scaffolding that are essential and the precise means through which its effects are accomplished—issues that, at present, are poorly understood (Packer 1993).

Furthermore, we must keep in mind that research on scaffolding is limited to Western children. As Rogoff and her collaborators emphasize, the "pedagogic" mode of finely tuned support inherent in the scaffolding metaphor may be especially suited to child-oriented, academic-related tasks that are common in Western cultures, since this form of communication does not characterize adult interactions with children everywhere. For example, Guatemalan Mayan caregivers are far less likely than are Americans to structure young children's learning situations. Instead, they expect children to take greater responsibility for their own learning through observation and participation in adult (rather than child-oriented) activities. Consistent with these values,

Guatemalan Mayan parents are less verbal in their interactions with young children; they rely more on demonstration, unobtrusive directing, and monitoring. Furthermore, they do not praise their children's performance, and they rarely display affection to the child publicly (Rogoff, Mistry, et al. 1993; Rogoff, Mosier, et al. 1993). These findings indicate that effective "scaffolding" may vary widely from culture to culture. Its characteristics can only be understood in terms of the values and requirements of the child's society as a whole.

The social origins of self-regulation: Children's private speech

Earlier we mentioned that in addition to fostering children's learning, scaffolding can promote the development of self-regulation; that is, besides acquiring more knowledge when their activities are scaffolded by others, children learn how to direct their own learning and behavior. A major means through which scaffolding exerts this effect is by prompting children to use private, or self-directed, speech to guide their actions.

Piagetian and Vygotskian views of children's private speech

During the early part of this century, Vygotsky, Piaget, and several other theorists noticed an interesting phenomenon in preschool children—that they talk to themselves as they go about their daily activities. This self-talk, or overt speech that does not seem to be addressed to another person, is referred to as *private speech.* Today, private speech continues to interest researchers and students of education and child development; over the past quarter-century, an increasing number of articles on the topic have appeared (for a review, see Berk 1992). Although Vygotsky and Piaget studied children's private speech at about the same time, they differed sharply in their interpretations of the nature and function of such speech in children's development.

In his earliest work, *The Language and Thought of the Child* ([1923] 1926), Piaget described three types of speech not clearly adapted to the needs of a listener or even expressed in such a way that others could understand its meaning. As children moved about the classroom and engaged in activities, they sometimes repeated syllables and sounds playfully, a form of speech Piaget called *repetition.* For example, one 6-year-old budding artist named Lev punctuated several of his strokes with a sing-song commentary that went something like this: "Luloid . . . le le loid . . . ." More often, children engaged in *monologues,* or verbal soliloquies. One day, while alone at the art table, Lev remarked, "I want to do that drawing, there . . . I want to draw something, I do. I shall need a big piece of paper to do that." Piaget's final speech type, *collective monologues,* referred to soliloquies in the presence of others. On another occasion, while working alongside a group of children, Lev blurted out, "I've already done 'moon' so I'll have to change it," a statement completely unrelated to the prior remarks of his companions.

Piaget called these utterances *egocentric,* a term expressing his view that they were a symptom of cognitive immaturity. According to Piaget, private speech reflected the preschool child's inability to take the perspectives of others. Because he emphasized the logical limitations of the "pre-operational" mind, Piaget viewed private speech as ineffective social speech. He suggested that as children's cognitive abilities develop—as they are better able to understand others' viewpoints—egocentric speech should decline and be replaced by more mature and effective social interaction. Thus, for Piaget, private speech was an unimportant side effect, or a residual characteristic, of the mind of the preoperational child—a phenomenon that had no positive function in development.

Vygotsky's interpretation of the nature and function of private speech differed markedly from Piaget's. In *Thought and Language* ([1934] 1962, [1934] 1986), Vygotsky criticized Piaget's perspective and made several important observations about children's private speech. First, children use more private speech while working on difficult tasks than on either easy tasks or no task at all. This finding led Vygotsky to surmise that children must use this speech for a different purpose than communication with others. Second, Vygotsky noted that with age, the frequency of private speech shows an inverted U-shaped pattern—peaking during the middle to end of the preschool years and then declining as children's overt private speech is replaced by whispers and inaudible muttering. Third, private speech does not become more social with age, as Piaget suggested. Instead, it becomes less understandable to others as it is abbreviated and internalized. Finally, also contrary to Piaget's prediction, Vygotsky noted that the more opportunities for social interaction the child has, the more private speech that occurs. Rather than private speech giving way to social speech, social and private speech seem to go together.

On the basis of these findings, Vygotsky concluded that private speech

With private speech, children do for themselves what caregivers have done for them during joint problem solving.

Scaffolding Children's Learning

plays a special and critical role in child development. He believed that children's self-talk originates in and later differentiates from social speech, at which time it takes on a unique form and function. According to Vygotsky, the primary goal of private speech is not communication with others but *communication with the self* for the purpose of *self-regulation,* or guiding one's own thought processes and actions. Vygotsky ([1934] 1986) argued that the most significant moment in cognitive development occurs when the preschool child begins to use language not only for communication with others but also as a tool of thought—a means to direct his or her own attention and behavior. It is at this point, when children internalize the cultural tool of language and rely on it to structure their own thinking, that human development differs from the development of lower animals. The resulting reorganization of thought and language allows all human higher mental functions to emerge.

Vygotsky's theory indicates that at first, language and cognition develop separately. As children acquire speech in the context of social communication, language and cognitive development merge to form a new level of organization whereby children start to guide their behavior verbally, using the meanings of their particular culture. Eventually private speech is internalized to form inner verbal thought. In sum, language is first used for social communication. It then turns inward, becoming a tool of the mind for speaking to the self and guiding behavior. This self-regulatory language is first overt (private speech) and then gradually becomes covert (inner speech or verbal thinking). In this way, language branches off from the social world and enters the individual cognitive world. Private speech is the intermediate stage in this internalization process.

The process of internalizing language is a clear example of Vygotsky's general genetic law of cultural development—that mental functions are first shared between people and then become part of an individual's psychological functioning. Just as adult speech once served to regulate children's actions during social interaction, now children's speech to themselves begins to affect their own behavior. In other words, with private speech, children do for themselves what caregivers did for them during joint problem solving. Therefore, Vygotsky regarded private speech as the primary means through which children transfer the regulatory role from others to the self. Through private speech, young children, whose behavior was once limited to rigid and unreflective reactions to stimuli, gain distance from stimuli in their environment and function at a more "executive," or planful, level (Diaz, Neal, & Amaya-Williams 1990).

Research on children's private speech

Today, Vygotsky's perspective on children's private speech is preferred over Piaget's, and practically all contemporary studies of the phenomenon are conducted within the Vygotskian framework (Berk 1992). Nevertheless, it is important to note that Piaget was not entirely wrong in his observations of young children's verbalizations. In highly demanding communicative situations (for example, when a preschooler converses on the telephone without the concrete support of face-to-face interaction and objects to talk about), children occasionally display egocentric speech—utterances that are poorly adapted to the needs of their listeners (Berk & Garvin 1992; Warren & Tate 1992). But in line with Vygotsky's theory, the consensus of current evidence is that the large majority of children's self-directed speech serves the function of self-regulation. In the following sections, we discuss major themes to emerge from Vygotsky-inspired research, including the developmental course of private speech, contextual influences on private speech, and the relationship between adult–child communication, private speech, and task performance.

Developmental course of private speech. Vygotsky's theory predicts that private speech undergoes four changes with development: (1) it becomes progressively internalized—that is, overt private speech decreases as it is replaced with partially internalized forms; (2) it increases over the preschool years and then begins to decline in the early years of elementary school, in an inverted-U pattern; (3) it undergoes structural/grammatical changes as it is abbreviated and internalized; and (4) with development, the timing of children's self-speech, with respect to their ongoing behavior, changes such that speech moves from following behavior to preceding behavior, as it takes on a planning and regulating function. Research has mostly confirmed these predictions.

Consistent support has been obtained for Vygotsky's first prediction—that movement from overt, externalized private speech to covert, partially internalized forms takes place over the preschool and elementary school years. Whether studying children of different ages or observing the same children longitudinally over time, researchers

report that 3- to 5-year-olds typically use audible private speech, whereas slightly older children (5- to 10-year-olds) tend to replace their overt speech with partially internalized manifestations of inner speech, such as whispers, inaudible muttering, and silent lip movements (Kohlberg, Yaeger, & Hjertholm 1968; Berk & Garvin 1984; Frauenglass & Diaz 1985; Berk 1986; Bivens & Berk 1990; Berk & Landau 1993). Interestingly, this same transition from use of externalized to internalized forms is also seen when children are studied microgenetically—that is, as they get progressively better at a novel task (Berk & Spuhl 1995).

Vygotsky's second prediction—an inverted-U–shaped pattern of development from the preschool to early elementary school years—has received some support. Nevertheless, it is clear that this hypothesis needs to be modified. Some researchers have found that private speech peaks around 3 to 5 years of age and then decreases (Kohlberg, Yaeger, & Hjertholm 1968; Frauenglass & Diaz 1985; Diaz, Winsler, & Montero 1994; Berk & Spuhl 1995). However, other studies have shown that in cognitively challenging situations, elementary school children continue to use a great deal of self-talk, which gradually diminishes from first to fifth grade (Berk & Garvin 1984; Berk 1986; Bivens & Berk 1990; Berk & Potts 1991; Berk & Landau 1993; Winsler 1994). Taken together, the evidence suggests that private speech undergoes an original internalization process during the preschool years. Subsequently, Vygotsky's inverted-U pattern seems to repeat itself each time children tackle a major new area of cognitive skill, such as reading, writing, and mathematical reasoning during the first few years of formal schooling.

Peaks and troughs in private speech may be especially evident during the preschool and early school years because children must master so many new and diverse activities. While raising questions about the existence of a single, overarching developmental pattern, this revised idea is ultimately consistent with Vygotsky's theory. Private speech remains a central, self-regulatory tool throughout development, and children first think out loud and then internalize this language to form inner verbal thought (and higher mental processes) when engaged in tasks that are within their ZPD (Berk 1992, 1994c).

According to Vygotsky's third developmental claim, since private speech branches off from social speech and becomes speech-for-self, it should become more abbreviated and fragmented with age. As speech progressively merges with thought, less overt explicitness is needed and utterances are no longer stated as complete phrases. Although Vygotsky reported data from his own experiments to support this hypothesis, only a few recent investigations have systematically tested the idea. They provide only preliminary support (Manning & White 1990; Feigenbaum 1992; Goudena 1992). Feigenbaum, for example, observed 4-, 6-, and 8-year-olds while they completed a road-building construction task, and he categorized their private utterances as either complete or fragmented. Fragmented utterances were strings of speech that were not grammatically intact, such as utterances without a subject, a predicate, or connecting words. Although 66% of 6- and 8-year-olds' self-regulatory private speech was fragmented compared to 45% of the speech of 4-year-olds, this difference was not large enough to be considered statistically significant.

Goudena (1992) found the same (nonsignificant) trend with his sample of 4- and 5-year-old children. Both researchers were quick to note the limitations of their studies, including small sample sizes, use of tasks that might not have been optimal for eliciting private speech, and the fact that no children younger than 4 years had been observed. According to Vygotsky's theory, abbreviation and fragmentation of private speech begins around age 3; therefore, by the time children are 4 years old, much abbreviation may have already occurred. Clearly, to fully test this hypothesis, more research is needed with larger samples that include younger children.

Vygotsky's last hypothesis about how private speech changes with development concerns the timing of speech with respect to action. He predicted that at first, children's self-speech would occur after the behavior with which it is associated, then it would appear at the same time as the behavior, and only later would it appear before the action it was intended to regulate. This component of Vygotsky's theory has not been studied extensively, and what little research exists provides only limited support. Whereas one study reported this age-related pattern in the timing of private speech (Kohlberg, Yaeger, & Hjertholm 1968), others have not (Rubin 1979; Pellegrini 1981; Berk & Spuhl 1995). Although Vygotsky's hypothesis suggests that private speech becomes more self-regulatory as it moves from accompanying action to preceding action, in actuality this may not be the case. The majority of children's private utterances at any age tend to be simultaneous with their ongoing activity. Simultaneous speech that guides behavior certainly fulfills an important self-regulatory function; therefore, such speech should be recognized as less useful and adaptive.

Furthermore, it is possible that different tasks require different sorts of verbal regulation. Sometimes reflecting on an action (speaking after doing) is an effective strategy, sometimes speaking while one is doing something is best, and at still other times it is preferable to plan one's behavior in advance with words. Indeed, a growing research literature reveals that children's self-directed utterances are highly diverse and serve a wide range of purposes (see Table 2.1). The most effective speech–action relationship may depend on the child's momentary goal. For example, first-grade beginning readers can be seen carefully and cautiously sounding out words—utterances that predict successful reading comprehension (Roberts 1979). Here, speech and action (comprehending text) appear to be simultaneous. As the box on pages 42 and 43 reveals, while alone in their cribs, toddlers can be heard emitting a stream of utterances through which they re-enact recent experiences and imagine future ones as a way of understanding and controlling them (Nelson 1989). Similarly, socially isolated preschoolers have been observed using high rates of fantasy statements in which they talk to nonpresent others, a form of speech that may permit them to practice communication skills with a comfortable, non-threatening playmate in preparation for interacting with peers (Rubin 1982; Olszewski 1987). In these instances, private speech seems to occur far in advance of the social behavior it aims to guide. Self-directed language is also a vital means for regulating emotional arousal (Thompson 1990). Even 4-year-olds realize that an upsetting experience can be blunted through private speech,

Category
Egocentric communication
Fantasy play and comments addressed to nonhuman objects
Emotional release and expression
Describing one's own activity and self-guidance
Reading aloud
Inaudible muttering

Table 2.1: Varieties of Private Speech

Description	Examples
remarks directed to another that result in communication failure because they are not adapted to the perspective of the listener	David and Mark are seated next to each other on the rug. David says, "It broke," without explaining what or when.
remarks involving role play, talking to objects, and sound effects for objects	Nancy says in a high-pitched voice to no one in particular, "I'll feel better after the doctor gives me a shot." "Ow!" she remarks as she pokes herself with her finger (a pretend needle). Jay snaps, "Out of my way!" to a chair after he bumps into it.
remarks expressing feelings not directed to any particular listener, or remarks having no external stimulus that seem to be attempts to emotionally integrate a past event or thought	Paula looks at the colorful picture on the cover of her new reading book and exclaims to no one in particular, "Wow! Neat!" Rachel is sitting at her desk with an anxious look on her face. repeating to herself, "My mom's sick, my mom's sick."
remarks about the child's own activity, including descriptions of what the child is doing at the moment and "thinking out loud," or goal-directed plans for action	Carla, while doing a page in her math book, says out loud, "Six." Then, counting on her fingers, she continues, "Seven, eight, nine, ten. It's ten, it's ten. The answer's ten." Michael, looking through the dictionary, says to himself, "Now where do I find this?" referring to a word. As he begins to turn the pages, he responds to his own query, "I know, I know, under 'C'."
remarks involving reading written material aloud or sounding out words	Tommy is reading a book, when he begins to sound out a difficult name. "Sher-lock Holm-lock, Sherlock Holme," he repeats, leaving off the initial "s" in his second, more successful attempt.
remarks uttered so quietly that they cannot be understood by an observer	Angela mumbles inaudibly to herself as she works on a math problem.

Toddlers' Crib Speech

So far, our discussion has largely focused on how children use private speech to guide their thinking during problem-solving and academic activities. Although most private speech is task related, children often use self-talk in other creative ways. Fantasy play, for example, evokes a variety of private speech forms that are part of the playful activity itself, including narratives, sound effects, running dialogues between imaginary figures, and expressions of feelings (Rubin & Dyck 1980; Gillingham & Berk 1995).

Young children also talk to themselves in novel ways while going to sleep. Several investigators have carefully recorded "crib speech"—the extended, solitary monologues that some toddlers (between the ages of 2 and 3) engage in before taking a nap or retiring for the night (Weir 1962; Kuczaj 1983, 1985; Nelson 1989). This fascinating speech is a developmental precursor to the task-oriented private utterances that Vygotsky and his followers emphasized, and it has unique, self-regulatory functions.

Presleep narratives serve at least three purposes. First, this language play is clearly an enjoyable pastime for children. Second, crib speech provides an excellent opportunity for toddlers to practice their emerging language skills without interruption or interference from others. While speaking to themselves in their cribs, toddlers experiment with new pronunciations, word meanings, and grammatical structures (Kuczaj 1983;

Nelson 1989). Interestingly, observations of one African Grey parrot in the process of being trained to speak showed that he also experimented with language forms when alone (Pepperberg, Brese, & Harris 1991). Third, the content of crib speech suggests that most of the time, children use it to make sense of their world—to understand their emotions and surroundings and to interpret events that happen to them. Here is an example of the bedtime speech of Emily, a 2-year-old whose many "narratives from the crib" became the subject and title of a book by Katherine Nelson (1989):

1. We are gonna . . .
2. at the ocean.
3. Ocean is a little far away
4. baw, baw buh [etc.]
5. far away . . .
6. I think it's . . .
7. couple blocks . . . away
8. Maybe it's down, downtown
9. and across the ocean,
10. and down the river,
11. and maybe it's in,
12. the hot dogs will be in a fridge
13. and the fridge (would) be in the water over by a shore
14. and then we could go in,
15. and get a hot dog and bring it out to the river,
16. and then sharks go in the river and bite me,
17. in the ocean,
18. we go into the ocean

19. and ocean be over by . . .

20. I think a couple of blocks away.

21. But we could be,

22. and we could find any hot dogs,

23. um the hot dogs gonna be for the for the beach.

24. Then the bridge is gonna,

25. we'll have to go in the green car.

26. 'cause that's where the car seats are.

(Nelson 1989, 66–67)

Nelson reports that the themes of young children's crib talk can usually be divided into three categories: (1) anticipating an upcoming event, (2) recalling a prior event, or (3) discussing how to act according to behavioral scripts, rules, and norms. The excerpt just presented was of the first type—commentary on an upcoming visit to the ocean. In the next example we see how Emily interpreted events that took place during a recent trip to the store:

1. We bought a baby

2. . . . 'cause,

3. . . . the, well because,

4. when she, well,

5. we thought it was for Christmas,

6. but when we went to the s-s-store we didn't have our jacket on,

7. but I saw some dolly,

8. and I yelled at my mother and said

9. I want one of those dolly.

10. So after we were finished with the store,

11. we went over to the dolly and she bought me one,

12. so I have one.

(Nelson 1989, 72)

In a final example we see the language play and experimentation that sometimes occurs during crib speech. Here, 2½-year-old Anthony talks about an average-size person he knows named Bob; the other people he mentions do not exist. Anthony explores the meaning of the words "big" and "little" and practices his counting skills:

1. hi big Bob

2. that's Bob

3. that's Bob

4. big Bob

5. little Bob

6. big and little

7. little Bobby

8. little Nancy

9. big Nancy

10. big Bob and Nancy and Bobby

11. and Bob

12. and two, three Bobbys

13. three Bobbys

14. four Bobbys

15. six

16. tell the night, Bobby

17. big Bob

18. big Bob not home

(Weir 1962; cited in Levy 1989, 128–29)

Private speech clearly comes in many forms. Children use it in the service of diverse self-regulatory goals—including guiding behavior, learning language, interpreting emotional states, expressing themselves creatively, and making sense of their world.

as when they reassure themselves, "Mommy'll be back soon" or "That shot from the doctor will only hurt a little bit." In this case, private speech follows an emotional reaction in an effort to redirect and control it. Thus, most private speech, regardless of its timing, can be seen as self-regulatory in some way.

Contextual influences on private speech. Young children do not talk to themselves equally in all situations. Certain contexts seem to bring out private speech. Winsler and Diaz (in press), for example, observed children in kindergarten classrooms, recording under which conditions the children spontaneously used private speech. The researchers found that kindergartners engaged in a great deal of self-talk while involved in goal-directed, problem-solving, or academic activities and used less private speech in other contexts. Classroom-based research with older, elementary school-age children has yielded similar results (Berk & Garvin 1984). In addition, during solitary play, preschoolers engage in rates of private speech that are especially high and that remain so from 2½ to 6 years of age. As we will see in Chapter 3, young children at play constantly set challenges for themselves. Under these circumstances, self-directed speech is common (Gillingham & Berk 1995). Taken together, these findings support Vygotsky's claim that children systematically use private speech as a tool for self-regulation—for directing their thought processes and behavior during cognitively demanding activities.

Other studies have shown that while working on problem-solving tasks, children use more private speech when the task is difficult compared to when it is easy (Kohlberg, Yaeger, & Hjertholm 1968; Deutsche & Stein 1972; Zivin

1972; Beaudichon 1973; Murray 1979). This finding also suggests that children use private speech for self-regulation. When tasks become harder, children rely more heavily on this cognitive tool to accomplish their goals. However, Behrend and his colleagues (Behrend, Rosengren, & Perlmutter 1989, 1992) found that the positive relationship between task difficulty and use of private speech is present only up to a point. When tasks are too difficult and therefore outside the children's ZPDs, they do not use much private speech. Instead, they are likely to display disorganized behavior or to disengage from the task. In sum, children seem to use private speech preferentially during moderately challenging problem-solving activities that are within their range of mastery.

How scaffolding fosters self-regulation through private speech. Our earlier discussion of scaffolding revealed that certain adult–child interaction styles can promote children's cognitive development. Research suggests that an important way in which scaffolding affects children's cognitive performance is by stimulating their spontaneous use of private speech as a self-regulatory and problem-solving tool. Many studies report that young children use more private speech when they are working with an adult who sensitively supports their activity (Goudena 1987; Behrend, Rosengren, & Perlmutter 1989, 1992; Diaz, Winsler, & Montero 1994; Winsler 1994; Berk & Spuhl 1995).

Berk and Spuhl (1995), for example, measured maternal interaction as 30 4- and 5-year-olds collaborated with their mothers on challenging pyramid-building and matrix-construction tasks. After the mother–child session, the children worked individually on Lego-construction problems (requiring skills similar to those required by the mother–child tasks) over the course of three sessions. Findings revealed that maternal support, in the form of an authoritative style (warmth plus structure adjusted to the child's needs), was positively associated with children's appropriate use of private speech during the individual session, as well as with gains in children's task performance over the course of the sessions. Also, using a statistical procedure that examines the relationship between two variables while controlling for a third, the researchers found that the positive relationship between authoritative parenting and children's task performance was stronger when children talked to themselves. In other words, when their mothers were warm and provided appropriate structure, children more often talked to themselves while working, which was associated with greater mastery of the task. In this study, private speech seemed to *mediate* the relationship between adult support and children's performance.

Diaz and his colleagues (Diaz, Winsler, & Montero 1994) have obtained additional support for the idea that scaffolding helps children develop their cognitive skills by augmenting private speech. These investigators observed 40 preschool children as they completed a 24-item selective-attention task (which involved deciding which of two dimensions, such as shape and color, several pictures had in common) with the aid of an experimenter who scaffolded the children each time they could not complete an item by themselves. Children who used private speech after scaffolding were much more likely to succeed on the subsequent task item than were children who did not talk to

When working on challenging tasks, children use private speech more heavily than they do when performing easy tasks.

themselves after scaffolding. It would appear, therefore, that children actively use private speech as a tool to transfer problem-solving knowledge and responsibility from the adult to the self. First, children collaborate with adults during a task, then they collaborate with themselves through self-talk, and later they are capable of independent, automatic performance without using speech.

Other studies reveal that adult scaffolding during a collaborative session affects children's private speech both during the adult–child session and afterward during independent problem solving (Behrend, Rosengren, & Perlmutter 1989, 1992; McCarthy 1992; Winsler 1994). For example, McCarthy (1992) found that the problem-solving strategies and types of private speech used by preschoolers were similar to those verbal strategies that mothers emphasized during previous scaffolding. Children whose mothers broke down the task into subgoals ("What shall we do first?") or tried to focus the child's attention ("Where is the clown?") made similar self-directed remarks when working by themselves. Winsler (1994) reported that children's use of private speech to take over regulatory responsibility was reduced when adults were verbally directive and did not relinquish control in accord with the child's increasing competence. He also found that the link between children's private speech and task performance was stronger after children collaborated with an experimenter specially trained to provide scaffolding than after children worked with their parents, who were not necessarily scaffolding.

Scaffolding seems to promote young children's private speech for a number of reasons. First, when an adult carefully regulates task difficulty through the amount of assistance provided to the child, the adult maintains the child in the ZPD. As discussed earlier, it is in this context, when children direct their own behavior on a challenging task, that they spontaneously use private speech.

Second, scaffolding influences private speech by bringing the task to a verbal level. When adults use questions and strategies to guide children and to help them discover solutions, they elevate language to the status of a primary problem-solving tool. This use of language by adults, combined with adult reduction of regulation as children's competence increases, leads children to use speech to solve problems. As a result, children realize that they can answer their own questions and scaffold themselves. Through private speech, children begin to create and expand their own ZPDs.

Third, through scaffolding, children learn how to regulate their own learning and behavior. Self-regulatory, or *metacognitive,* skills, such as knowing how to structure the environment for learning; choosing useful problem-solving strategies; and planning, guiding, and evaluating one's own thinking and behavior develop as children use speech to solve problems, first together with adults and then alone. All of these self-regulatory capacities predict academic achievement, as well as other positive psychological and behavioral outcomes in children (see Zimmerman & Schunk 1989; Schunk & Zimmerman 1994).

Relationship of private speech to task-related behavior and perfor- **mance.** Two main transitions characterize children's gradual attainment of independent functioning and competent performance. The first is the transition from other-regulation to self-regulation, which occurs as children use private speech, as we have just discussed. The second is the transition from active self-regulation with the help of overt private speech to silent, autonomous functioning. This latter transition concerns the dynamic relationship of children's private speech to task-related behavior and performance.

Research reveals that the relation of private speech to children's behavior is consistent with Vygotsky's assumption that self-guiding utterances help bring action under the control of thought. In Bivens and Berk's (1990) longitudinal study, in which children were followed from first to third grade as they worked on mathematics tasks in their classrooms, gradual internalization of private speech went hand-in-hand with more effective channeling of task-related behavior. Children who used a great deal of task-irrelevant speech, such as wordplay and emotional release, often squirmed in their seats and chewed and tapped their pencils. They also had trouble staying attentive to the math assignments. In contrast, children who frequently used audible, task-relevant utterances engaged in more nonverbal behaviors directed at overcoming difficulties, such as counting on fingers, using a pencil to follow a line or read a word, and relying on objects to assist with counting. Finally, children whose private speech was largely internalized sat quietly at their desks and were highly attentive. Overall, children who progressed more rapidly from audible, self-directed utterances to inner speech were also advanced in their ability to inhibit self-stimulating motor activity and to focus attention.

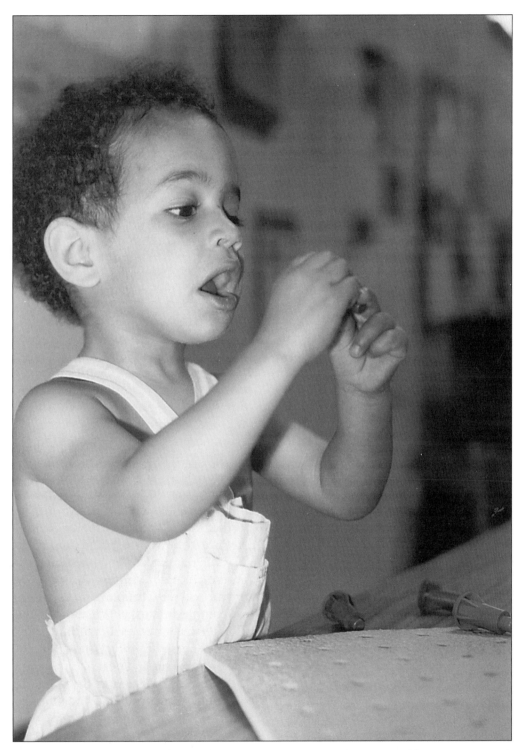

If a child is using overt, task-relevant private speech, then the activity is probably within the child's zone of proximal development: it is challenging enough for the child to need to use self-talk but not too difficult.

If private speech is a tool that children use to guide their behavior during problem solving, then we would expect it to be positively associated with task success. However, the relation between private speech and performance seems to be considerably more complex and dynamic than this straightforward prediction suggests. Since private speech increases when children face challenges, it may at times coincide with task failure. Children's use of private speech is a signal that they have encountered obstacles and difficulties in their efforts to master a task. But we must keep in mind that initially, children's private speech may not be efficient and effective enough to result in immediate task mastery. Instead, the beneficial effect of private speech on performance may take time to accumulate and only be apparent at some point in the future.

In support of this idea, private speech is typically unrelated or negatively related to performance when researchers observe children at only one point in time (Zivin 1972; Frauenglass & Diaz 1985; Berk 1986). But several studies show that children's use of private speech is associated with task *improvement* (Behrend, Rosengren, & Perlmutter 1989, 1992; Bivens & Berk 1990; Gaskill & Diaz 1991; Azmitia 1992; Berk & Spuhl 1995). The more private speech preschoolers and early elementary school children use, the greater their performance gains when assessed from two days to as much as a year after the initial observation (Berk 1992).

Supporting children's use of private speech. Research reveals that private speech is a problem-solving tool universally available to children who experience rich, socially interactive environments. Several interdependent factors—the demands of a task, its social context, and individual characteristics of the child—govern the extent and ease with which children use private speech to guide their behavior (Berk 1994b). Consistent with these findings, adults foster children's self-guiding private speech when they provide tasks at the upper end of the child's current abilities (in the ZPD), as well as patient, encouraging assistance and feedback coordinated with the child's self-regulatory efforts (that is, scaffolding).

Despite this evidence, many adults continue to regard private speech as meaningless, socially unacceptable conduct. As a result, they often discourage children from engaging in audible self-talk. We now know that private speech is healthy, adaptive, essential behavior, and (as we will see in Chapter 4) some children need to use it more often and over a longer age span than do others. At home, parents can listen to the private utterances of their children, gaining insight into their plans, goals, and difficulties. At school, teachers can be mindful of private speech, recognizing that when children use it to a greater extent than is typical for their age, they may need extra support and guidance.

Teachers can also design learning environments that permit children to be verbally active while solving problems and completing tasks. When new goal-oriented activities are being integrated into the curriculum, self-guiding private speech can serve as one indicator of the appropriateness of the tasks for fostering learning and self-regulation. If a child is using overt, task-relevant private speech, then the activity is probably within the child's ZPD. It is challenging enough for the child to need to use self-talk but not too difficult—a judgment that can also be verified by the child's active engagement with and attentiveness to the task (Diaz et al. 1992; Winsler & Diaz in press).

Once viewed as inconsequential activity, today private speech is recognized as a central force in development (Diaz & Berk 1992). In talking to themselves, children build a bridge between their social and psychological worlds as they strive to become competent, autonomous beings.

Play in Vygotsky's Theory

Three-year-old Nancy and her mother are in the basement playroom fixing decorations for a Halloween party. When Nancy begins to show signs of boredom, her mother suggests that she drive her car. Nancy retrieves a child-size red plastic dashboard with steering wheel and seatbelt, and positions herself for driving. "Be sure to fasten your seatbelt, right?" reminds her mother. "Buckle up for safety!" Nancy fastens her seatbelt, turns the steering wheel, and pushes the horn. To her mother's queries, "Where are you going? Are you taking a trip?" Nancy replies, "To Havana." . . . She explains that Havana is far away and discusses with her mother how many stops will be needed en route and how old one has to be to get a driver's license.

Eventually Nancy's mother ceases to be a spectator to her daughter's play and actually enters the pretend world in the role of passenger. Nancy tells her to sit in the back seat and buckle her seatbelt. Her mother then asks, "Are you the mom?" and Nancy says, "Yes." . . . The pretend child proceeds to badger the placidly driving pretend mother: she wants to open the car window and stick her feet out, complains that a bug flew in the window, whines about being hungry, and finally announces an urgent need to go to the bathroom. The pretend mother utters an exasperated, "Ohhhh!," stops the car, and shows the child to the bathroom (the area to the left of the sofa). Toileting accomplished, complete with sound effects and enacted flushing, the pair get back into the car and resume their journey. (Adapted from Haight & Miller 1993, 1)

This chapter is an expanded version of an article by Laura E. Berk, entitled, "Vygotsky's Theory: The Importance of Make-Believe Play," that appeared in the November 1994 issue of *Young Children*.

Vygotsky's works contain only a brief, 12-page statement on play and its role in child development, written in 1933. Despite the brevity of his treatment of the topic, Vygotsky's ideas on the development and significance of play are provocative, innovative, and ahead of his time. In accord with his emphasis on children's use of signs as a pivotal stepping stone to higher cognitive processes, Vygotsky ([1933] 1966) neglected the sensorimotor play of infancy and, instead, emphasized representational play—the make-believe that emerges at the end of toddlerhood, blossoms during the preschool years, and evolves into the games with rules that dominate middle childhood. Vygotsky accorded fantasy play a prominent place in his theory, granting it the status of a "leading factor in development" ([1930–1935] 1978, 101), as the following frequently quoted remarks reveal:

[P]lay creates a zone of proximal development in the child. In play, the child always behaves beyond his average age, above his daily behavior; in play it is as though he were a head taller than himself. As in the focus of a magnifying glass, play contains all developmental tendencies in a condensed form and is itself a major source of development. ([1930–1935] 1978, 102)

In this chapter, we consider Vygotsky's ideas on the functions of play in the life of the young child, his vision of how play develops, and why he viewed play as leading development forward, contributing greatly to children's capacity to engage in planful, self-regulatory activity.

Unfortunately, Vygotsky-inspired research on play is limited, largely because Vygotsky wrote so little on the topic. Investigators have focused much greater attention on the social-interactional and sign-mediational aspects of his theory, which are far more extensively addressed in his writings. Nevertheless, the literature stimulated by Vygotsky's approach to play is growing, and research not directly intended to test his ideas has also provided considerable support. We will discuss these findings as we explore Vygotsky's ideas, along with additional evidence that situates make-believe squarely within a sociocultural context. We will see that adults and peers scaffold young children's representational play, nurturing the transition to fantasy and make-believe and its elaboration over the preschool years. Representational play, in turn, serves as a unique but broadly influential zone of proximal development within which *children advance themselves* to ever higher levels of psychological functioning.

Development and significance of imaginative play

Vygotsky began his consideration of the importance of play in children's development by suggesting that if we can identify its defining features, we can gain insight into its essential functions in development. To isolate the distinctiveness of play, Vygotsky explored characteristics regarded by other theorists as central to playful activity and found them wanting.

For example, the common assumption that play is pleasurable activity is neither specific to play nor characterizes all playful circumstances. Many other experiences, such as eating a favorite treat, being granted the undivided attention and affection of a parent, or listening to an exciting story, are at least as gratifying and sometimes more so than play. Furthermore, certain playful

In play the child behaves beyond his age, above his daily behavior—it is as though he were a head taller taller than himself.

experiences—games that can be won or lost—are not pure fun for the child when they result in disappointing outcomes.

A second way of understanding play is to highlight its symbolic features, as Piaget ([1945] 1951) did in his characterization of the blossoming of make-believe at the beginning of the preoperational stage. Although the young child's burgeoning capacity to represent the world contributes to the emergence of make-believe during the second year, symbolism is yet another feature that is not exclusive to play. Both Piaget and Vygotsky noted that it also characterizes language, artistic, and literacy activities that develop during the preschool years.

Vygotsky concluded that play has two critical features that, when combined, describe its uniqueness and shed light on its role in development. First, all representational play *creates an imaginary situation* that permits the child to grapple with unrealizable desires. Vygotsky pointed out that fantasy play makes its appearance at a time when children must learn to postpone the gratification of impulses and accept the fact that certain desires will remain unsatisfied. In contrast to infancy, when the interval between desires and their fulfillment is short, during the second year caregivers begin to insist that toddlers delay gratification and acquire socially approved behaviors.

To illustrate this change, consider a recent study in which mothers were asked to indicate which things they require their young children to do and which things they insist they not do between 13 and 30 months of age (Gralinski & Kopp 1993). The researchers found that rules for behavior received increasing emphasis during the second year. Initially, mothers focused on rules involving safety, property, and respect for others. Young toddlers were admonished not to get too close to dangerous situations, such as steep staircases, hot stoves, and busy streets, and not to harm their own or others' belongings—for example, by tearing up books, coloring on walls, or handling breakable objects. Considerate behavior—not taking toys from or being too rough with other children—was also stressed. Over time, mothers' expectations expanded. They added rules related to family routines (putting toys away, helping with simple chores), self-care (washing hands, brushing teeth, dressing), and delay of gratification (waiting for a turn, eating dessert at the end of a meal), until by 30 months all types of rules were emphasized to the same degree. Just as Vygotsky noted, during the very period in which children must learn to subordinate their momentary desires to the rules of social life, imaginative play begins to flourish.

The creation of an imaginary situation in play, however, has often been assumed to be a way in which children attain immediate gratification of desires that they cannot satisfy in real life. Vygotsky believed that this commonly held view is incorrect. A second feature of all representational play is that it *contains rules for behavior* that children must follow to successfully execute the play scene. Games that appear in the late preschool period and preoccupy children during the school years are clearly rule based. But even the simplest imaginative situations created by very young children always proceed in accord with social rules, although these rules are not laid down in advance. For example, a child pretending to go to sleep follows the rules of bedtime behavior. Another child imagining himself to be a father and a doll to be a child conforms to the rules of parental behavior. Yet a third child playing astronaut observes the rules of shuttle launch and space walk. Vygotsky concluded, "Whenever there is an imaginary situation, there are rules" ([1930–1935] 1978, 95). A child cannot behave in an imaginary situation without them.

These attributes of play—an imaginary situation governed by rules—provide the key to its role in development. According to Vygotsky, make-believe supports the emergence of two complementary capacities: (1) the ability to separate thought from actions and objects, and (2) the capacity to renounce impulsive action in favor of deliberate and flexible self-regulatory activity. The following two sections elaborate on these ideas.

Separating thought from actions and objects

In creating an imaginary situation, children learn to act not just in response to external stimuli—the immediate objects and events before them—but also in accord with internal ideas, or the *meaning* of the situation. Infants and very young children, Vygotsky explained, are reactive beings; momentary perceptions trigger and dictate their behavior. A baby who sees an attractive toy grabs for it without delay; a toddler runs after a ball that has rolled into the street without considering consequences. "[I]n play, things lose their determining force. *The child sees one thing but acts differently in relation to what he sees. Thus, a condition is reached in which the child begins to act independently of what he sees*" ([1933] 1978, 97).

Just how does imaginative play help children separate thought from the surrounding world and rely on ideas to guide behavior? According to Vygotsky, the object substitutions that characterize make-believe are crucial in this process. When children use a stick to represent a horse, or a folded blanket to represent a sleeping baby, their relation to reality is dramatically changed. The stick becomes a pivot for separating the meaning "horse" from a real horse; similarly, the blanket becomes a pivot for distinguishing the meaning "baby" from a real baby. This separation of meaning occurs because children change the substitute object's usual meaning when they behave toward it in a pretend fashion.

Vygotsky emphasized that it is very difficult for young children to sever thinking, or the meaning of words, from the objects to which they refer; they do so only gradually. Indeed, research reveals that the flexibility of children's object substitutions increases with age. Between 18 months and 2 years of age, make-believe becomes more detached from the real-life conditions associated with it. In early pretense, toddlers use only realistic objects—for example, a toy telephone to talk into or a cup to drink from. Around age 2, use of less-realistic toys, such as a block for a telephone receiver, becomes more frequent. Sometime during the third year,

*E*ven the very simplest imaginative situations created by very young children always proceed in accord with social rules, although these rules are not laid down in advance.

children can imagine objects and events without any direct support from the real world, as when they say to a play partner, "I'm calling Susie on the phone!" while pretending to dial with their hands or without acting out the event at all. By this time, a play symbol no longer has to resemble the object or behavior for which it stands (Bretherton et al. 1984; Corrigan 1987; McCune 1993; Tamis-LeMonda & Bornstein 1993).

Vygotsky viewed play as a transitional "stage between the purely situational constraints of early childhood and adult thought, which can be totally free of real situations" ([1930–1935] 1978, 98). In helping children separate meaning from objects, pretense in early childhood serves as vital preparation for the much later development of abstract and imaginative thinking, in which symbols are manipulated and propositions evaluated without referring to the real world (Vygotsky [1930] 1990). And in detaching meaning from behavior, make-believe also helps teach children to make deliberate choices from among alternative courses of action. Consequently, fantasy play is an additional factor—beyond those discussed in the previous chapter—that promotes self-regulation. The capacity to think in a self-regulatory fashion is also strengthened by the rule-based nature of play, as we will see in the next section.

Renouncing impulsive action

Vygotsky pointed out that the imaginative play of children contains an interesting paradox. In play, children do what they most feel like doing, and to an outside observer, the play of preschoolers appears free and spontaneous. Nevertheless, play constantly demands that children act against their immediate impulses because they must subject themselves to the rules of the make-believe context or the game they are playing. In this sense, free play is not really 'free,' since renouncing impulsive action—that is, *not* doing just what one wants to do at the moment—is the route to satisfying, pleasurable make-believe. Vygotsky stated,

Play continually creates demands on the child to act against immediate impulse. At every step the child is faced with a conflict between the rules of the game and what he would do if he could suddenly act spontaneously. In the game he acts counter to the way he wants to act. A child's greatest self-control occurs in play. He achieves the maximum display of willpower when he renounces an immediate attraction in the game (such as candy, which by the rules of the game he is forbidden to eat because it represents something inedible). Ordinarily the child experiences subordination to rules in the renunciation of something he wants, but here subordination to a rule and renunciation of action on immediate impulse are the means to maximum pleasure. ([1930–1935] 1978, 99)

In sum, according to Vygotsky, the essential feature of play is self-restraint—willingly following social rules. In play, subordinating momentary desires to a role in a make-believe scene and its rules becomes *"a new form of desire."* In this way, play creates a zone of proximal development through which the young child realizes many achievements that "will become her basic level of real action and morality" in the future ([1930–1935] 1978, 100). By enacting rules in make-believe, children come to better understand societal norms and expectations and strive to behave in ways that uphold them. For example, a child occupying the role of parent in a household scene starts to become dimly aware of parental responsibilities in real situations and gains insight into the parent–child relationship (Haight & Miller 1993).

When we look at the overall course of the development of play from early to middle childhood, the most obvious way in which it changes is that it increasingly emphasizes rules. According to Vygotsky, rules are brought to the forefront of the games that preoccupy school-age children, while the imaginative side of play recedes over time. Nevertheless, every game with rules, from board games to baseball, contains an imaginary situation in concealed form, and both components of play are retained throughout development. The greater stress on the rule-oriented side of play over time means that children gradually become more conscious of the goals of their play activities. During early childhood, the self-regulatory properties of play are exercised without the child even noticing that he or she is renouncing impulsive action in favor of rule-based behavior. In this way, play promotes the development of voluntary intentions—the formation of real-life plans and goals—quite effortlessly, making it, for Vygotsky, "the highest level of preschool development. The child moves forward essentially through play activity" ([1930–1935] 1978, 102–03).

Vygotsky summarized, "The development from games with an overt imaginary situation and covert rules to games with overt rules and a covert imaginary situation outlines the evolution of children's play" ([1930–1935] 1978, 96). From this perspective, the fantasy play of the preschool years is essential for further development of play in middle childhood—specifically, for movement toward game play, which provides additional instruction in setting goals, regulating one's own behavior in pursuit of those goals, and subordinating action to rules rather than impulse—in short, for becoming a cooperative and productive member of society. Play, in Vygotsky's theory, is the preeminent educational activity of early childhood.

Impact of imaginative play on development

In contrast to Piaget, who regarded play as the purest form of assimilation, a means through which children practice newly formed representational schemes, Vygotsky emphasized the development-enhancing, forward-moving consequences of pretense. Was Vygotsky correct that make-believe has a far-reaching impact on development, supporting the emergence and refinement of a wide variety of competencies? A close look at his theory reveals that the

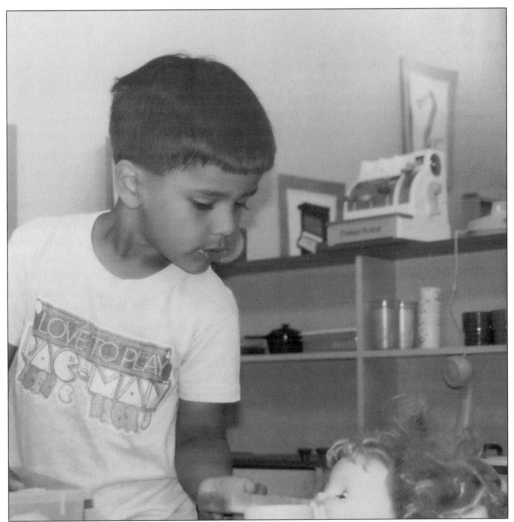

Play, in Vygotsky's theory, is the preeminent educational activity of early childhood.

benefits of play are seen as complex and indirect; they may take years to be realized (Nicolopoulou 1993). Still, there is considerable support for Vygotsky's view that play contributes to the development of a diverse array of higher mental functions.

General cognitive and social skills

Many studies indicate that play not only reflects but contributes to general cognitive and social development (Singer & Singer 1990). Sociodramatic play, the coordinated and reciprocal make-believe with peers that first appears around age 2½ and increases rapidly until age 4 to 5, has been studied most thoroughly. In contrast to social nonpretend activities (such as drawing or putting puzzles together), during social pretend, preschoolers' interactions last longer, show more involvement, draw larger numbers of children into the activity, and are more cooperative (Connolly, Doyle, & Reznick 1988). When we consider these findings from the standpoint of Vygotsky's emphasis on the social origins of higher mental functions, it is not surprising that preschoolers who spend more time at sociodramatic play are advanced in general intellectual development, show an enhanced ability to understand the feelings of others, and are seen as more socially competent by their teachers (Burns & Brainerd 1979; Connolly & Doyle 1984). Young children who especially enjoy pretending also score higher on tests of imagination and creativity. When play objects are used in novel ways, they encourage the discovery of new relationships and may enhance children's ability to think flexibly and inventively (Freyberg 1973; Dansky 1980; Pepler & Ross 1981; Saltz & Brodie 1982).

Memory

Additional evidence indicates that fantasy play strengthens children's memory. Recall for both list-like and narrative information is promoted by make-believe. For example, Newman (1990) instructed one group of 4- and 5-year-olds to play with a set of toys and another group simply to remember the toys. The play condition produced far better recall. Rather than just naming or touching the objects (strategies applied by preschoolers in the "remember" condition), children instructed to play engaged in many spontaneous organizations of the materials that enabled them to memorize effortlessly. These included functional use of substitute objects (pretending to eat the toy banana or putting shoes on the doll) and narrating their activities (as in "I'm squeezing this lemon" or "Fly away in this helicopter, doggie!"). When children embed an object in meaningful make-believe, they increase its memorableness. In this way, play may provide a vital foundation for more sophisticated memory strategies mastered throughout middle childhood that depend on establishing meaningful relationships among to-be-remembered information.

In another investigation addressing the role of thematic fantasy play in memory development, 5- and 6-year-olds' recall of an unfamiliar story was tested after exposure either to a pretend condition, in which they enacted themes of a story they had just heard, or to a control condition, in which storytelling was immediately followed by a return to regular classroom activities. Each week, for a period of six weeks, some children listened to the teacher read a story, selected roles and props, and then acted out the story. Other children gathered to hear a story and then returned to their usual lessons. Children who engaged in thematic fantasy play performed better when asked to recall a story they had not heard before (Silvern et al. 1986). Other research confirms that children's storytelling and story memory are promoted by opportunities to engage in fantasy play (Saltz & Johnson 1974; Saltz, Dixon, & Johnson 1977; Pellegrini & Galda 1982).

Language

Effective story recall requires elaborate facility with language, a capacity that is also enriched by play experiences. As Ervin-Tripp (1991) notes, young children engaged in play hear speech embedded in actions on objects that are talked about at the moment. This helps ensure that language is understandable because it is highly redundant with the immediate context. When new words and expressions arise in the course of a fantasy scene or game, children can guess their meaning easily from concrete cues in the situation.

Furthermore, as children engage in play talk, they often correct one another's errors, either directly or by demonstrating the acceptable way to speak. For example, in enacting a telephone conversation, one kindergartner said, "Hello, come to my house please." Her play partner quickly countered with appropriate telephone greeting behavior: "No, first you've got to say 'what are you doing?" (Ervin-Tripp 1991, 90). Vocabulary also extends during make-believe as children introduce new words they have heard during recent experiences. One 4-year-old playing nurse remarked to an agemate, "I'm going to give you a temperature." Although her first use of the term was not correct, active experimentation increases the chances that she will notice more about

the context in which 'temperature' is applied in the future and move toward correct usage. And as she brings new words to the play situation, they become available to others. Finally, the linguistic skills required to express different points of view, resolve disputes, and persuade peers to collaborate so play can continue are numerous. Play offers an arena in which all facets of conversational dialogue can be extended.

Reasoning

Make-believe also fosters young children's ability to reason about impossible or absurd situations—a finding highly consistent with Vygotsky's emphasis that play assists children in separating meanings from the objects for which they stand, thereby permitting the meanings themselves to be manipulated in flexible and innovative ways. A repeated finding in the cognitive development literature is that through much of middle childhood, children's thinking is tied to the here and now—to the concrete reality before them. But under certain conditions, a "theoretical" mode of reasoning is attained by young children. Dias and Harris (1988, 1990) explored 4- to 6-year-olds' capacity to follow logical propositions even when the context in which they are conveyed defies real-world knowledge. Consider the following syllogism:

All cats bark.

Rex is a cat.

Does Rex bark?

Dias and Harris had some children act out problems like this with toys that represented the content of each premise. A second group of children were told that the events were taking place on a pretend planet rather than Earth. A control group

Playing together helps children to acquire the many linguistic skills they need to express different points of view, resolve disputes, and persuade peers to collaborate so that play may continue.

of children merely listened and answered the question. Children in the two "play" conditions gave more theoretical than factual responses and were also able to justify their answers with theoretical ideas—for example, "In the story, cats bark, so we can pretend they bark."

The authors concluded that entering the *pretend mode* enables children to reason with contrary facts as if they were true—findings that provide striking verification of Vygotsky's assumption that under play conditions, the child is well "beyond his average age, above his daily behavior" ([1930–1935] 1978, 102). Treating verbal statements as a logical basis of deduction independent of their content is a capacity that does not emerge in the *reality-oriented mode* until adolescence.

The boundary between appearance and reality

Yet another way in which children's thinking is advanced in the pretend mode over the reality-oriented mode has to do with the distinction between appearance and reality. Many parents of preschoolers are familiar with calls like this from the bedroom after the lights have been turned out: "Mommy, Daddy, monsters are in my room again!" To rid the room of scary creatures, animal pictures may have to be removed from the walls and mobiles from the ceiling, and a search may have to be conducted inside the closet and under the bed.

Recent empirical evidence confirms that in certain situations, preschoolers are easily tricked by the outward appearance of things; they erroneously conclude that the way things look is the way they are. Flavell, Green, and Flavell (1987) presented children with appearance–reality problems in which objects were disguised in various ways. The children were asked what the items were, "really and truly." Preschoolers were easily tricked by sights and sounds. When asked whether a white piece of paper placed behind a blue filter is "really and truly blue" or whether a can that sounds like a baby crying when turned over is "really and truly a baby," they often responded "yes!" Not until age 6 to 7 did children do well on these tasks.

Yet in make-believe, children display object substitutions in which play symbols are substantially different from the things they represent. Often we hear children say such things as, "Pretend this ball is an apple" or "Let's use this block for a walkie-talkie." However, preschoolers do not conclude that these imaginary symbols are real. Indeed, children can tell the difference between pretend play and real experiences long before they answer many appearance–reality problems correctly (DiLalla & Watson 1988; Woolley & Wellman 1990). Make-believe play may be important in helping children master distinctions between appearance and reality in daily life because of the repeated experience it provides in transforming a wide variety of objects from real to pretend meaning and back again.

Imaginative inner speech

In addition to viewing fantasy play as instrumental for the development of nonplay skills, it can also be examined on its own terms—as imaginative activity that draws on and expresses salient aspects of the child's cognitive, emotional, and social lives (Nicolopoulou 1991). Indeed, the storylike narrative of fantasy play may foreshadow the playful stream of verbal commentary that characterizes our inner psychological experience and that seems to be as important for adapting to everyday existence as the logical thinking emphasized by Piaget.

In line with this interpretation, Vygotsky proposed that the impulse for fantasy and role enactment does not fade away by adolescence. Instead, he argued, the imaginative thinking of later years is an internalized, abbreviated form of the make-believe of early childhood that can be understood as "play without action" ([1930–1935] 1978, 93). Constraints imposed by society along with advances in cognition lead externalized, imaginative play to go underground. Gradually it is transformed into images and silent self-talk and eventually into "an elaborate stream of consciousness that meanders along with an inner 'voice over,' [remarking] wrily on new experiences, reflecting on the past, and predicting the future during wakefulness and sleep" (Singer & Singer 1990, 232–33). By introducing fantasy elements into consciousness, this inventive, private commentary probably helps us cope with the mundane, repetitive aspects of our daily lives by opening new horizons that extend beyond actual possibilities. Few would deny that this playful form of thought is a ubiquitous and necessary feature of human experience. It may also be the basis of the creative mental combinations displayed by adult artists and scientists. Vygotsky ([1930] 1990) speculated that creative imagination has its roots in the pretend scenarios and object substitutions of early childhood (Smolucha 1992a).

In sum, fantasy play contributes to social maturity and to the construction of diverse aspects of cognition—to overall intellectual performance, the generation of creative ideas, memory for diverse forms of information, language competence, the capacity to reason theoretically, the differentiation of appearance and reality, and the playful stream of verbal narrative that comments on and assists us in coping with our daily lives. For those who have questioned whether play activities, so indigenous and absorbing to children, must be curbed in favor of more "productive" activity or whether they constitute a powerful zone of proximal development, the findings just reviewed clearly grant play a legitimate and fruitful place in children's lives.

Scaffolding children's play

The Piagetian view of symbolic play, dominant for the past three decades, claims that make-believe emerges spontaneously when children become capable of representational thought. Much like the way in which Piaget interpreted egocentric speech (see Chapter 2), he and his followers assumed that very young children lack the cognitive competencies to share play symbols with others—either adults or peers—until well into the preschool period. Consider, for example, the following statement by a leading researcher summing up the literature on play prior to the early 1980s: "It is unlikely that parents play pretend games with their young children or model such games" (Fein 1981, 1106).

Because the Piagetian perspective has been so widely accepted, not until recently have investigators seriously ad-

dressed the social context of children's play experiences. Their findings challenge the notion that fantasy play is an unprompted phenomenon, arising solely from tendencies within the child. Instead, new evidence suggests that make-believe, like other higher mental functions, is the product of social collaboration. More expert members of the culture *scaffold* children's pretending, facilitating its early emergence and elaboration. Once pretend capacities are in place, children quickly establish shared playful understandings with one another, jointly creating imaginative scenes with rules that guide their activity in pairs and small groups. These scenes serve as microcosms of cooperative activity, mirroring social relations and productive, goal-oriented activity within the larger society.

Adult–child play

(Twenty-four-month-old Elizabeth is being carried upstairs for a diaper change by her mother.)

Elizabeth: My going Sherman Dairy. *(Sherman Dairy is the family's favorite dessert restaurant.)*

Mother: You're going to Sherman Dairy?

Elizabeth: Yeah.

Mother: Is Andrew the cook? *(Andrew is a 4-year-old friend who is playing with Elizabeth's sister.)*

Elizabeth: Yep. *(Pause) My* cook.

Mother: *(Putting Elizabeth on the changing table and beginning to change her)* You're the cook? You can cook with your dishes, right? Do you have some pots and pans?

Elizabeth: Yep.

(Adapted from Haight & Miller 1993, 46)

In the play sequence just described, 2-year-old Elizabeth initiates a make-believe scenario in which a trip upstairs for a diaper change is transformed into a journey to buy ice cream. In response to Elizabeth's make-believe initiative, her mother encourages her to expand the imaginative theme and act it out with toys. The play episode is elaborated and sustained as her mother asks questions that help Elizabeth clarify her intentions and think of new ideas.

Vygotsky-based research on play emphasizes that make-believe is, from its beginnings, a social activity (El'konin 1966; Garvey 1990; Smolucha 1992a; Haight & Miller 1993). In Western industrialized societies, play first appears between caregivers and children; pretense and games are initially learned under the supportive guidance of experts. From these interactions, children appropriate the communicative conventions, social skills, and representational capacities that permit them to carry out make-believe on their own.

Studies documenting caregiver support and shaping of play during infancy are plentiful. For example, around the middle of the first year, turn-taking games, such as pat-a-cake and peekaboo, appear. At first, the parent starts the game and acts out both roles, and the infant is an amused observer. By 12 months, the infant becomes an active participant, exchanging roles with the parent. As she does so, she practices the turn-taking pattern of human conversation and begins to internalize the dialogic structure of play interactions (Ratner & Bruner 1978; Sachs 1980; Trevarthen 1989). In addition to playing turn-taking games, both mothers and fathers engage in physical play with babies during the first two years, but fathers do so more often. Beyond age 2, only fathers play highly charged bouncing, lifting, and wrestling games with children—typically with their sons (McDonald & Parke 1986). Research suggests that through such play, children

begin to learn to regulate emotional arousal and "read" the emotions of others in ways that facilitate play with peers in early childhood (Carson, Burks, & Parke 1993). Thus, infant–caregiver play contributes importantly to early communicative, emotional, and social skills that make later representational play with others possible.

More recent literature reveals that caregiver scaffolding of play extends beyond infancy to the make-believe activity of young children. Haight and Miller (1993) have conducted the most extensive of these investigations. Their research was sparked by the observation that pretense requires a specialized set of communicative conventions. For example, players must agree on role assignments ("How 'bout you be the teacher, and I'll be the student") and transformations of objects and locations ("Hey, we can use the block corner to make a classroom"), and they must also inform one another about shifts in scenes ("Let's pretend it's time to go home now") (Garvey & Kramer 1989). In view of the conventionalized nature of pretend talk, Haight and Miller speculated that the skills that contribute to effective make-believe must be learned through interaction with more experienced partners.

To find out, the researchers traced the development of pretend play at home in nine children growing up in middle-class American families, following them longitudinally from 1 to 4 years of age. Their findings contradicted the Piagetian view that pretense is individually generated and only later becomes social. Instead, make-believe was predominantly social across the entire age span, consuming from 68 to 75% of children's total pretend time. Furthermore, mothers were the children's principal play partners until 3 years of age. By age 4, the children

> *When the important adults in the child's life establish a climate for make-believe, encouraging and accepting the child's imaginings with enthusiasm and respect, they foster creativity.*

played about equally with mothers and other children (siblings and peers). Overall, mother–child pretend declined with age, whereas child–child play increased.

Pretending with mothers, however, was not caused by lack of child playmates at the youngest ages. Of those children who had fairly continuous access to other children, 0 of 4 pretended with those children at 12 months, 2 of 4 at 24 months, 3 of 4 at 36 months, and 4 of 4 at 48 months. Similarly, Dunn and Dale (1984) observed a group of 2-year-olds, all of whom had siblings, and reported that although the children played with both their mother and their sibling, at this young age they preferred their mother. These findings, as well as others, support the notion that caregivers prompt pretense initially (Miller & Garvey 1984). And they confirm the Vygotskian view that play with caregivers gradually gives way to play with peers as children's competence increases.

Further evidence that caregivers teach their toddlers to pretend stems from Haight and Miller's (1993) observation that at 12 months, make-believe was fairly one-sided; almost all play episodes were initiated by mothers. From age 2 on, when pretending was better established, mothers and children displayed mutual interest in getting make-believe started; half of pretend episodes were initiated by each, a finding confirmed by other investigators (Dunn &

Wooding 1977). At all ages, mothers typically followed the child's lead and elaborated on the child's contribution. In response, children continued to seek out their mothers as play partners even after they had become competent at play with other children. Thus, although pretending was first introduced to 12-month-olds by their mothers, it quickly became a joint activity in which both partners participated actively in an imaginative dialogue and in which mothers gradually released responsibility to children for creating and guiding the fantasy theme.

Additional research extends Haight and Miller's (1993) findings. Building on work by Vygotsky's colleague El'konin (1966, 1978), Smolucha (1992a, 1992b) reported that children's object substitutions during make-believe are traceable to episodes in which their mothers showed them how to engage in object renaming or suggested a pretend action to the child. Although spontaneous object substitutions do occur as early as 12 months, the majority of very young children's pretending with objects is initiated by their mothers (Smolucha 1991). By age 2, mothers talk more about nonexistent fantasy objects, a change that may prompt children to widen the range of object substitutions in their play (Kavanaugh, Whittington, & Cerbone 1983). Furthermore, many parents in industrialized societies surround their children with toys designed to stimulate pretend themes— miniature cars, dolls, pretend people, and animal figures, to name just a few. By offering an array of objects specialized for make-believe, caregivers communicate to children that pretense is a valued activity and maximize opportunities to collaborate with them by integrating play props into fantasy scenes (Sutton-Smith 1986; Haight & Miller 1993).

As we saw earlier in this chapter, object substitutions are an aspect of pretense that provides an essential foundation for abstract and imaginative thought, and Smolucha demonstrates that they originate in early childrearing contexts that foster play. In line with this idea, Singer and Singer (1990) argue that for creativity to develop at its best, important people in the child's life must establish a climate for make-believe, encouraging and accepting the child's imaginings with enthusiasm and respect. These researchers examined the life histories of famous writers, artists, and scientists and discovered that in many instances, a significant individual—a parent, an older sibling, an extended-family relative, or a teacher—promoted imaginative experimentation by telling fantastic stories, initiating joint pretend, or offering gifts (such as books and puppets) that inspired make-believe.

For example, in his autobiography, the Russian author Vladimir Nabokov described his mother bringing out jewelry for his amusement at bedtime, an experience that inspired the images of "mystery and enchantment" and glorious celebrations that later appeared in his novels (Singer & Singer 1990). Edith Wharton recalled a friend of her father's who, after dining with the family on Sunday, would take her on his knee and recount marvelous tales of mythology. She regarded these storytelling episodes as critical in her development as a writer of fiction. Charlotte Bronte remarked on a gift of toy soldiers to her brother. Together with her three older siblings (two of whom also became writers), she transformed the tiny men into make-believe authors and publishers and invented games in which enchanted islands were populated with fanciful creatures. According to Singer and Singer, this "sense of wonder," woven out of socially guided play in childhood,

is found not only in the autobiographies and biographies of famous writers, artists, and scientists but also in the recollections of those ordinary people who are creative and imaginative—or who could be if they would get in touch with their earliest [experiences] of play. (1990, 1)

Consequences of supportive adult–child play

In their longitudinal study, Haight and Miller (1993) carefully examined the play themes of mother–child pretending and found that it seemed to serve a variety of everyday functions—communicating feelings, expressing and working through conflicts, enlivening daily routines, teaching lessons, and influencing the behavior of play partners. These diverse social uses of caregiver–child play are illustrated in Table 3.1. Haight and Miller suggest that adult support and expansion of preschoolers' make-believe should facilitate all of the developmental outcomes discussed earlier in this chapter, although, as yet, no systematic research on the topic exists.

Accumulating evidence *does* show that make-believe with mothers is more sustained and involves more fantasy transformations than does solitary make-believe. In line with Vygotsky's zone of proximal development, very young children, for whom make-believe is just emerging, act more competently than they otherwise would when engaged in play with a mature partner. In several recent studies, researchers compared 1- to 3-year-olds' solitary pretend with their make-believe while interacting with their mothers. In each investigation, children engaged in more than twice as much make-believe when mothers were involved. In addition, caregiver support led early make-believe to move toward a more advanced level (Dunn & Wooding 1977; O'Connell & Bretherton 1984; Zukow 1986; Slade 1987; Fiese 1990; Tamis-LeMonda & Bornstein 1991; Haight & Miller 1993; O'Reilly & Bornstein 1993). For example, when mothers actively took part, children were more likely to combine representational schemes into more complex sequences—for example, as part of putting teddy bear to sleep, they would brush his teeth, tuck him into bed, sing him a lullaby, and kiss him good night. Play themes were also more varied and diverse during mother–child sequences, and maternal verbal commentary was especially effective in raising both the duration and the level of play. In Haight and Miller's study, suggestive evidence emerged that mother–child play does, in fact, promote child–child play. One-year-old children whose mothers engaged in a great deal of pretending ranked high in peer play at 4 years. And children of the most enthusiastic and imaginative parents were among the most highly skilled preschool pretenders.

Critical features of adult–child play

Although parent–child play has been granted considerable research attention, a search of the literature did not turn up a single study addressing adults' participation in children's play in preschool and child care. Although teachers have always engaged in pretense to some extent, exactly how often and in what ways they join in young children's make-believe are not yet known. Nevertheless, evidence on the social origins and facilitating impact of adult–child play

Table 3.1.
Function
Communicating feelings
Arguing
Enlivening daily routines
Teaching
Managing others
Having fun

Adapted and paraphrased from W.L. Haight & P.J. Miller, *Pretending at Home: Early Development in a Sociocultural Context* (Albany, NY: State University of New York Press, 1993), 73–80. (Used by permission of the publisher)

Everyday Functions of Caregiver–Child Make-Believe Play

Description	Example
Some caregivers and children use pretending to communicate about emotionally charged topics, for regulation of affect.	Four-year-old Joe often moved into make-believe with his mother to express complex feelings about his baby brother. In one instance, he climbed onto a wardrobe in the basement and taunted his mother by reaching toward a hot pipe, much like his brother would do. Feigning severity, Joe's mother restrained his arm and warned, "Don't! You'll get burned!" Then she lifted him down as he pretended to scream like a baby.
Occasionally, joint make-believe incorporates serious caregiver–child conflicts and serves as a means to defuse them.	Three-year-old Nancy and her mother engaged in real conflicts without abandoning the pretend frame. One had to do with the efforts of Nancy's mother to get her to give up her pacifier. As each spoke through a hand puppet, Nancy announced, "I want a pacifier." Her mother's puppet responded, "Little girl, you just have a red dot on your face for a mouth, I don't think you can fit a pacifier in your mouth."
Caregivers and children sometimes collaborate in make-believe to relieve the mundane quality of daily routines.	While 2-year-old Molly sat on the floor of her bedroom folding socks with her mother, she put a pair together, held it up, and exclaimed, "Mommy, look what I made. I made us something to eat."
Caregiver–child pretend may serve as a vehicle for teaching nonplay lessons.	Michael's mother used pretend to encourage him to use the toilet. Reluctant at first, he became an eager learner when put in charge of toilet training his baby bear.
Joint make-believe often functions strategically in pursuit of interactional goals.	Molly, at 2½ years, hesitated as she stood at the top of a slide and appealed to her mother for help. After her mother encouraged her to slide down and she refused, Molly stepped into the pretend mode: " A shark come . . . . There's a shark come . . . . There's a shark in the sand." Molly's mother helped her down.
Most of the time, adults and children engage in imaginative play just for fun.	Justin regularly visited a playground, where his mother often joined his pretending, occasionally assuming the role of monster. Laughing as she ran after him, Justin's mother said, "Here comes the monster!" Justin squealed with delight. After a chase, his mother continued, "Ahhhhhh! Now the monster's got you!" while she grabbed and kissed him.

suggests that it is vital for adults in early childhood settings to engage in joint play with children. Indeed, given the increasing numbers of infants and pre-schoolers whose mothers are employed, caregivers need to supplement the parental "play function" in the young child's life, just as they help fulfill a wide variety of other childrearing roles.

Effective playful involvement with children, however, requires early childhood environments that are developmentally appropriate. Especially important are generous adult–child ratios, a stable staff that relates to children sensitively and responsively, and settings richly equipped to offer varied opportunities for make-believe (National Association for the Education of Young Children 1991). These factors are critical because they ensure that caregivers have the necessary time, rapport, and props to stimulate and build on children's imaginative contributions and scaffold them in the direction of more complex, social pretend with peers.

At the same time, adults walk a fine line in making effective contributions to children's pretense. The power of adult–child play to foster development is undermined when teachers communicate in ways that are too intrusive, overpowering, or one-sided. In a book on play written for parents more than two decades ago, Brian Sutton-Smith (1974) anticipated Vygotsky's influential statement that "[i]n play, the child always behaves beyond his average age, above his daily behavior; in play it is as though he were a head taller than himself" (Vygotsky [1930–1935] 1978, 102). Sutton-Smith explained that make-believe permits children who are still acquiring language to represent their everyday lives and inner thoughts and feelings more completely than is possible through any other symbolic medium.

Refer again to the examples in Table 3.1, and note how difficult it would be for children to construct such well-articulated statements in words alone or in their drawings. Pretense seems to be far ahead of other forms of representation. Consequently, adults do not need to use didactic means to promote it, as they sometimes do when helping preschoolers master puzzles or other cognitive tasks. Instead, adult participation is most helpful when it responds to, guides, and elaborates on the child's behavior with demonstrations and suggestions.

In support of the idea that interactional reciprocity is best suited to stimulating the development of make-believe, Fiese (1990) found that maternal intrusiveness (initiating a new activity unrelated to the child's current pattern of play), questioning, and instructing led to immature, simple exploratory play in 15- to 24-month-olds. In contrast, turn taking and joint involvement in a shared activity were far more likely to result in high levels of pretense. In play, adults need to set clear limits on their own degree of control over the make-believe situation.

Furthermore, a study by O'Connell and Bretherton (1984) indicates that adult intervention that coincides with aspects of play the child is in the process of acquiring at the moment is most effective in engaging children. Observing 20- and 28-month-olds engaged in joint play with their mothers, the researchers reported that younger children were more likely to follow maternal suggestions to explore the environment or arrange and combine toys. Although 20-month-olds sometimes made use of prompts for symbolic play, 28-month-olds did so much more often. In a similar vein, Lucariello (1987) found that when 24- to 29-month-olds were famil-

By offering an array of objects specialized for make-believe, caregivers communicate that pretense is a valued activity and maximize opportunities to collaborate with the children in integrating play props into fantasy scenes.

iar with a play theme suggested by their mother, both partners displayed advanced levels of imaginative activity and constructed the scenario together. When the theme was unfamiliar, the mother took nearly total responsibility for pretense. Consistent with Vygotsky's concept of the zone of proximal development, these findings remind us that adult guidance that recognizes children's current level of competence, communicating in ways that build on it, is most effective. As O'Connell and Bretherton note, "Children must have reached some state of readiness in order to incorporate any new, socially constructed knowledge" (1984, 362).

When children grow up in households that are economically stressed, pretend play is substantially reduced, at least in the preschools in which such children have been observed (Garvey 1990). Nevertheless, low-income and poverty-stricken children vary considerably in their fantasy engagement. Freyberg (1973) interviewed parents of six children, three of whom showed a high level of pretense and three of whom showed a low level. Her findings suggested that the difference had social origins—specifically, in parental support, raising the question of whether make-believe should be directly taught to preschoolers who rarely engage in it. Many experts say yes, provided the teaching is responsive to children's interests and current cognitive capacities. Research shows that tutoring economically disadvantaged preschoolers in pretense enhances their competence, both in play and in a wide variety of school-related activities (Rubin, Fein, & Vandenberg 1983). The evidence is consistent enough to justify sociodramatic training as an important part of the curriculum in all preschools and primary-grade classrooms.

In one of the most extensive projects aimed at promoting play among disadvantaged children, Phyllis Levenstein intervened indirectly, by teaching parents to play with their preschoolers. She confirmed that parental playfulness rather than directiveness predicted children's later cognitive and social maturity. In addition, Levenstein found that teaching and learning during caregiver–child play appears to be most effective when it is embedded in a warm, affectionate relationship—one that creates "a non-didactic climate of light spontaneity and fun" (Levenstein & O'Hara 1993, 243).

In sum, when early childhood environments are developmentally appropriate, they are likely to encourage critical features of adult–child make-believe that advance both play and nonplay competencies. A developmentally appropriate environment includes consistently available staff members who model and suggest play themes within the child's range of understanding, who react to children's play initiatives with acceptance and enthusiasm, and who offer ideas that help children extend their imaginative creations.

Social pretend play with peers

At nursery school, 4-year-old Jason joins a group of children in the block area for a space shuttle launch. "That can be our control tower," he suggests to Vance, pointing to a corner by a bookshelf.

"Wait, I gotta get it all ready," states Lynette, who is still arranging the astronauts (two dolls and a teddy bear) inside a circle of large blocks, which represents the rocket.

"Countdown!" Jason announces, speaking into a small wooden block, his pretend walkie-talkie.

Joint Adult–Child Make-Believe Should Take Its Cues from the Child

For adult–child play to be most effective in capturing children's interest and fostering development, teachers and caregivers need to be responsive to the child's contributions and build on them. The following excerpts of joint make-believe recorded in a high-quality child care center accredited by the National Academy of Early Childhood Programs serve as examples. A richly equipped physical setting, small group sizes, ready availability of adults, a daily program in which children select many of their own activities, and well-trained teachers provide the sociocultural context for verbally stimulating but nondirective adult interaction that scaffolds children's play and, in turn, many aspects of their psychological development.

*   *   *

Three-year-old Kathy wanders over to the rug where Mrs. N. is seated, reading a story to Casey and Tangie. Nearby in a box lies a doll covered by a small blanket.

"Can I take this?" asks Kathy, pointing to the doll.

"Sure," responds Mrs. N. "I think the baby is ready to get up and listen to the story."

Kathy picks up the doll, moves in closer to Mrs. N., and responds, "I think the baby's hungry." She pretends to put food in the baby's mouth.

Tangie joins in, "Kathy is feeding Georgie."

Mrs. N. confirms and elaborates, "Yes, Kathy is feeding Georgie. The baby needs to be fed before we go home." Then she asks Kathy, "What's the baby's name? Do you remember what we named her?"

"Georgie," answers Kathy. Then Kathy makes some squeaking sounds as she moves the doll's head. "She wants to hear it," says Kathy, interpreting the sounds for Mrs. N.

Mrs. N responds, "Oh, you mean her nursery rhyme?"

"Yes!" the children chorus. With Mrs. N, they begin to chant, "Georgie, Porgie, Puddin' and Pie" while Kathy makes Georgie dance to the rhythm.

*   *   *

Four-year-old Towanda is seated in a small wagon that Diane is pulling around the room.

"Stop the bus!" shouts Towanda, who jumps out, puts on her hat, and goes over to the housekeeping corner, where Mrs. B is seated.

Mrs. B. says, "Hi, Towanda. Where have you been? Where did you go in the bus?"

Towanda answers, "I've been for a ride."

Mrs. B responds inquisitively, "You went for a ride?"

Towanda explains, "I went to the store."

"Well, what did you buy at the store?" Mrs. B encourages.

Towanda whispers.

"Oh, Christmas candy!" exclaims Mrs. B. "Where is this Christmas candy?"

"I left it on the bus," replies Towanda.

"When the bus driver comes back, maybe you can get it," says Mrs. B. Then Mrs. B invites Towanda to join the activity in the housekeeping corner by saying, "Would you like to cook dinner now? What are we going to have for dinner?"

Towanda answers, "Some food and some popcorn."

"Popcorn for dinner? Oh, I'm very hungry, Towanda. I need more than popcorn."

"Okay, how 'bout some pork chops and some beans and some applesauce," offers Towanda.

Mrs. B exclaims, "Sounds yummy!"

Towanda goes over to the stove, where Hal and Kristie are playing with the pots and pans. The children begin to talk about cooking dinner.

L. Berk, personal observation, 1990.

Intervening to Promote Adult–Child Play

Phyllis Levenstein's Mother–Child Home Program (MCHP) is a preventive educational and mental health program for poverty-stricken preschoolers at risk for developmental difficulties. Conceived in 1965 during the time period in which early intervention first became a national policy in the United States, the MCHP received its inspiration from two sources. First, it drew from the complementary theories of Lev Vygotsky ([1934] 1962) in Russia and Jerome Bruner (1964, 1984; Bruner, Olver, & Greenfield 1966) in the United States, both of whom stressed the importance of verbal interaction and negotiation of shared meaning between mothers and young children for optimum cognitive development. Second, the work of American psychologist Robert White served as a major impetus for the program. According to White's (1959) theory of effectance motivation, competence is achieved through children's sense of being able to master the environment (effectance) and their joy at this mastery (efficacy). Combining these ideas, Levenstein and her co-workers argued that a warm, involved, verbally rich parent–child relationship is best suited to promote such mastery and that this relationship is best realized in the context of play.

The MCHP involved twice-weekly half-hour home sessions with the mother and child for two years prior to school entry. Gifts of play materials (toys and books) selected to be intrinsically motivating to the parent–child pair were brought to the home by a visitor called the "toy demonstrator," who modeled verbal interaction techniques for the mother. The adult–child dialogue, however, was designed to be nondidactic. Toy demonstrators discouraged mothers from bombarding children with a large quantity of information. Instead, mothers were encouraged to have fun while interacting with their child.

Follow-ups of the children's development revealed that the MCHP succeeded in its goals. In comparison to controls, participating children displayed short-term gains in IQ and lasting gains in academic achievement, meeting the national norms in first through eighth grade (Levenstein 1988; Levenstein & O'Hara 1993). A close look at maternal interaction behaviors lent insight into the reasons for the program's success. A subsample of program and control mothers were asked to go twice to a laboratory, where 10 minutes of their play with their children at age 3½ and two years later at 5½ was videotaped. Over the two-year period, the children's development was also followed. Program mothers scored markedly higher than did the controls in stimulating verbal behavior—a difference that persisted after their children entered kindergarten and were no longer participants in the MCHP. Furthermore, the maternal behaviors that best predicted intellectual, academic, and social competence were responsiveness to the child's verbalizations, warmth (expressed in smiles and other affectionate gestures), and stimulation of creative thinking. In contrast, maternal information-giving behaviors in the context of play were negatively related to school-related cognitive and social skills.

In line with Vygotsky's theory, Levenstein concluded that responding to children with lighthearted, pleasurable conversation that promotes involvement and imaginative thinking during play is especially well suited for fostering the effectance motivation and self-regulatory capacities necessary for success in school (Levenstein & O'Hara 1993). In contrast, presenting a relentless barrage of information that communicates "at" rather than "with" children fails to involve them in the play dialogue and interferes with optimal development.

"Five, six, two, four, one, blastoff!" responds Vance, commander of the control tower.

Lynette makes one of the dolls push a pretend button and reports, "Brrrm, brrrm, they're going up!" (Berk 1993, 311)

Among children who have regular opportunities to associate with agemates, sociodramatic play—or make-believe with peers—is under way by age 2½, and it quickly blossoms over the preschool years. As the preceding excerpt reveals, by age 4, children can create and coordinate several roles in an elaborate plot, and they display a sophisticated understanding of role relationships and story lines.

Pretending with peers makes use of the diverse competencies children develop in playing and conversing with adults. Yet it, too, must be responsive, harmonious, and cooperative to result in satisfying play experiences and to contribute to children's development. According to Göncü (1993), social play with peers requires *intersubjectivity*—the process whereby individuals involved in the same activity arrive at a shared understanding. In Chapter 2 we noted that intersubjectivity is essential for adult scaffolding of children because it creates a common ground for communication as each partner adjusts to the perspective of the other. Intersubjectivity is also necessary for sociodramatic play to be sustained and for it to serve as a zone of proximal development in which children advance their skills and understanding (Corsaro 1983). In the play episode just described, the three children display a high level of intersubjectivity as they jointly construct a complex scenario and respond in a smooth, complementary fashion to each other's contributions.

The importance of intersubjectivity for peer social play is suggested by the work of many play theorists. Piaget noted that for children to play together, they must collectively construct play symbols ([1945] 1951). Likewise, Vygotsky claimed that in pretense with peers, children jointly develop rules that guide social activity ([1930–1935] 1978). And Parten labeled the most advanced form of peer social participation *cooperative play*, in which children orient toward a common goal through negotiation of plans, roles, and division of labor (1932).

Recent evidence indicates that intersubjectivity among peer partners increases substantially over the preschool years, as the amount of time children devote to sociodramatic play increases (Rubin, Fein, & Vandenberg 1983). Göncü (1993) observed the play dialogues of 3- to 4½-year-olds, noting the occurrence of the following four broad categories of acts, of which two reflect an intersubjective state and the other two indicate lack of intersubjectivity:

1. *Expanding play interaction:* introducing new elements into the play interaction, such as toys, themes, and talk about the nature of play (e.g., asking the partner what he or she wants to do); adding new information to the partner's ideas; and adding information to one's own previously expressed ideas to contribute to the shared play activity (build-ons).

2. *Expressing agreement:* directly expressing agreement with the partner's ideas by accepting the partner's statements, revising the partner's ideas, and trying to resolve differences of opinion.

3. *Emphasizing one's own ideas:* engaging in egocentric repetitions of one's own interests; failing to take into account the partner's viewpoint.

4. *Irrelevant acts:* expressing disinterest in the partner's idea or failure to understand it.

With age, children showed a greater degree of shared understanding during play. Older preschoolers used more extensions, build-ons, and affirmations of a partner's play messages to maintain interaction. Furthermore, with age, children more often responded to expansions with extensions, introductions, or acceptances rather than with disagreements, repetition of their own interests, and irrelevant acts. Indeed, by age 4½, children were considerably less likely to emphasize their own opinions and much more likely to elaborate on the ideas of their partners. Göncü concluded that the "ability to take into account another's viewpoint reflects itself in, and is probably promoted by, the growing tendency to engage in dialogue with peers" (1993, 113).

When we look at these features of child–child play, we see even more clearly that warm, responsive caregiver interaction is important in encouraging such play. Yet even after sociodramatic play is well under way and adults have started to reduce their play involvement, teachers and caregivers need to guide children toward effective relations with agemates. Interestingly, observational evidence indicates that teachers rarely mediate peer interaction except when intense disagreements arise that threaten classroom order or children's safety (Neuman & Roskos 1991; Howes & Clemente 1994). In instances in which adults do step in, they do not always tailor their intervention to children's current capacities or use techniques that help children regulate their own social behavior. For example, when peer conflicts occur in preschool, teachers almost always use directive strategies, in which they tell

---

Table 3.2. **Three Questions to Help Teachers Decide How Much Guidance to Offer Children During Play with Peers**

Question	Goal
1. What have I seen this child do before in situations simular to this one?	Focus on the developing skills of individual children.
2. How much, or little, of my help is required for the child to be "successful" in meeting his or her goals in this situation, as well as the goals I have for the classroom?	Think in terms of what level of support is necessary, without taking away from children responsibility that they are capable of assuming.
3. How can I keep children focused on each other rather than on me?	Intervene soon enough to prevent escalation of peer difficulties, thereby avoiding high levels of intrusion by the teacher.

From N. File, "The Teacher as Guide of Children's Competence with Peers," *Child and Youth Care Forum* 22 (1993): 357–58. (Used by permission of the publisher)

children what to do or say ("Ask Daniel if you can have the fire truck next") or solve the problem for them ("Jessica was playing with that toy first, so you can have a turn after her") (File 1993, 352). Less-directive approaches—for example, asking questions that prompt children to come up with solutions—occurred infrequently. Furthermore, the strategies teachers used were not related to children's age or the maturity of their social play. Teachers rarely fostered social competence by providing assistance within the child's zone of proximal development, gradually shifting responsibility for mature social behavior to the child.

File recommends a Vygotskian approach to facilitating peer relations, in which teachers acquire detailed knowledge of individual children's social skills—the type of information they typically gather only for the cognitive domain. When intervening, teachers must use a range of teaching strategies, since (as with cognitive development) the support that is appropriate for scaffolding social development varies from child to child and changes over time. At times the adult might model a skill or give the child examples of strategies (e.g., "You could tell Paul, 'I want a turn'"). At other times she might ask the child to engage in problem solving ("What could you do if you want a turn?") (1993, 356). In each instance the teacher selects the level of support that best matches the child's abilities and momentary needs and then pulls back as the child acquires new social skills within his zone of proximal development. File suggests that teachers consider three questions, listed in Table 3.2, that can help them decide on the most effective communication in each situation.

Many teachers hesitate to intercede in children's play with peers, perhaps because the teachers fear being too intrusive or believe (erroneously) that children pick up social skills on their own. When adults do intervene, children's behavior may have become so extreme that the adult's first impulse is to be directive and forceful. However, a Vygotsky-based teaching framework applied to the social arena regards the adult as an active agent in the child's social development, providing individualized guidance that grants each child as much responsibility for negotiating interactions with peers as he or she is capable of handling at the moment.

In contrast to their behavior during play interactions, preschoolers have greater difficulty establishing a cooperative, shared framework in "closed-end" problem solving, in which they must orient toward a single correct solution to a task (Tudge & Rogoff 1987). Here, again, is an example of how children's social competence is more advanced in play than in other contexts. The social skills mastered during sociodramatic activities gradually generalize to peer interactions in nonplay activities (Vygotsky [1930–1935] 1978).

The "physical" side of the social context of play

Adults affect children's play not just through their influence on social interaction but also through their arrangement of the play environment. The physical context of play is important because it can shape and direct the opportunities children have to interact with peers, as well as the play themes that they select, providing mediating frameworks from the surrounding culture. Pretending clearly emerges within and is influenced by particular physical ecologies, as the following examples reveal.

Consider an investigation in which two researchers, in collaboration with a teacher, changed the physical arrange-

The physical context of make-believe play shapes and directs the opportunities that children have to interact with peers, as well as the play themes that they select.

ment of preschool activity centers and observed the impact of this change on children's selection of play spaces and props and their peer interaction. Kinsman and Berk (1979) were interested in factors that cause preschoolers' behavior to conform to gender stereotypes of their culture at an early age. At the same time, a preschool teacher wondered how to arrange her classroom to enhance the social and play experiences of 4- and 5-year-olds. Together, the researchers and the teacher selected two activity centers—the housekeeping and block areas—for special interest, since these centers united their respective interests. A plan was devised in which children were observed for a three-week period under usual conditions, in which the

two centers, located next to each other, were separated by a high wall of shelves. Then the shelves were removed, and changes in children's use of each area and the quality of their play were noted.

Findings revealed that boys and girls did not differ in time spent in the two settings, either before or after the shelves were removed. In fact, under each condition, children of both sexes preferred the block area. But changes in aspects of their play were dramatic. Before the shelves were removed, play was highly gender stereotyped. Children largely interacted with same-sex peers, a pattern that was particularly pronounced for boys in blocks and for girls in housekeeping. In addition, when boys entered the housekeeping area, they generally did not use its play materials. Instead, they tended to play in ways that were irrelevant to the basic purpose of the setting, such as by acting out themes of King Kong or Batman.

Behavior after the divider was removed was strikingly different. Instead of playing primarily with same-sex peers, boys and girls frequently played together. And girls, especially, engaged in more complex play, integrating materials from both settings into their fantasy themes. Finally, negative interactions between children declined after the divider was removed, perhaps because the more open play space reduced crowding and competition for materials. Kinsman and Berk's study highlights how play spaces reflect as well as inculcate attitudes and values of the surrounding culture—often in ways of which teachers are not consciously aware.

Adults also influence children's everyday pretending through the play props they provide. Some evidence suggests that less-realistic objects promote more inventiveness in play. In one study, McLoyd, Warren, and Thomas (1984) brought together small groups of preschoolers for two play sessions—one with highly realistic toys (trucks, dolls, and tea sets) and the other with materials that had unclear functions (pipe cleaners, cardboard cylinders, and paper bags). Children used the specific toys to act out familiar roles, such as mother, doctor, and baby. In contrast, the nonspecific materials encouraged fantastic role play, such as pirate and creature from outer space. Fantastic roles, in turn, led to more complex social interaction, especially planning statements, as in "I'll be the pirate and you be the prisoner" or "Watch out! Now I'm going to jump ship!" Since fantastic make-believe does not follow

Children's make-believe play thrives when a variety of substitute objects—some realistic and some nonrealistic—are available.

familiar everyday scripts, children devoted more time to planning each episode and explaining to peer companions what they were doing.

McLoyd, Warren, and Thomas's findings suggest that teachers make sure that a variety of substitute objects—some realistic and some nonrealistic—are available to children. Realistic toys prompt children's exploration of their everyday social world, the role possibilities offered by their society, and the myths that are an integral part of popular culture (superheroes, Jurassic Park creatures, and Ninja Turtles). Nonrealistic toys seem to trigger less-standard as well as other-worldly themes. Still, throughout the preschool years children prefer replica objects when engaged in make-believe (McLoyd 1983; Haight & Miller 1993). At first, this seems to be because very young preschoolers need to use realistic pivots to pretend; later, it may result from the fact that realistic toys provide touchstones of ready contact with peers, who are familiar with the everyday roles and cultural myths they represent.

Finally, when a limited assortment of play objects is available, adults can encourage a flexible relationship between toys and children's play themes by demonstrating and suggesting new play possibilities. Once a play scenario is under way, object and setting substitutions can bend to the requirements of the plan, as well as redirect the story line. In one such instance, a pair of children out to destroy a monster beamed a toy flashlight at the invisible creature (which paralyzed him), put him in the oven in the housekeeping corner, and pronounced themselves heroes of the day!

Play in broader sociocultural context

Vygotsky-influenced research on Western middle-class children indicates that caregivers scaffold young children's emerging pretense by arranging play situations, providing props, and suggesting and modeling make-believe themes. Older siblings—and, by implication, those siblings' playmates—also foster imaginative play in young children, although how effectively they do so depends on the quality of the relationship between sibling pairs. Dunn and Dale (1984) found that when 2-year-olds and their older preschool siblings got along well, siblings offered the younger child a unique context for acquiring play skills. Whereas mothers usually acted as interested and involved spectators, offering relevant comments and suggestions but avoiding adoption of pretend identities themselves, siblings invited their younger brothers and sisters to join in their plots and play scenes. As a result, the younger child was expected to coordinate role actions with that of the older child, and 2-year-olds did so with surprising sophistication.

In some cultural groups, children are not regarded as suitable social partners for adults; consequently, they do not interact as equals in conversation, and parents rarely play with them. Instead, children speak when spoken to, replying to requests for information or complying with an adult's directives. Under these conditions, older siblings and cousins serve as first playmates and also as caregivers while mothers tend to new babies or work responsibilities (Whiting & Edwards 1988). Observations of toddlers in rural India, Guatemala, and central Mexico reveal that parent involvement in pretense seldom occurs, but toddlers often pretend in the company of older siblings who encourage and instruct them (Zukow 1989; Rogoff, Mosier, et al. 1993).

Recently, Farver (1993) compared the quality of maternal and sibling play with 2- and 3-year-olds in an American and a Mexican community, which differed strikingly in the amount of time mothers and older siblings spend in direct interaction with young children. In each culture, mother–child and sibling–child pairs were videotaped in their homes as they played with a bag of wooden shapes suggestive of make-believe. In line with expectations, 3-year-old American children experienced more complex play with mothers, and Mexican children engaged in more complex play with their 3½- to 7-year-old siblings. Furthermore, Farver observed that American siblings tended to rely on intrusive tactics; they more often instructed, directed, and rejected their younger partner's play. In contrast, Mexican siblings used more behaviors that gently facilitated pretense—invitations to join, comments on the younger child's actions, suggestions, and positive affect. In this respect, the Mexican siblings were similar to American mothers in their scaffolding, a skill that appeared to be fostered by the Mexican culture's assignment of caregiving responsibilities to older brothers and sisters.

These findings suggest that children can be socialized into pretense by a variety of expert partners. In preschool and child care settings, mixed-age groupings that permit older and younger children to spend time together provide additional opportunities to promote make-believe. The evidence to date suggests that older siblings from some ethnic-minority families may be particularly adept at such scaffolding—indeed, as capable as many adults! Because of their limited experience with the caregiving role and their more-conflictual relationships with siblings, ethnic-majority children may need more assistance in learning how to play effectively with younger peers. Teachers and caregivers can provide this guidance by observing children's play, intervening when necessary, and demonstrating and suggesting sensitive, responsive strategies. In classrooms with a multicultural mix of children, skilled ethnic-minority children can serve as models and scaffolders for agemates, showing them how to engage younger children in play.

Conclusion

The vast literature on children's play reveals that its contributions to child development can be looked at from diverse vantage points. Psychoanalytic theorists have highlighted the emotionally integrative function of pretense, pointing out that anxiety-provoking events, such as a visit to the doctor's office or discipline by a parent, are likely to be revisited in the young child's play, but with roles reversed so that the child is in command and compensates for unpleasant experiences in real life (Erikson 1950). Piaget underscored the opportunities that make-believe affords for exercising symbolic schemes. And both Piaget and Vygotsky recognized that pretense allows children to become familiar with social role possibilities. In cultures around the world, young children act out family scenes and highly

visible occupations—police officer, doctor, and nurse in Western nations; rabbit hunter and potter among the Hopi Indians; and hut builder and spear maker among the Baka of West Africa (Garvey 1990). In this way, play provides children with important insights into the link between self and wider society.

Vygotsky's special emphasis on the imaginative and rule-based features of play adds an additional perspective to the viewpoints just mentioned—one that reminds us of the critical role of make-believe in developing reflective thought as well as self-regulatory and socially cooperative behavior. For those teachers who have always made sure that play is a central feature of the early childhood curriculum, Vygotsky's theory offers yet another justification for play's prominent place in preschool and primary-grade learning environments. For other teachers whose concern with academic progress has led them to neglect or eliminate play from the young child's school life, Vygotsky's analysis offers a convincing argument for change—a powerful account of why make-believe is the ultimate activity for nurturing capacities that are crucial for academic as well as later-life success.

Research amply verifies that fantasy play provides a broad foundation for developing skills that are essential for attaining personal goals and becoming a responsible and productive member of society. The unique features of make-believe help children understand the meaning and function of significant cultural roles while promoting the formation "of voluntary intentions, . . . real-life plans and volitional motives" (Vygotsky [1930–1935] 1978, 102)—in short, all the competencies that make it the ideal instructive context for mature, cognitively and socially competent behavior.

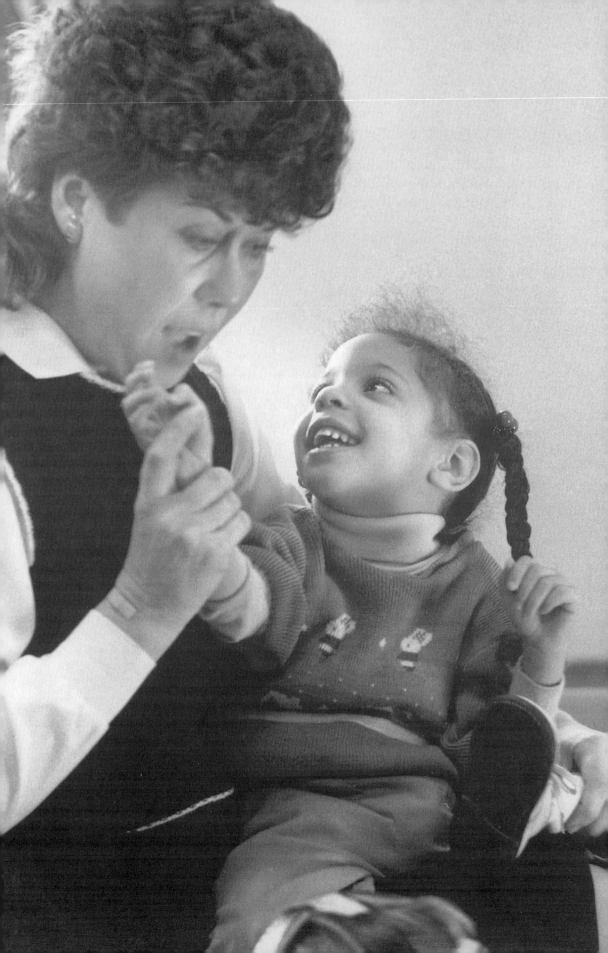

Children with Serious Learning and Behavior Problems

While the other children worked quietly on math problems, 8-year-old Calvin squirmed in his seat, dropped his pencil, looked out the window, fiddled with his shoelaces, and talked out. "Hey Joey," he yelled to a classmate over the top of several desks, "wanna play ball after school?" Joey didn't answer. He and the other children weren't eager to play with Calvin. Out on the playground, Calvin was a poor listener and failed to follow the rules of the game. When at bat, he had difficulty taking turns. In the outfield, he tossed his hat up in the air and looked elsewhere when the ball came his way. Calvin's desk at school and his room at home were a chaotic mess. He often lost pencils, books, and other materials necessary for completing his schoolwork. At the end of math period, Calvin's paper was still a blank.

Calvin is one of the 3 to 5% of school-age children with attention-deficit hyperactivity disorder (ADHD). Children diagnosed with this condition have great difficulty staying on task for more than a few minutes. In addition, they often act impulsively, ignoring social rules and lashing out with hostility when frustrated. Many (but not all) are hyperactive. They charge through their days with excessive motor activity, leaving parents and teachers frazzled and other children annoyed. (Adapted from Berk 1994a)

As we will see in this chapter, Calvin's behavior elicits from adults and peers negative reactions that limit full cultural development and higher mental functions. In the Vygotskian view, improving the quality of Calvin's social life—by providing effectively scaffolded learning activities and positive interactions with adults and peers—is critical to successful intervention.

In this chapter, we discuss Vygotskian insights into the development and education of young children with disabilities and/or serious learning and behavior problems. Vygotsky became interested in children with special needs early in his career, a concern that grew steadily until his death. As we noted in Chapter 1, he was instrumental in establishing a research laboratory for the study of abnormal child development in the Soviet Union in 1925. Toward the end of his life, Vygotsky served as director of this institute, and today the Russian Institute of Defectology, as it is currently called, continues to be the major national center for research on children with disabilities.

The best English-language source on Vygotsky's original writings in this area is a recently translated book (Vygotsky 1993), published within a collection of his works relating to *defectology,* the Russian term for abnormal child psychology and learning disabilities. Although Vygotsky focused on children with physical, and especially sensory, disabilities (e.g., blind and deaf children) and persons with major psychological disorders (e.g., severe mental retardation and schizophrenia), his basic principles of abnormal psychology apply to children with any type of physical or psychological difficulty. This chapter begins by outlining Vygotsky's main ideas on the development of children with special needs. Then, we briefly discuss what little work has been done to apply Vygotskian principles to children with sensory deficits. Next, we explore an area of special education that has been more heavily studied from the Vygotskian perspective: the self-regulatory difficulties of impulsive, inattentive, and hy-

Unless children with disabilities get many opportunities to interact positively with adults and peers, they are likely to develop secondary, more serious problems in their "cultural development."

peractive children. Finally, we consider the implications of Vygotsky's ideas for teachers and parents of children with such difficulties.

Vygotsky's approach to children with special needs

One of Vygotsky's (1993) core ideas related to children with disabilities (either psychological or physical) is that the most debilitating consequence of the problem for the child's development is not so much the original disability but rather how the defect changes the way the child participates in the activities of his or her culture. Consistent with Vygotsky's idea that higher mental functions have their roots in social interaction and collaborative activities, children whose disability interferes with their opportunities to experience positive interaction with adults and peers will develop a secondary, more serious problem in their "cultural development." This lack of full participation in social activities limits the development of higher mental functions, such as self-regulation. According to Vygotsky,

Why do the higher functions fail to develop in an abnormal child? Not because the defect directly impedes them or makes their appearance impossible . . . . [T]he underdevelopment of the higher functions is a secondary structure on top of the defect. Underdevelopment springs from what we might call the isolation of an abnormal child from his collective . . . . Any given defect in a child produces a series of characteristics which impede the normal development of his collective relations, cooperation, and interaction with others. Isolation from the collective or difficulty in social development, in its turn, conditions underdevelopment of higher mental functions, which would otherwise arise naturally in the course of normal affairs . . . . " (1993, 199)

Take, for example, blind or deaf children. As we will see shortly, such children can adequately compensate for their original problem as long as they remain in sensitive environments where they are treated as participating members and are integrated into the social and collective activities of their culture. If, however, they are prevented from interacting with others and, therefore, from acquiring effective social and language skills, their cultural, social, and psychological development will suffer.

Interestingly, although Vygotsky saw the social difficulties—and ultimately the deficits in higher mental functions—of children with disabilities as more problematic than the original problem, he also emphasized that these aspects are more amenable to treatment. Vygotsky stated,

[T]he underdevelopment of the higher processes is not primarily, but secondarily conditioned by the defect. And consequently, they represent the weakest link in an abnormal child's chain of symptoms. Therefore, this is where all educational efforts should be directed, in order to break the chain at its weakest point . . . . unlike the defect itself, which is a factor in the failure of the elementary function's development, the collective, as a factor in the development of the higher psychological functions, is something which we can control. As hopeless as it is in practical terms to battle with the defect and its natural consequences, it is valid, fruitful, and promising to struggle with difficulties in collective activities. (1993, 199)

According to Vygotsky, most important in the education of children with psychological or physical problems is improving social interactions with adults and peers. This means that children with difficulties should be included as much as possible in the regular activities of the primary culture. Thus, Vygotsky was an early advocate of mainstreaming in early childhood education. Furthermore, he assumed that the same general laws and processes of development that apply in normal development also apply to children with special deficits or disabilities. The path of development of such children is altered because of compensatory behaviors that emerge because of the defect and the defect's impact on the child's interactions with the environment. For this reason, carefully designed social environments and scaffolded learning experiences that promote the development of higher mental functions play an even more critical role in maximizing the potential of such children. In sum, Vygotsky believed that the education of children with special needs must have the same general goals as that of typically developing children. In some cases, the means used to achieve the goals might have to be modified, but the general approach should be the same.

Vygotsky's views on assessment of the zone of proximal development (ZPD), described in detail in Chapter 6, are particularly important for children with learning and behavior problems. Too often, educational planning for these children is based on an evaluation of what they cannot do. Standard, static individual testing naturally reveals that such children have difficulty with many tasks. As a result, they are likely to be labeled in terms of their limitations, and those with the greatest difficulties are likely to be isolated in special classrooms. This special classroom for "defective" children creates a different culture, with distinct social interactions and expectations for behavior, thereby compromising the development of higher mental functions.

Since children with mental or physical problems have developed in unique ways, their repertoire of abilities is more complex than that of their unaffected agemates, with weaknesses in some areas and compensatory strengths in others. Standard testing procedures are unlikely to adequately assess the true abilities of such children—nor can such procedures assess their potential to learn. Therefore, Vygotsky's concept of the ZPD, with its implications for dynamic and flexible assessment, is especially crucial for children with disabilities. Rather than focusing on what such children cannot do, the more important and challenging question for Vygotsky was what these children *can* do, both independently and with the assistance of others. Consequently, Vygotsky emphasized that teachers and parents should focus on the strengths of these children rather than being preoccupied with their weaknesses. In emphasizing strengths, adults are more likely to provide effective scaffolding and tasks within the ZPD. The deficient abilities, or weaknesses, that these children display will improve with time, if they are ever to change, in the context of scaffolded activities.

Children with sensory deficits: The case of deaf children

To Vygotsky, deaf children, who are completely or almost completely devoid of access to sound, posed particularly challenging problems. Given the importance of language and social interaction in Vygotsky's view of the developing mind, it is not surprising that he wrote about the education of deaf children (Vygotsky 1925). Vygotsky's great concern was that not being able to understand and use the language of their culture would seriously interfere with children's internalization of language as a tool of thought. Under these conditions, higher mental functions, including self-regulation, would not develop normally.

Vygotsky found himself caught in a fundamental dilemma about how best to

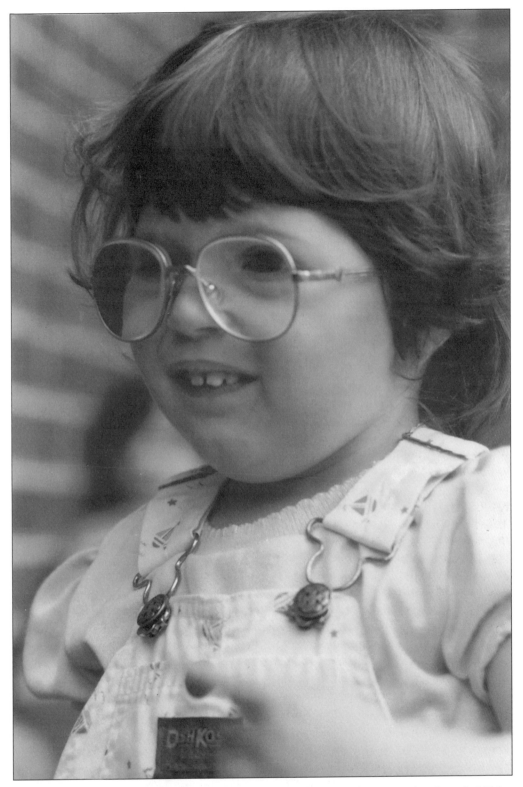

Because a child with a mental or physical disability is apt to have a repertoire of abilities even more complex than those of unaffected agemates—with weaknesses in some areas and compensatory strengths in others—standard testing procedures are unlikely to assess the child's true abilities or learning potential.

educate deaf children. On one hand, he believed that deaf children needed to learn how to speak and understand oral language (through lip reading) to become regular, participating members of the larger culture. For this reason, Vygotsky searched for effective methods to train lip reading and language production. On the other hand, he soon realized that teaching these skills to deaf children was so unnatural, physically invasive, and labor intensive that the resulting language acquisition process deviated sharply from that of hearing children (Vygotsky 1925; Knox & Stevens 1993). Also, the isolation that resulted from sending deaf children to special schools to learn oral language violated one of Vygotsky's main principles—that children with learning difficulties should be educated in the same basic way as children who do not have learning problems.

Interestingly, sign language, called "mimicry" in Russia during Vygotsky's time, was poorly understood and almost uniformly rejected as a primitive, animalistic gesture system that did not approximate real language. For this reason, Vygotsky was originally opposed to teaching deaf children a manual linguistic system. However, as some Vygotskian scholars have noted, he began to change his mind in later writings (Knox & Stevens 1993). Today, it is widely recognized that sign languages (such as American Sign Language [ASL]) are complete symbol systems with all the characteristics of any other human language, including a full vocabulary and complex grammatical and pragmatic rules. If Vygotsky had known what we currently know about sign language, he probably would have been a staunch advocate for its use, since it is the most efficient and effective route to enhancing the social interactions of deaf

children and permitting full cultural development of higher mental functions.

Consistent with this view, modern research reveals that optimal psychological development of deaf children depends on opportunities to experience supportive parent–child interaction. An important approach to exploring this issue has been to compare deaf children of deaf parents with deaf children of hearing parents. Deaf children of deaf parents are typically identified as hearing impaired in infancy. Since their parents use sign language at home, these children acquire it as their native tongue during early childhood. In contrast, deaf children of hearing parents may not be identified as deaf until long after birth. Since their hearing parents usually do not use sign language (and it takes time to learn if they so choose), these children are not exposed to the same rich language environment as either deaf children with deaf parents or hearing children with hearing parents. As Vygotsky's theory suggests, the development of these three groups of children varies considerably.

Deaf children of deaf parents resemble hearing children of hearing parents in quality of parent–child interaction, including reciprocity of communication and scaffolding (Meadow et al. 1981; Jamieson 1994; Jamieson & Pedersen in press). In addition, language acquisition among deaf children of deaf parents is quite typical in timing and sequence, and these children's spontaneous use of self-directed signs resembles hearing children's use of overt private speech. As long as deaf children's early social experiences resemble those of their hearing counterparts and they become fluent in sign language, the transition from other-regulation to self-regulation seems to occur normally for this group (Jamieson 1994).

Parent–child communication, language acquisition, and the development of self-regulation in deaf children of hearing parents are strikingly different. A large number of studies show that hearing parents of deaf children are (1) less positive in interaction; (2) less effective at achieving joint attention, reciprocity, and intersubjectivity; (3) less sensitive to the child's cues; and (4) more directive and controlling than are deaf parents of deaf children and hearing parents of hearing children (Brinich 1980; Meadow 1980; Wedell-Monning & Lumley 1980; Meadow et al. 1981; Lederberg & Mobley 1990; Spencer & Gutfreund 1990; Meadow-Orlans 1993; Jamieson 1994; Jamieson & Pedersen in press).

These differences appear as early as 12 months of age, as a study by Meadow-Orlans (1993) reveals. She compared the parent–child interactions of 9 deaf infants of deaf parents, 12 deaf infants of hearing parents, and 10 hearing infants of hearing parents. Videotapes of two free-play sessions in a laboratory—the first taken at 12 months and the second at 18 months—were coded for maternal behaviors (sensitivity, involvement, flexibility, positive affect, and consistency), infant behaviors (compliance, positive affect, involvement, and gentleness), and dyadic behaviors (mutuality, shared understanding, and shared turn taking). No differences were found between hearing parents of hearing children and deaf parents of deaf children. However, compared to these two groups, hearing mothers of deaf children scored lower in maternal sensitivity, positive affect, shared understanding, and shared turn taking. These differences increased in magnitude from the first to the second session. In addition, although infants in all three groups displayed similar behaviors at 12 months, by 18 months three of the four child measures showed differences in a negative direction for deaf children of hearing par-

> *Deaf mothers of deaf children have been found to engage in the same types of maternal teaching strategies and scaffolding techniques as hearing mothers of hearing children.*

ents. Meadow-Orlans pointed out that mother and child contributed jointly to the quality of interaction. However, on the basis of the longitudinal nature of the investigation, she concluded that ineffective parent–child communication was probably responsible for negative child behavior, rather than the other way around.

Other investigators have explored parental scaffolding of deaf children from a specifically Vygotskian perspective (Jamieson 1994; Jamieson & Pedersen in press). Jamieson and her colleagues, for example, found that deaf mothers of deaf children engaged in the same types of maternal teaching strategies and scaffolding techniques as did hearing mothers of hearing children. Once again, however, hearing mothers of deaf children, compared to the other two parent–child groups, had trouble modifying their verbal and nonverbal exchanges to match the child's behavior and competence. This outcome is at least partly due to the child's difficulty in evoking supportive maternal behaviors. The deaf child cannot respond to the auditory messages of hearing parents, who rely heavily on auditory responsiveness and feedback to sustain effective social interaction; consequently, intersubjectivity (shared understanding of events between parent and child) is limited. Jamieson also measured the degree of transfer from other-regulation to self-regulation in deaf children's interactions with their mothers. While mothers and

Vygotsky's theory suggests that intervention and education for deaf children be designed to give them many opportunities to use sign language in the context of activities with others, to stimulate both language and cognitive development.

their preschool children worked on a wooden three-dimensional puzzle task, she recorded the proportion of puzzle-construction attempts that were child initiated at the beginning and end of the five-minute session. Unlike the deaf mother–deaf child and hearing mother–hearing child groups (in which children increased their attempts from the beginning to the end of the session), hearing mothers of deaf children did not gradually relinquish responsibility for the task to the child. Consequently, children in this group did not increase their puzzle-construction attempts over time.

According to Vygotsky, since children with limited parent–child communication and few opportunities to participate in scaffolded task activities internalize language less effectively, they should display self-regulatory difficulties. Indeed, deaf children of hearing parents have repeatedly been found to have behavioral and impulse-control problems, relative to both deaf children with deaf parents and hearing children with hearing parents (Schlesinger & Meadow 1972; Harris 1978; Chess & Fernandez 1980). Vygotsky's theory suggests that intervention and education for deaf children be based on the goal of giving them many opportunities to use sign language in the context of activities with others, to stimulate both language and cognitive development.

The studies just described illustrate Vygotsky's point that more devastating than the original defect are its consequences for the child's participation in collective activity. The absence of hearing per se is not a major problem for the psychological development of deaf children. When granted the opportunity, these children easily acquire an alternative symbol system through social interaction and compensate for their deficit. Difficulties emerge only when limited parent–child communication prevents full development of linguistic and cognitive skills.

In considering these findings, our goal is not to blame hearing parents of deaf children. Most do the best they can, in view of the difficulties of communicating with a child unable to hear speech. In fact, some investigators point out that hearing parents of deaf children invent some effective strategies for conversing with their children. For example, the directive statements of such mothers are often well intended—aimed at evoking a response from the child so a dialogue can be extended (Caissie & Cole 1993). Hearing parents of deaf children also must make the difficult decision of whether or not to learn and use sign language and, if so, to what extent. Those parents who choose to master signing go through the even more arduous task of acquiring a second language in adulthood and figuring out how to use it effectively in the home. A complicating factor in this decision is that in reality, deafness is a continuum: children range from slightly hearing impaired to completely deaf. For those children who fall somewhere in the middle of this continuum, it is often unclear whether hearing problems will improve or worsen with age. In these cases, it is especially difficult for parents to decide whether to foster verbal English or sign language as the child's predominant linguistic system. In instances of severe hearing loss, in which normal acquisition of spoken English is unlikely, Vygotsky-based research indicates that learning and using sign language is vital for safeguarding and nurturing deaf children's linguistic, cognitive, and psychological potential.

Nevertheless, Vygotsky's fundamental dilemma pertaining to the education of deaf children returns: Maximizing opportunities to interact with others using sign language generally means that separate schools for deaf children are necessary. Given the choice of (1) limited participation in cultural activities, awkward social interactions, and impoverished language and cognitive abilities versus (2) functioning well within a subculture of individuals who communicate with sign language and offer the child a stimulating social world, the Vygotskian perspective clearly favors the second option.

Children with self-regulatory problems

The majority of research applying Vygotskian principles to children with special needs focuses on the large number of children who are difficult to manage in early school settings because of their inattention, impulsivity, hyperactivity, disruptive behavior, and/or learning difficulties. By school entry, many such children are diagnosed with attention-deficit hyperactivity disorder (ADHD) (American Psychiatric Association 1994). ADHD affects 3 to 5% of the elementary school population, with rates approaching 6 to 10% in boys (Barkley 1990). There is now evidence for moderate stability in symptoms of inattention, high activity level, and difficult behavior from early to middle childhood and into adolescence. Children identified by their

*High activity level, inattention, and disruptiveness in young children are typical for preschool children; it is only when these behaviors are **severe** and **frequent** that the child is at risk for future problems.*

teachers as extremely "difficult to manage" in the preschool years are at considerable risk for the attention and behavior problems associated with ADHD when they reach elementary school, and many children with serious problems in elementary school continue to show difficulties in secondary school and into the adult years (Campbell et al. 1986; Campbell & Ewing 1990; Barkley et al. 1991; Weiss & Hechtman 1993).

However, we must keep in mind that the mere presence of inattention, high activity level, and disruptiveness in young children is not a predictor of lasting difficulties. These behaviors are normal and typical for preschoolers, who are just beginning to bring action under the control of thought. Instead, the *severity* and *frequency* of these symptoms are critical in determining whether or not a preschool child is at risk for future problems (Barkley 1990; Campbell 1990; Campbell et al. 1994).

Over the past 25 years, investigators have turned to Vygotsky's theory for help in understanding and treating inattentive and impulsive children, because their problems involve self-regulation. Children diagnosed with ADHD have (1) difficulty in planning and organizing their actions; (2) trouble modulating their attention, arousal, and activity to the appropriate level called for in the environment; and (3) difficulty resisting and inhibiting impulsive responding to stimuli (Douglas 1983, 1988; Barkley 1990, 1994; Landau & Moore 1991). Each of these problems is closely related to the self-regulatory processes of guiding, monitoring, and controlling attention and behavior to reach goals.

Scaffolding Children's Learning

Although clinicians agree that many children with ADHD are deficient in self-regulation, little is known about the self-regulatory strategies they use when trying to focus their attention and behavior (Berk 1992; Diaz & Berk 1995). As a result, several researchers have explored the verbal self-regulatory capacities of ADHD children from a Vygotskian perspective. In the following sections, we first discuss early attempts to apply Vygotsky's theory to the treatment of ADHD. Then we consider the relationship between children's social environments and their self-regulatory problems. Finally, we summarize what is currently known about the private speech of children with learning and behavior problems and the implications of our current knowledge for classroom practices.

Self-instructional training: Is it effective?

Early attempts to apply Vygotsky's ideas to children with learning and behavior problems began in the late 1960s when several researchers devised cognitive-behavioral interventions for impulsive/hyperactive children (Palkes, Stewart, & Kahana 1968; Meichenbaum & Goodman 1971). Today, these programs are known as *self-instructional training*. Although originally designed to ameliorate the learning difficulties of impulsive, non–self-controlled, and inattentive children, these procedures have also been extended to children whose most evident difficulties are frequent aggression or learning disabilities (Camp et al. 1977; Wong 1985; Hughes 1988).

The rationale for self-instructional training is heavily grounded in behaviorism, which regards development as externally motivated by modeling and reinforcement. In addition, designers of these treatments drew on the Vygotskian assumption that speech addressed to the self allows children to master their own actions. Consequently, they reasoned that if normally achieving children use private speech to regulate their behavior, and children who are inattentive and impulsive have behavior regulation problems, then such children need to be taught how to talk to themselves. A major assumption of the approach is that children with serious learning and behavior problems do not spontaneously use private speech when engaged in goal-directed activities (Kendall & Braswell 1985).

In a typical program, the therapist acts as a model, talking aloud while performing a task. Next, the child is asked to perform the task while speaking to him- or herself, using statements similar to those used by the therapist. Then, fading of self-instructions occurs; the child is asked to perform the task using no sound, only lip movements. Finally, the child is asked to verbalize covertly. In this way, the treatment tries to induce, through modeling and direct instruction, the natural course of private speech internalization during an activity, as originally described by Vygotsky.

Despite the intuitive appeal of self-instructional training, evaluations of its effectiveness in reducing impulsivity and improving task accuracy have been disappointing. When positive outcomes do occur, they are limited to tasks on which children were trained or to very similar tasks. Maintenance or generalization across situations and over time—especially to academic performance in classrooms—has not been demonstrated (Dush, Hirt, & Schroeder 1989; Abikoff 1991; Hinshaw & Erhardt 1991). Recently, several investigators have concluded that intervention with self-instructional train-

The behavior of children with ADHD often elicits controlling and negative communications from others, thus reducing the help these children get in learning to regulate their own behavior.

ing was probably premature. Although the procedures were motivated by a sincere effort to relieve the intractable learning problems of targeted children, they were not grounded in systematic research on the social experiences and quantity and quality of spontaneous private speech of these children (Diaz, Neal, & Amaya-Williams 1990; Berk & Potts 1991; Berk 1992; Berk & Landau 1993; Winsler 1994; Diaz & Berk 1995).

Adult–child communication and children with ADHD

Given the crucial role that social interaction plays in fostering optimal development, it is not surprising that relationships between adults and children play a role in children's self-regulatory problems. Since self-regulation emerges from other-regulation and social environments differ in the extent to which they provide effective scaffolding (which promotes children's takeover of the regulatory role through private speech), children's self-regulatory capacity is influenced by the quality of other-regulatory support in adult–child communication, to which (as we have mentioned before) both partners contribute.

Although many causal explanations of ADHD have been proposed over the years, current evidence favors a strong biological contribution (Barkley 1990, 1994). In support of a genetic basis, par-

ents and siblings of children with ADHD are more likely to have the disorder; identical twins more often share it than do fraternal twins; and adopted children with ADHD are likely to have a biological parent (but not an adoptive parent) with similar symptoms (O'Connor et al. 1980; Alberts-Corush, Firestone, & Goodman 1986; Biederman et al. 1990). In addition, damaging environmental influences during the prenatal period, such as maternal smoking, alcohol use, and lead exposure, are linked to increased risk for ADHD (Landau & Moore 1991; Barkley 1994). At present, "there is no evidence to suggest that parenting or childrearing is in any way [the cause of] the primary symptoms of the disorder" (Landau & McAninch 1993, 52). However, through transactions between the child and the social environment, poor parenting can exacerbate the child's symptoms, and it can also lead to secondary problems associated with ADHD, such as oppositional and defiant behavior, severe discipline problems, and low self-esteem.

Children with ADHD have parents who are consistently more controlling and negative than do children without the disorder (Campbell 1975; Cunningham & Barkley 1979; Mash & Johnston 1982; Barkley, Cunningham, & Karlsson 1983; Tallmadge & Barkley 1983). Parents of ADHD-diagnosed children use more verbal directives, issue more commands, more often physically direct the child during an activity, give more suggestions and corrections, and are less responsive to their child's behavior than parents of children (for a review, see Danforth, Barkley, & Stokes 1991). In classrooms, these negative messages are often extended. Teachers find themselves directing and commanding these children throughout the day and offering them little praise. Indeed, the presence of a single child with ADHD can catalyze substantially more teacher-given negative feedback to all children in the classroom (Campbell, Endman, & Bernfeld 1977).

The current consensus of research is that because of their off-task behavior and noncompliance, ADHD-diagnosed children play a major role in eliciting these controlling and negative styles of adult communication. Teachers offer the following descriptions of such children: "doesn't seem to listen," "fails to finish tasks," "can't concentrate," and "requires more redirection" (Barkley 1990, 1994). During problem solving, children with ADHD are quick to respond without considering alternatives. They constantly get up and sit down, fidget, and manipulate objects unrelated to the task at hand (Landau & Moore 1991); as a result, their work is often careless and inaccurate. In class, they blurt out responses, fail to take turns, and display a low tolerance for frustration and poor cooperation with agemates during joint tasks and games. Not surprisingly, they typically have few friends and are rejected by their peers (Barkley 1990; Landau & Moore 1991).

As children with ADHD elicit maladaptive interaction patterns from parents, teachers, and peers, they reduce the capacity of the social environment to help them make an optimal transition from other-regulation to self-regulation. Consistent with Vygotsky's theory, the characteristics of these children affect the social experiences they have with other members of their culture and, in turn, the degree to which they actively participate in collaborative activities that promote the development of higher mental functions. From a Vygotskian perspective, therefore, it is crucial to improve the adult–child interactions these children experience.

A recent study of children with ADHD explored the relationship between parent–child interaction and children's use of private speech. Winsler (1994) videotaped 39 6- to 8-year-old boys, 19 of whom were clinically diagnosed with ADHD, as they worked on selective attention and Lego construction tasks under several social conditions. On one day, children worked together with their parents on one of the tasks and then completed a similar but not identical task alone. Parents were instructed to "help him learn this task so that afterward he can do a similar one by himself." On a different day, the same boys worked on the other task, once in collaboration with an experimenter trained to implement the scaffolding procedures described in Chapter 2 and then on a similar task individually.

As expected, parents of children with ADHD were more directive and engaged in less effective scaffolding than did the experimenter while working with the same children. Correspondingly, the ADHD-diagnosed children used significantly more private speech during the collaborative session with the scaffolding experimenter, compared to the session with the parent, and the amount of private speech during collaboration with the experimenter increased linearly as the experimenter sensitively engaged the child in the task and turned over responsibility to the child as he demonstrated mastery. This pattern of increasing a child's private speech by decreasing adult control was not found in the parent–child sessions. Overall, the findings suggested that children with ADHD can respond to changes in social context. In this study, children were found to use more self-regulatory language when they received highly sensitive scaffolding by an adult knowledgeable about ADHD and its implications for learning.

Private speech of children with self-regulatory problems

During the past two decades, investigators have observed children who display impulsive or hyperactive behavior to see whether their private speech is similar to that of other children in terms of quantity, quality, and developmental course. Four conclusions can be drawn from these studies:

• Contrary to assumptions underlying self-instructional training programs, impulsive, inattentive, and hyperactive children use *more* overt, task-relevant private speech while working on tasks than do same-age peers without behavior problems (Zivin 1972; Campbell 1973; Dickie 1973; Copeland 1979; Zentall, Gohs, & Culatta 1983; Zentall 1988; Berk & Potts 1991; Berk & Landau 1993; Winsler 1994).

• In addition to including more overt, task-relevant private speech, the self-speech of ADHD-diagnosed children often contains more irrelevant and off-task comments (Zivin 1972; Dickie 1973; Copeland 1979; Berk & Potts 1991; Diaz et al. 1992; Winsler 1994).

• Children with ADHD use fewer of the partially internalized forms of self-speech (whispers and inaudible muttering) than do children of the same age without behavior problems (Berk & Potts 1991; Berk & Landau 1993; Winsler 1994).

• The private speech of children with ADHD is less-strongly related to their task performance and on-task attention than is the speech of children without behavior problems (Berk & Potts 1991; Berk & Landau 1993; Winsler 1994).

These findings indicate that the form, function, and developmental course of private speech in impulsive, inattentive, and hyperactive children is similar to that of other children—an outcome in agreement with Vygotsky's assumption that private speech is a universal human problem-solving tool. At the same time, compared to their unaffected agemates, the private speech of children with ADHD remains externalized over a longer developmental period, as evidenced by their reduced use of the most mature, internalized private-speech forms. According to Berk and her collaborators, this delay in private-speech internalization can be understood in terms of yet another common factor influencing private speech—that it increases under conditions of cognitive challenge. Since a deficient attentional and/or motor control system introduces extra obstacles to task success, it limits the extent to which private speech helps ADHD-diagnosed children to gain efficient mastery over their behavior. Therefore, children with such deficits need to use externalized task-relevant utterances over an extended developmental period and take longer to move toward inaudible forms (Berk & Potts 1991; Berk 1992, 1994c; Berk & Landau 1993).

In support of this interpretation, factors on both the child's side and the adult's side that reduce impediments to self-regulation (1) increase the maturity of ADHD children's private speech, and (2) strengthen the relationship of such speech to task-related behavior and performance. With respect to child characteristics, Berk and Potts (1991) examined the relationship between private speech and behavior among 19 ADHD and 19 normally achieving 6- to 11-year-old boys engaged in mathematics tasks in their classrooms. Findings indicated that only among the least distractible boys with ADHD did audible self-guiding speech predict improved attention to math assignments. Furthermore, the researchers tracked a subsample of ADHD-diagnosed children while they were both taking and not taking stimulant drug medication, the most widely used treatment for the disorder. Although stimulants are not a complete remedy for ADHD, research indicates that they augment attention and performance in approximately 70% of clinically diagnosed school-age children who take them (Pelham 1987, 1993; Barkley 1990).* Berk and Potts reported that medication sharply increased the maturity of private speech of boys with ADHD, leading them to rely less on externalized task-relevant utterances and more on inaudible muttering. In addition, only under the medicated condition was children's inaudible muttering strongly associated with improved self-regulation, in the form of reduced self-stimulating behavior and greater attention to mathematics tasks.

On the adult's side, Winsler (1994) found that quality of adult scaffolding predicted the extent to which private speech was related to attention and task performance in children with ADHD. After boys with ADHD experienced scaf-

folding by a trained experimenter aware of their diagnosis and its debilitating consequences for social interaction, their partially internalized forms of private speech were better connected with task performance than was the case after a collaborative session with their parent, during which scaffolding was less optimal. Furthermore, research indicates that the quality of adult communication with ADHD-diagnosed children can be augmented through medication therapy. When gains in attention and impulse control occur as a result of stimulant medication, relations with parents, teachers, and peers improve. As children listen and cooperate more, adult commands and negative discipline diminish, and the need for intensive supervision and control declines. Still, the majority of such children continue to require substantial external control and limit-setting, since their behavior remains less self-regulated and organized than that of their agemates without behavioral problems (Pelham 1987, 1993; Landau & Moore 1991; Landau & McAninch 1993).

Finally, although our discussion has focused on learning and behavior problems associated with ADHD, a few investigations have been carried out on children identified as having learning disabilities—specific learning impairments that lead them to achieve poorly in school despite average or above-average intelligence. A similar pattern of findings—less optimal parent–child interaction, more externalized private speech, a delay in private-speech internalization, and less-effective integration of private speech with behavior—emerges in these studies (Berk & Landau 1993; Lyytinen et al. 1994). One reason that children identified as having learning disabilities may engage in higher rates of audible private speech than do their normally achieving classmates is that they rely on develop-

---

* Use of stimulant medication to treat preschoolers who are inattentive and display poor impulse control is usually not warranted. Research indicates that 4- to 5-year-olds do not respond as favorably to stimulants as do older, school-age children (Barkley 1989). In addition, preschoolers show more side effects to stimulant drugs, such as clinging and decreased solitary play, that can actually interfere with cognitive and social development. Finally, the beneficial impact of medication is short term. Behavior improves only while the child is taking the drug; there are no lasting benefits of drug therapy per se (Campbell 1985; Landau & McAninch 1993; Pelham 1993). Drug therapy is useful because in ameliorating the child's attentional and behavior problems even temporarily, it improves children's social environments and capacity to engage in academic activities.

mentally less-mature, time-consuming cognitive strategies when engaged in academic tasks (Geary et al. 1987). In other words, the content of their private speech renders it less effective in helping them gain control over their behavior. Although the cognitive strategies of children with ADHD have yet to be systematically investigated, their overriding difficulty in sustaining attention and inhibiting impulsive action may also lead their strategies to be less flexible and accurate than those of their classmates (Berk & Potts 1991). These observations suggest that both groups of children would benefit more from instruction in effective, efficient problem-solving strategies than from generic training in use of private speech—a capacity they already possess.

Enhancing educational environments for children with serious learning and behavior problems

According to Vygotsky's theory, social experiences that enhance self-regulation and higher mental functions in typically developing children should also foster these same outcomes in children with serious learning and behavior problems. Vygotsky-based interventions rely on adult–child dialogues that focus on tasks within the child's ZPD. Adult scaffolding, in which the assistance provided is adjusted to the child's momentary behavior and gradually reduced as the child takes over responsibility for the task, is vitally important.

Yet we have seen that children with attentional deficits, impulsivity, and other learning difficulties are far less likely than their agemates to experience this finely nuanced communication. Research shows that the opportunities of children

with ADHD to participate in such discourse are limited by the stress they bring to the adult–child relationship. Consequently, help for these children often must begin with fairly directive efforts to reduce their inappropriate behavior. Giving specific instructions and requests, keeping expectations for task-oriented and social behavior clear and highly consistent, following through to make sure the child complies, and praising the child for attending and cooperating have been shown to improve behavior, reduce adult and peer reprimands, and provide the child with initial successes, which help mend their shattered sense of self-esteem (Barkley 1990; Pelham 1992). For children who are on medication, these intervention procedures can reduce the necessary dosage and, consequently, minimize the possibility of undesirable side effects (Landau & McAninch 1993).

The techniques just described have been found to interrupt negative cycles of communication between adults and children with behavior problems, thereby creating a context in which development-enhancing interaction is possible. Once these conditions are in place, parents can be taught to respond with sensitive, scaffolded instruction while their children work on challenging cognitive tasks (such as homework assignments)—social experiences that are vital for prompting self-regulatory private speech and learning gains. Teachers, too, may need to be reminded to provide scaffolded assistance, as well as activities that are appropriately challenging (within the children's ZPD). Gradually transferring responsibility from the adult to the child is essential for helping children with self-regulatory deficits overcome their difficulties. Because of the aversive behaviors of inattentive and impulsive children, adults often conclude that these children are incapable of self-

In environments that permit children to move about and collaborate with others and to take frequent breaks during sedentary activities, the behavior of children with self-regulatory problems is less distinctive and disturbing.

management. As a result, parents and teachers may overlook improvements in behavior and fail to grant such children a greater measure of control when they become ready for it.

Finally, setting demands affect the extent to which inattentive and impulsive children present problems in classrooms. Developmentally inappropriate environments—ones that are excessively structured, that emphasize adult input to the neglect of child participation, and that require children to do all work by themselves at their seats—place special strains on the resources of these children. As a result, their behavior is especially troublesome. Not surprisingly, diagnoses of ADHD tend to increase as children move from less-structured preschool and kin-dergarten classrooms into formal primary schooling (Pellegrini & Horvat 1995). In contrast, in environments that offer a balance of adult and child control by permitting children to move about and collaborate with others and to take frequent breaks during sedentary activities, the behaviors of children with self-regulatory problems are less distinctive and disturbing (Jacob, O'Leary, & Rosenblad 1978; Pellegrini & Horvat 1995). The Vygotsky-based curricular innovations we will take up in Chapter 6—each of which depends on joint participation of adults and children and scaffolded mastery of developmentally appropriate, challenging tasks—are as essential for children with deficits and disabilities as they are for their typically developing peers.

The Relation between Learning
and Development:
Comparing Vygotsky's Theory with
Other Prominent Perspectives

As far as education is concerned, the chief outcome of [Piaget's] theory of intellectual development is a plea that children be allowed to do their own learning. Piaget is not saying that intellectual development proceeds at its own pace no matter what you try to do. He is saying that what schools usually try to do is ineffectual. You cannot further understanding in a child simply by talking to him. (Duckworth 1964, 20)

[According to Vygotsky], psychological development occurs through teaching/learning and upbringing . . . . [through] various types of spontaneous and specially organized interactions of the child with adults, of one person with other people—interactions through which a human being assimilates the achievements of historically shaped culture . . . . [A]n essential role in this process . . . is played by systems of signs and symbols. (Davydov 1995, 15, 18)

In previous chapters we discussed central aspects of Vygotsky's sociocultural theory, making note along the way of how it differs from other prominent approaches to child development and education—especially the cognitive-developmental theory of Jean Piaget. In Chapter 2 we saw how Vygotsky's view of the role of language in cognitive development is at odds with the Piagetian view. According to Vygotsky, language, in the form of private speech, is the centerpiece of development—the pivotal means through which culturally adaptive cognitive strategies are transferred from the social to the psychological plane of functioning. Vygotsky regarded the inner dialogues derived from external- ized, self-directed utterances as the seat of human consciousness. Because the human mind is formed through the in- ternalization and transformation of so- cial interactions, it is permanently im- bued with its social origins. In contrast, Piaget viewed language as a secondary, emergent phenomenon—as an out- growth of the sensorimotor activity in- volved in infants' and young children's independent exploration of the physical world. Private speech was seen as a symptom of the preschooler's imma- ture, egocentric, nonsocially adapted thought; it served no positive, adaptive purpose in the life of the young child. Similarly, in Chapter 3 we discussed the Vygotskian view of make-believe play as socially generated and inherently communicative. To Piaget, however, symbolic play, like private speech, was initially a solitary activity made up of idiosyncratic symbols. It only gradu- ally became social with cognitive matu- rity and the decline of egocentrism.

In this chapter, we address more fully the unique features of the Vygotskian approach in relation to other major theo- ries of this century, making explicit its profound implications for early child- hood teaching and learning. Vygotsky explained that the distinctiveness of his perspective could be understood by analyzing the connection between learning and development ([1930– 1935] 1978; [1934] 1986). He identi- fied three major perspectives on this relationship, each of which remains alive in contemporary theory:

1. learning and development as sepa- rate entities,

2. learning and development as identical, and

3. learning as leading development.

These views are summarized in Table 5.1. When examined together, they clarify the reasons that Vygotsky's theory offers a new, integrative frame- work for designing developmentally appropriate practices preeminently suited to meeting the educational needs of young children.

To characterize and illustrate the three positions, Vygotsky discussed the ac- quisition of children's spontaneous and scientific concepts. Spontaneous, or ev- eryday, concepts are those that are mas- tered in the course of daily life. They include common knowledge—for ex- ample, familiar objects (ball, bicycle), actions (run, fall), human relationships (brother, aunt, friend), basic numerical ideas (counting), and a sense of time (yesterday, today, and tomorrow). The development of spontaneous concepts

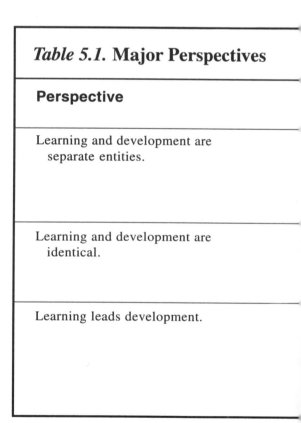

Table 5.1. Major Perspectives

Perspective
Learning and development are separate entities.
Learning and development are identical.
Learning leads development.

is not conscious and deliberate. Children acquire them with ease and with little or no awareness that they are thinking conceptually. In contrast, scientific, or school-taught, concepts are typically learned as the result of instruction—out of interaction between a naive child and a knowledgeable teacher. Examples are history, causality, multiplication, and nations of the world. Once children master these concepts, they are consciously aware of what they know and can articulate their understanding with verbal definitions. Vygotsky argued that theorists' ideas about the relation between spontaneous and scientific concepts reflect basic assumptions about the link between development and learning in the child. Let us see how this is the case.

Learning and development as separate entities

The first position states that learning and development are separate entities—that development is the dominant process, and that learning follows after it and has little impact on the structure or maturity of children's thinking. From this perspective, development is viewed as largely internally controlled; what comes from within the child is most important for directing cognitive change. The environment, including the social environment, is available for children to interact with as they make sense of experience, but it does not play a central role in the evolution of the child's capacities. Instead, children are largely in charge of revisions in their own think-

on the Relation between Learning and Development

Description	View of Child and Social Environment	20th-Century Theory
Development is the dominant process; learning follows after it and refines and improves on structures that have already emerged.	active child; social environment refrains from interfering with natural development	Piaget's cognitive-developmental theory
Development results entirely from learning; the social environment provides input, which is absorbed, ready-made, by children.	passive child; social environment takes full responsibility for development	Behaviorism
Learning plays a major role in development, leading it forward as children receive instruction from more-expert partners on tasks within their zones of proximal development.	active child and active social environment collaborate to produce development	Vygotsky's sociocultural theory

> *Vygotsky acknowledged that some development may occur as the result of "the child's thought bump[ing] into the wall of its own inadequacy," but he questioned whether such experiences are the major teacher of the child.*

ing, with biological readiness being the major determinant of change. Development is seen as a process of maturation under the control of biological laws; learning involves applying new skills made possible by development.

For those who adhere to this view, instruction does not make a substantial contribution to children's basic understandings and ways of interpreting the world. Instead, it refines those capacities that emerge spontaneously from children's explorations of their surroundings. According to Vygotsky, the "separatist" position assumes that

[development] creates the potentialities, [learning] realizes them. Education is a superstructure erected over maturation, or education is related to development as consumption to production. Learning depends on development, but the course of development is not affected by learning. ([1934] 1986, 174–75)

Vygotsky explained that there is a basic element of truth to the separatist perspective, since it rests on the observation that the child must be developmentally ready if instruction is to be successful. It would be counterproductive and foolish to try to teach a 1-year-old to tie shoes or a 2-year-old to read and write. But the separatist position overemphasizes the importance of development and underemphasizes the contribution of learning, since it as-

sumes a one-sided, dependency relationship between them: Instruction, although separate from development, depends on it, but development is largely unaffected by instruction. In terms of the distinction between spontaneous and scientific concepts, only the former—the child's interpretations of the world, uninfluenced and unprompted by adults—are assumed to inform us about characteristics of children's thinking.

Vygotsky ascribed the separatist view to the cognitive-developmental theory of Piaget, who regarded the study of children's spontaneous reasoning as the route to illuminating the special qualities of their thought. Nonspontaneous concepts, Piaget believed, reflect the imposition of adult categories on children. Children may memorize or learn these categories superficially, but they tell us little about children's true understanding. Consequently, Piaget chose to interview young children about situations in which they were unlikely to have received direct instruction—conservation, seriation, hierarchical classification, and such natural phenomena as rivers flowing into lakes and the sun moving across the sky ([1923] 1926, [1926] 1930). School learning, in the form of direct teaching of scientific concepts, was assumed to have little determining effect on development.

Instead, Piaget assumed that the child's thought becomes more like that of the adult when children become developmentally ready to notice deficiencies in their immature, illogical reasoning and abandon it in favor of a logical approach to the world. Indeed, Piaget regarded the thought of the young child and that of more mature peers and adults not as collaborative and complementary but rather as in conflict (Tudge & Winterhoff 1993). At each stage, children are jarred into noticing that their spontaneous concepts provide incomplete or inadequate representations of reality. As a result, they modify those concepts in such a way that adult modes of reasoning win out. Eventually, children extend their new, logical approach to the world to the mastery of scientific concepts taught in school.

Vygotsky acknowledged that some development may occur as the result of "the child's thought bump[ing] into the wall of its own inadequacy," but he questioned whether such experiences are the sole, or even the major, teacher of the child ([1934] 1986, 165). According to Vygotsky, Piaget's theory establishes "a principle of antagonism between development and learning" (p. 157). The conflict is resolved by development achieving domination and control over learning.

Piaget's view of the child as actively striving to make sense of experience was revolutionary when it first reached the United States in the middle of the 20th century. By the 1960s, educators embraced it with enthusiasm, designing Piaget-based curricula that emphasized *discovery learning*—children's spontaneous interaction with the environment. In a Piaget-based classroom, teachers de-emphasize conveying knowledge verbally, through didactic instruction. Instead, they provide a rich variety of activities designed to promote exploration and encourage children to choose freely from among them. In addition, classrooms based on Piagetian principles promote sensitivity to children's readiness to learn by means of a concerted effort not to speed up development through instruction. New skills are not imposed before children indicate that they are interested or ready. Because Piaget's theory stresses the supremacy

of development over learning, the teacher's contribution to the process of acquiring new knowledge is reduced relative to the child's. In sum, the Piagetian approach to education is one of an active organism taking responsibility for change in a social environment that refrains from interfering with natural development.

Learning and development as identical

A second position is that learning and development are essentially the same—a perspective that reflects the associationistic, environmental-contingency approach to education. From this vantage point, concepts have no inward history within the child and do not undergo spontaneous development. Instead, they must be imposed from without, and they are absorbed, ready-made, by children. The social environment provides input in the form of explicit instruction in values and knowledge, which accumulate within the child through imitation and through rewards for correct responses and punishments for incorrect responses. The underlying psychological theory of this approach is behaviorism; it can be traced to the work of John Watson, Edward Thorndike, and B.F. Skinner, who assumed that development results entirely from learning (Kohlberg & Mayer 1972).

Vygotsky explained the futility of regarding development in this way. A wealth of evidence reveals that when young children acquire a new word from listening to adult speech, the concept underlying it is not fully mature. To the contrary, such concepts are incompletely formed and undergo many changes with age. Furthermore, children do not imitate and absorb information ready-made from the environment. Instead, they are selective learners. For example, children rarely imitate skills they have fully mastered or those that are far beyond their current capacities. Instead, they imitate ones that are currently in the process of formation—that are within range of their developmental level (Bloom, Hood, & Lightbown 1974; Kaye & Marcus 1981). The identity perspective ignores the truth at the heart of the separatist approach: Instruction that pays no attention to developmental readiness is fruitless and results only in meaningless parroting of adult-transmitted knowledge.

The identity position characterizes traditional classrooms in which teachers regard their primary objective as transmission of information and view children as respondents whose major task is to absorb academic knowledge and skills. In academic preschools based on this model, teaching is oriented toward acquisition of facts, emphasizes low-level cognitive functions, and depends on adult-structured materials and worksheets. The approach is adult centered rather than child centered (Goodlad 1984). Since it denies the existence of the child's spontaneous development, it is antithetical to current conceptions of developmentally appropriate practice that advocate providing activities suited to children's developmental level, with the aim of fostering an active mind that thinks, reasons, questions, and experiments (National Association for the Education of Young Children 1991). In sum, the identity viewpoint is one of a passive child in a social environment that takes full responsibility for children's psychological growth. Since development and learning are regarded as identical, the position dismisses any consideration of the relation between them.

The Vygotskian view: Learning leads development

The Vygotskian position is one in which learning and development are neither separate nor identical processes. Instead, they combine in a complex, interrelated fashion such that *instruction leads, or elicits, development.* How is this possible? The answer lies in the zone of proximal development, the difference between what a child can achieve independently and what he or she can achieve in conjunction with another person. Vygotsky explained,

In the child's development, imitation and instruction play a major role. They bring out specifically human qualities of the mind and lead the child to new developmental levels. . . . What the child can do in cooperation today he can do alone tomorrow. Therefore the only good kind of instruction . . . must be aimed not so much at the ripe as at the ripening functions. It remains necessary to determine the lowest threshold at which instruction in, say, arithmetic may begin, since a certain minimal ripeness of functions is required. But we must consider the upper threshold as well; instruction must be oriented toward the future, not the past. ([1934] 1986, 188–89)

According to Vygotsky, educative environments for children must utilize the zone of proximal development. When teachers continually offer children (or permit them to choose) problems that they are able to handle without assistance or provide experiences that are too distant from children's independent mastery, then they fail to orient instruction so it enhances development. Instead, Vygotsky emphasized that teachers must collaborate with children in joint cognitive activities carefully chosen to fit the child's *level of potential development,* thereby advancing the

In the Vygotskian view, learning and development are neither separate nor identical processes; rather, they combine in complex, interrelated fashion such that instruction leads, or elicits, development.

child's actual development (Wertsch & Rogoff 1984). As Vygotsky underscored,

instruction is good only when it proceeds ahead of development. It then awakens and rouses to life those functions which are in a stage of maturing, which lie in the zone of proximal development. It is in this way that instruction plays an extremely important role in development. (1956, 278)

Vygotsky argued that as instruction leads to new knowledge and skills, it also permits children to move to a new level of understanding in which they become aware of and achieve control over their mental activities. That is, as children integrate into their private speech the strategies conveyed through dialogue with more expert partners about challenging tasks, they begin to engage in "verbalized self-observation" in which they reflect on those strategies and apply them in a deliberate fashion ([1934] 1986, 170). Therefore, for Vygotsky, instruction is a major contributor to children's growing consciousness and regulation of their own thought processes; it prompts a shift to a higher level of cognitive activity.

Vygotsky drew on research into the link between scientific and spontaneous concepts by his colleague Zhozephina Shiff to illustrate the connection between instruction and development. Shiff made up two sets of stories to go along with pictures that showed the beginning of an action, its continuation, and its end. The material for one set dealt with scientific concepts taught in school and was drawn from the primary social studies curriculum. The other set of stories focused on spontaneous concepts—situations that occur often in everyday life. After hearing each story, second- and fourth-graders were asked to complete a concluding sentence expressing a logical relation about story

events (e.g., "The boy fell off his bicycle because . . . ")—a task that indicated the extent to which they could consciously reflect on each type of knowledge.

Shiff found that conscious comprehension of the material was considerably advanced for scientific (school-taught) concepts over spontaneous (naturally acquired) concepts. Children did much better on the sentence-completion task when the information they were reasoning about had been learned through instruction rather than through their own independent activity. Also, the age difference in performance was greater for spontaneous concepts than for scientific concepts. With age, reflection on spontaneous concepts caught up with awareness of scientific concepts.

Vygotsky reasoned that when children develop on their own, their awareness centers on the goal of their mental activities. They rarely stop to reflect on the mental activity itself—the means they use to get to the goal. A preschooler tying a knot, working a puzzle, or drawing a picture focuses on the results of thinking (the knot, the puzzle, or the picture), not on how to go about thinking. But when instruction is imposed on an activity within the child's zone of proximal development, the adult breaks down the task into component parts and suggests routes to mastery (e.g., "First you do this one, and then you do the next one"), supports the child's efforts, and helps the child evaluate them (e.g., "If you try it this way, I think you'll find that it works better"). As a result, children not only acquire new knowledge but step up to a higher level of mental development in that they begin to think about their own thinking. This change permits them to regulate their behavior more effec-

Instead of discovery learning or didactic teaching, the Vygotskian approach to education is one of **assisted discovery.**

tively, since it produces awareness and mastery of their own thoughts. Eventually the cognitive advances achieved through instruction are extended to spontaneous concepts, the ones children have acquired on their own. In this way, learning is a powerful force in directing development, bringing systematic reasoning and reflective consciousness to the child. Vygotsky summarized,

learning is a necessary and universal aspect of the process of developing culturally organized, specifically human psychological functions . . . . [T]he developmental process lags behind the learning process. ([1930–35] 1978, 90)

The Vygotskian view that learning leads development implies a very different approach to classroom practice than either the separatist or the identity perspective. Rather than proposing an active child who takes charge of his or her own development (separatist) or a passive child controlled by the surrounding world (identity), the sociocultural vision proposes that an *active child* and an *active social environment* collaborate to produce developmental change. Growth occurs in the zone of proximal development—a phase of mastery created in the course of social interaction in which the child has partially acquired a skill but can successfully apply it only with the assistance and supervision of an expert partner. The child actively explores, tries out alternatives, and orients to the partner for help, while the partner guides and structures the child's activity, scaffolding the child's efforts to extend current skills and knowledge to a higher level of competence. As children internalize features of this interaction, they operate on and reconstruct it, striving to understand and adapt it to new but similar situations (Wood 1980; Bruner 1983; Wertsch 1985a). In the process, they not only use the acquired skills adaptively but become capable of invent-

ing new skills. In the words of Giyoo Hatano, children who experience this type of educational system become "adaptive experts" (1993, 155).

In sum, instead of advocating either discovery learning in its purest form or didactic teaching, the Vygotskian approach to education is one of *assisted discovery*. In the educational literature, this way of teaching has been referred to in diverse ways—as guided practice, responsive teaching, assisted performance, and Socratic dialogue, among others. Tharp and Gallimore sum up applications of Vygotsky's theory to education as

[child performance] through assistance and cooperative activity, at developmental levels quite beyond the individual level of achievement . . . . Through this process, the child acquires the "plane of consciousness" of the natal society and is socialized, acculturated, made human. (1988, 30)

Vygotsky and Piaget: A meeting of minds

In the preceding sections, we compared the Vygotskian sociocultural perspective to other major views. In doing so, we accentuated their differences. The tenor of our discussion reflects the current split between theorists, researchers, and educators who identify themselves as primarily Vygotskian or primarily Piagetian—a division that one writer recently described as "tumultuous" (Glassman 1994, 186).

Yet, as Vygotsky ([1934] 1986) made clear, Piaget's work served as a major impetus for Vygotsky's theorizing about the role of self-directed speech in cognitive development. Similarly, Piaget ([1962] 1979), in responding to Vygotsky's critique of his interpretation of egocentric speech, stated that he found much of value in Vygotsky's writings on thought and language. Although important differences between Vygotsky's and Piaget's theories exist, there are also vital commonalities that could serve as the foundation for building fruitful bridges (Tudge & Winterhoff 1993; Cobb 1994; Glassman 1994). A close look reveals that in their visions of the role of natural or biological change and of historical and social circumstances in development, the contrast between the two great thinkers is more one of emphasis than of irreconcilable division.

For example, late in his career Piaget addressed the impact of social context on development, commenting that he regarded variations in social experience as contributing to (but not as the sole determinant of) the child's construction of knowledge (1985). Similarly, Vygotsky proposed a biologically based, natural course of development as one of two major lines of change, the other being the cultural line that transforms biologically determined structures into complex, reflective forms. As we pointed out in Chapter 2, Vygotsky did not ignore the organismic foundation for development, and there are universal aspects to his theory—the most important being the joining of thought and language in the early preschool years, which paves the way for the emergence of higher psychological functions. Thus, Piaget and Vygotsky each devised theories with natural and social dimensions and regarded neither as sufficient by itself to explain development. Piaget, however, stressed the natural side in his account of general structural change in children's thinking, and Vygotsky stressed the social side in highlighting the transforming impact of dialogues with expert partners on children's naturally formed concepts.

The contrast between the two great thinkers, Vygotsky and Piaget, is more one of emphasis than of irreconcilable division.

In sum, Piaget and Vygotsky both started with the same basic view of the child as a biological organism. Piaget focused on what it is within the organism that leads to cognitive change. Vygotsky explored how social experience might cause important revisions in the child's thinking to come about. Although Vygotsky's emphasis on the role of instruction in development highlights the importance of verbal dialogue ([1934] 1986), he explicitly indicated that children sometimes revise their thinking by stumbling across challenges in the environment. Similarly, Piaget accepted the notion that members of the child's culture can aid development through instruction and dialogue, although not in the radically transforming way that Vygotsky proposed. For Piaget, instruction can refine and improve structures that have already emerged, but it cannot lead to the development of concepts, as Vygotsky believed it does.

Because Piaget and Vygotsky share a set of basic beliefs about development, their theories are best viewed as not in opposition but rather as complementing one another. Glassman (1994) sums up their common features as follows:

• There are two lines of development—the natural and the social—that interact continuously in the development of thinking. Each is important, and cognitive change cannot be understood without both.

• Development is the result of experience in an environment; eventually, children become capable of transform-

Piaget focused on what it is within the organism that leads to cognitive change; Vygotsky explored how social experience might cause important revisions to the child's thinking.

ing their experiences mentally, through internal reflection.

• The course of cognitive development involves major, qualitative transformations in thinking. For Piaget, children everywhere move through a series of four stages. For Vygotsky, thinking is radically transformed when (1) children become capable of linguistic communication, and (2) instruction leads them to become aware of and to master their own thoughts.

• The pace of an individual's development can be influenced by the social milieu.

By remaining cognizant of similarities between Piaget and Vygotsky, researchers and practitioners can use the theories' points of departure as checks and balances in their own work. As Glassman suggests,

[A teacher] concerned with cultural influences but also aware that cognitive structures " . . . cannot be forced on the child from the outside . . . " (Vygotsky 1929, 421) might turn to the ontological processes developed by Piaget to check on whether it is possible to teach a child something at a certain age. A developmental researcher concerned with universal development can balance what seem to be universal findings against social histories. (1994, 212)

The differences between Piaget and Vygotsky should not lead to ruptures between those who prefer one perspective over the other. Recognition of shared as well as unique features allows for constructive dialogue and the likelihood of an expanded, unified perspective that incorporates the best features of both in the near future. Indeed, it is intriguing to speculate about the broader conception that might exist today had these two giants of cognitive development had the chance to meet and weave together their extraordinary accomplishments.

6

Vygotsky's Theory in
Early Childhood Classrooms

In programs that are consistent with Vygotsky's framework, such as the Reggio Emilia program in Italy, the role of the teacher is seen as "provoking occasions of discovery through a kind of alert, inspired facilitation and stimulation of children's dialogue, co-action, and co-construction of knowledge. Because intellectual discovery is believed to be an essentially social process, the teacher assists even the youngest children to learn to listen to others, take account of their goals and ideas, and communicate successfully." (Edwards 1993, 154)

As expressed by one of the Reggio pedagogistas, "We [teachers] must be able to catch the ball that the children throw us, and toss it back to them in a way that makes the children want to continue the game with us, developing, perhaps, other games as we go along." (Filippini 1990, as cited in Edwards, Gandini, & Forman 1993, 153)

In this chapter we address applications of Vygotsky's theory to teaching and learning in early childhood classrooms. We will see that the sociocultural perspective assumes that besides presenting necessary information, extended opportunities for discussion and problem solving in the context of shared activities are essential for learning and development. In the words of two Vygotskian scholars, education must be thought of in a new way—not in terms of the transmission of knowledge but in terms of "transaction and trans-

formation" (Chang-Wells & Wells 1993, 59). Through its emphasis on the social origins of higher mental functions and its ideas on how culturally constructed tools of the mind are internalized by the individual, Vygotsky's theory has provided a provocative framework for instructional innovation. Several themes are ever-present in contemporary efforts to apply Vygotsky's ideas to the education of young children.

First, Vygotsky-based curricular reform places a heavy emphasis on classroom discourse—both teacher–child and child–child interaction. Vygotsky regarded the discourse of schooling as qualitatively different from everyday interaction. In school, words serve not only as a means of communication but also as objects of study, as children begin to talk about reading and writing as well as linguistically mediated topics in mathematics, science, social studies, and other subjects. Recall from Chapter 5 that Vygotsky viewed instruction as the means whereby children become aware of and develop the capacity to consciously manipulate and control the symbolic systems of their culture. Mastery of written language is especially important in this process. Vygotsky ([1930–1935] 1978) pointed out that written expression must be more precise and expanded than verbal expression because it cannot rely on supplementary elements, such as tone of voice and gesture, to clarify meaning. Consequently, it is especially well suited to support children's appreciation of language as a system and its use as a tool for thought. Therefore, a major portion of this chapter centers on forms of classroom discourse that foster facility with textual material.

Not surprisingly, most efforts to promote development-enhancing classroom discourse have focused on elementary school, the period during which "formal" education is initiated. In accord with this emphasis, our discussion centers on the primary grades. Nevertheless, the examples we will describe and the principles that underlie them can be adapted for use with younger children. In the final section of this chapter, we will discuss a unique, contemporary approach to preschool education that is highly consistent with sociocultural theory. Vygotsky's major pedagogical message for preschool teachers was to provide many opportunities for scaffolded activities within the young child's zone of proximal development (ZPD) and, especially, for imaginative play—the ultimate means of promoting the self-regulatory skills required for cooperative endeavors with peers and for successful mastery of academic tasks after school entry (see Chapter 3). Overall, developmentally appropriate preschool and primary classrooms should differ in the relative balance of play versus academic-related experiences they provide; with age, children become cognitively equipped to handle more of the latter.

A second, related theme that pervades Vygotskian curricular innovations is an emphasis on literacy. We have already noted that according to Vygotsky ([1930–1935] 1978), literate activities play a major role in the development of conscious awareness of mental functions and in bringing them under voluntary control. Once children become aware of the symbolic and communicative systems of language, thinking starts to become an object of attention and reflection. Consequently, teachers in Vygotsky-based classrooms transform the environment into a highly literate setting in which many different types of symbolic communication can be used, integrated with one another, and mastered by children. Reading, writing, and quantitative reasoning are not transmitted in isolation or in a rigid, step-by-step manner in which children are drilled on component skills in ways devoid of sense or meaning. Instead, literacy as understanding and communication of meaning in authentic social contexts is central. The "whole-language" movement, a current approach to early childhood literacy education influenced by Vygotsky's theory, embodies these ideas. In this chapter we discuss a variety of educational practices, many of which are consistent with the tenets of whole language. We will illustrate these practices with examples from several subject-matter areas, thereby underscoring their broad applicability. Readers specifically interested in pursuing the whole-language philosophy should consult works by Goodman (1986), Watson (1989), and McGee and Richgels (1990).

Third, throughout this chapter we will revisit a concept central to Vygotsky's theory: the zone of proximal development. Providing assistance to children that is responsive to their current level of progress and that spurs their development by capitalizing on momentary instructional opportunities is seldom seen in North American classrooms. Yet sociocultural theory tells us that without sensitive intervention adapted to individual children's ZPDs, they learn at less-than-optimum rates. The idea of *emergent curriculum*—which means that early childhood teachers make plans based on children's evolving interests and competencies rather than mapping out classroom experiences months ahead of time, is highly consistent with Vygtosky's theory, since this approach integrates child spontaneity with flexible but deliberate teacher guidance (Jones & Nimmo 1994). And as we will see, Vygotsky's notion of the ZPD has not only inspired development-enhancing instructional procedures but led to new "dynamic" techniques for assessing children's readiness to learn.

Finally, a sociocultural approach to education requires shaping the classroom into a community of learners—a sociocultural system created from within by teachers and children and supported from without by its surrounding social context. The interdependence of adults

> *Teachers in Vygotsky-based classrooms transform the environment into a highly literate setting in which many different types of symbolic communication are used and integrated.*

and children in contributing to emergent understandings through joint involvement in culturally meaningful activities is at the heart of Vygotskian school experiences (Moll & Greenberg 1990). In this respect, several investigators have argued that Vygotsky's original conception of the ZPD needs to be broadened, from a view of a single child in collaboration with a more expert partner to a vision of collective, interrelated zones (Moll & Whitmore 1993). In the final section of this chapter, we consider several successful attempts to restructure schools so that the reorganization of goals and the external supports necessary to design classrooms as sociocultural learning communities can take place.

The importance of activity settings in which children are required to function

If collaboration with others is so essential for cognitive development during schooling, then why does it seldom occur? Sociocultural theory emphasizes that the nature of the activities in which adults and children engage influences the quality of their verbal interaction, which, in turn, molds their thinking (Tulviste 1991). From this perspective, a major reason that interactions directly assisting children's learning are rare in many classrooms is that with the transition to kindergarten and first grade, teacher–child interaction is often driven by familiar, well-learned preselected activities designed for the class as a whole. Furthermore, many teachers rely on scripts from teaching manuals to guide discourse related to these activities. Not surprisingly, the resulting interaction tends to alternate between the teacher's questions and the expected responses of the children. This style permits total-class lessons to flow smoothly but largely restricts children's involvement to low-level cognitive processing, such as rote, repetitive drill, and memorization of facts. Indeed, up to 20% of questions in classrooms that emphasize recitation discourse can be answered with a simple "yes" or "no" (Goodlad 1984; Gallimore, Dalton, & Tharp 1986; Oakes 1986). Unfortunately, more often than not an unexpected remark from a child during a recitation sequence leads teachers to terminate the interaction and move on to another child in search of the predicted response. Only when large-group activities veer off their preplanned course do teachers seem to engage children in higher-level thinking, such as analyzing, synthesizing, and applying ideas and concepts.

For at least two reasons, whole-class instruction—the most common activity setting in American and Canadian classrooms—works poorly to achieve the negotiation of shared meaning necessary to guide children through successive ZPDs. First, the teacher cannot adequately attend to the instructional needs of individual children. If he or she stops to assist one or two children, management difficulties quickly surface among the remainder of the class (Tharp & Gallimore 1988). Second, to maintain order and a smooth flow of class-

room events, whole-class teaching requires constant asymmetry of power between teachers and children. When children are granted no more than a reactive voice in classroom dialogues, they have little opportunity to experiment with strategies under the watchful eye of an adult expert and to indicate (through verbal or behavioral cues) the kind of assistance they need to achieve meaningful understanding. It is not surprising that in classrooms in which instruction is largely confined to the whole-class setting, interactive experiences that permit children to move beyond acquisition of "a basket of facts" are virtually nonexistent (Anderson 1984).

When is whole-class instruction appropriate?

Most Vygotsky-based curricula include short periods in which teachers gather the whole class in a meeting area, since the success of other activity settings rests on effective functioning of the entire class. Sometimes teachers may want to use a whole-class session to orient children to small-group and individual lessons and to convey any special procedures necessary to perform those tasks, such as rotation through different areas of the classroom. At other times, the whole group may be used for classwide instruction addressing content that many children are ready to master at the same time. Occasionally, teachers assemble the whole class to solve social problems and teach values essential for forming a community of learners. And once in a while, they may take a moment to share their philosophy of instruction with the entire class, granting children insight into exactly why they arrange classroom experiences as they do. For example, at the conclusion

Small-group and dyadic interactions that occur in activity centers permit children to assume an active voice and teachers to impart a voice to them through dialogue.

of an activity, one teacher of third-graders remarked to her class after they had gathered on the rug, "Talking is probably the most important thing we do here, because you learn the most when you can talk while you work" (Moll & Whitmore 1993, 28). This statement sums up simply and elegantly a central Vygotskian tenet of education. It contrasts sharply with the messages admonishing children to be silent that have peppered whole-class instruction for centuries.

Activity centers

Activity centers are thematically structured areas of the classroom that permit children to work in various ways to accomplish individual and group academic goals. Small-group and dyadic interactions that occur in activity centers permit children to assume an active voice and teachers to impart a voice to them through dialogue. Activities are best arranged so that limits are not placed on what children can learn about the themes addressed by the materials and props of the center. Because of the diversity of experiences possible in activity centers, each participant can make useful contributions to the understanding of others that often move beyond the confines of the activity area. For example, in one classroom, center-based activities were eventually extended throughout the room, and children collectively reached heights not possible without the combination of teacher guidance and the cooperative involvement of other children that was generated by the activity setting. A center with thematic props on Egypt eventually led the

> *In reciprocal teaching, a teacher and several children form a learning group in which they take turns leading a discussion aimed at helping the children understand and learn from a text passage.*

classroom to be transformed into a museum, through which the children guided children from other classes in their school (Moll & Whitmore 1993).

Activity centers are ideally suited for joint construction of meaningful goals through rich classroom talk that promotes higher-order, literate modes of communicating and thinking. Small-group and dyadic interaction surrounding common tasks enable teachers to fulfill their crucial role of assisting children in explaining their ideas, raising questions, overcoming fears of risk taking when new challenges arise, and working together despite differences in language, cultural background, and abilities.

Individual child activities

A final activity setting important in Vygotsky-based classrooms involves the individual child interacting with texts—written either by other authors or by the children themselves. Children transfer the understandings and skills they have gleaned from dialogues with others to their own literacy-related discourse. In these settings, they converse not just with themselves but also with the text narrative. As Tharp and Gallimore (1988) point out, a literate life involves continuous interaction with written materials. Time, space, and resources for carrying out discourse with text should be made available early in a child's development. Eventually, dia-

logue with others speaking through text becomes the most common activity setting for learning, offering a lifetime of occasions to acquire new knowledge and symbolic tools.

Teacher–child discourse

What kind of teacher–child discourse is best suited to developing active, self-confident learners with a firm grasp of the literate modes of expression of their cultural communities? In the following sections, we answer this question by considering three innovative instructional programs stimulated by Vygotsky's ideas. At the heart of each program are efforts by teachers to engage in interactive teaching with respect to a diverse array of challenging tasks. In doing so, teachers communicate their firm desire to foster children's active involvement in and control of their own learning.

Reciprocal teaching

Reciprocal teaching is a method of instruction inspired by Vygotsky's theory that was originally designed to improve reading comprehension among older elementary school children who are at risk for academic difficulties or who are already experiencing such difficulties (Palincsar & Brown 1984). Recently, the approach has been extended to younger children and to other subject-matter areas, such as social studies and science lessons. In reciprocal teaching, a teacher and two to four children form a learning group in which they take turns leading a discussion aimed at helping the children understand a text passage and acquire new knowledge from it. The role of the teacher is to scaffold children's involvement in the discussion in ways that eventually lead to full participation in the dialogue, as well as mastery of the text at hand.

To reach these goals, group members apply four cognitive strategies in sequential order: *questioning, summarizing, clarifying,* and *predicting.* At first, the teacher explains and models the strategies to prompt children's entry into the interaction. As children become more proficient, the teacher supports and provides feedback while gradually reducing his or her own role in the discussion. Systematic use of the four cognitive strategies ensures that children will grasp new knowledge by linking it to previously acquired information, retain clear direction to the discussion, elaborate their ideas, and rework what they have learned so it can be used to solve new problems.

Once group members have read a passage, a dialogue leader (initially the teacher, later a child) begins by *asking questions* about its content. Children pose answers, raise additional questions, and, in case of disagreement, reread the text. Next, the leader *summarizes* the passage, and discussion takes place to achieve consensus on the summary. Then participants *clarify* ideas that are ambiguous or unfamiliar to any group members. Finally, the leader encourages children to *predict* upcoming content based on prior knowledge and clues in the passage (Palincsar & Klenk 1992).

In reciprocal teaching, children meet for many sessions and read a variety of passages that contain analogous themes so that their understanding of important concepts can be deepened through examination of similarities. By using texts with recurrent themes, children quickly learn that they can use information gleaned from one to grasp the meaning of another—that is, to process new text more efficiently and effectively than

they could without the previously acquired relevant knowledge.

Here is an excerpt of a reciprocal teaching episode that ensued after a small group of first-graders and their teacher had begun to read a series of stories addressing the theme of animal survival. Just before this dialogue, the teacher read a passage about the snowshoe rabbit to the children that described the birth of baby rabbits and the ways in which the mother rabbit cared for them:

Kam (dialogue leader): When [were] the babies born?

Teacher: That's a good question to ask. Call on someone to answer that question.

Kam: Robby? Milly?

Milly: Summer.

Teacher: What would happen if the babies were born in the winter? Let's think.

Several children make a number of responses including: "The baby would be very cold." "They would need food." "They don't have no fur when they are just born."

Kam: I have another question. How does she get the babies safe?

Kris: She hides them.

Kam: That's right but something else . . . .

Teacher: There is something very unusual about how she hides them that surprised me. I didn't know this.

Travis: They are all in a different place.

Teacher: Why do you think she does this?

Milly: Probably because I heard another story and when they're babies they usually eat each other or fight with each other.

Teacher: That could be! And what about when the lynx comes?

Several children comment that that would be the end of all the babies.

Travis: If I was the mother I would hide mine, but I would keep them all together.

Kris: If the babies are hidden and the mom wants to go and look at them, how can she remember where they are?

Young children need to have time, space, and resources to engage in discourse with text.

Teacher: Good question. Because she does have to find them again. Why? What does she bring them?

Milly: She needs to bring food. She probably leaves a twig or something.

Teacher: Do you think she puts out a twig like we mark a trail?

Several children disagree and suggest that she uses her sense of smell. One child, recalling that the snowshoe rabbit is not all white in the winter, suggests that the mother might be able to tell her babies apart by their coloring.

Teacher: So we agree that the mother rabbit uses her senses to find her babies after she hides them. Kam, can you summarize for us now?

Kam: The babies are born in the summer . . . .

Scaffolding Children's Learning

Teacher: The mother . . .

Kam: The mother hides the babies in different places.

Teacher: And she visits them . . .

Kam: To bring them food.

Travis: She keeps them safe.

Teacher: Any predictions?

Milly: What she teaches her babies . . . like how to hop.

Kris: They know how to hop already.

Teacher: Well, let's read and see.

(Palincsar, Brown, &
Campione 1993, 47–48)

As this segment of discourse reveals, reciprocal teaching evokes an impressive array of higher-order cognitive processes in children, including analysis of text content, synthesis with previous knowledge, question asking, and inference making. Children's contributions to the dialogues are rich in clarifications and extensions of the story theme and full of discoveries and speculations based on information read in previous texts. Designers of the technique remarked that as children make these connections, they often voice them with great excitement, expressed through "squeals of delight" (Palincsar, Brown, & Campione 1993, 49).

Research reveals that compared to control children (who listened to the same stories but did not engage in dialogue about their content), first-graders who experienced reciprocal teaching over as little as 20 consecutive days showed impressive gains in comprehension of passages thematically related to but different from the ones used in the discussions. In addition, when given a sorting task in which they were asked to group pictures of animals into themes emphasized in the stories, children who participated in reciprocal teaching more often made classification decisions based on thematic similarities, whereas control children's groupings were largely limited to animals' physical characteristics. Underlying principles rather than obvious perceptual features more often guided the conceptual thinking of the children who experienced reciprocal teaching (Palincsar, Brown, & Campione 1993). Just as Vygotsky's theory suggests, the strategies conveyed through dialogues scaffolded by an adult expert led to impressive gains in higher mental functions.

Reciprocal teaching is probably the most structured of Vygotsky-based interventions, but designers of the technique comment that it is deliberately so. The strategies woven into reciprocal teaching were selected because they represent the cognitive activities in which successful comprehenders typically engage as they learn from text (Palincsar, Brown, & Campione 1993). Because of its structure, reciprocal teaching is an especially good technique for teachers to apply who are just beginning to integrate the sociocultural framework into classroom experiences. For all new learners (teachers and children alike), it is helpful to have a clear road map for a new practice—particularly one that is of such demonstrated success! Later, as the inquiry procedures of reciprocal teaching become well learned, teachers can adapt them to new curricular goals and to suit the needs of particular classroom situations. Indeed, observations reveal that both teachers and children start by labeling the four strategies of reciprocal teaching and using them in fairly rigid order. Gradually, all participants become more flexible. Teachers pause and children interject questions and clarifying remarks from the very outset of a session, even as the passage is read.

Just as children are cognitively stretched and stimulated by Vygotskian dialogic experiences, teachers are challenged in their efforts to activate and sustain them. Teachers who use reciprocal teaching find themselves calling on a diverse array of conversational devices to support children's discussions, including cueing ideas, paraphrasing children's contributions, selectively using praise, and even engaging in well-timed silence (Palincsar, Brown, & Campione 1993). But to use these strategies effectively, teachers are likely to find that their own inner dialogues about children and the process of instruction change, becoming more intense and effortful, as the box below reveals.

Inquiry in mathematics lessons

The teacher–child dialogic model we are about to discuss has elements in common with reciprocal teaching, since it focuses on developing inquiry skills in young children through active involvement with others in problem solving. It differs from reciprocal teaching largely in that its procedures are less structured—that is, not laid out in advance. Instead, negotiation of meaning takes place as teachers and children talk about and practice the subject matter at hand—in this instance, mathematics. As

---

Learning to Engage in Responsive Questioning: Teachers' Inner Speech

According to Vygotsky, behavior is first regulated through dialogue with a more capable individual surrounding challenging tasks, then by the self-directed utterances of the learner. As new skills become automatized, private speech goes underground and becomes more rapid, abbreviated, and silent. Although this process has been studied intensively in children (see Chapter 2), it can also be seen in adults during skill acquisition. Gallimore, Dalton, and Tharp (1986) asked teachers to describe their inner speech as they applied a new approach to dialogue in their classrooms called "responsive questioning," designed to replace the predictable question–correct answer sequences of the traditional recitation method.

Like reciprocal teaching, responsive questioning permits teachers to guide, assist, and regulate students' information processing, encouraging them to engage in higher-order thinking and more elaborate expression of ideas. To

help teachers master this form of discourse, they were taught a technique of question asking called "E-T-R" (experience, text, and relationship). For example, before a story is read, the teacher questions children to bring into awareness any prior experiences that might relate to it. Once reading begins, the teacher periodically returns to E-questions to extend the experiential background on which children can build an understanding of the story line. She also adds T-questions (those that guide text processing) directed at various levels of comprehension, from literal details to higher-order inferences. In addition, R-questions (those that prompt children to draw relationships) are introduced to assist children in connecting current knowledge and past experiences (E) with text information (T).

Gallimore, Dalton, and Tharp point out that responsive questioning creates interactions that resemble natural conversation. Consequently, besides fostering more-advanced cognitive processing, responsive questioning may fit quite well

---

Scaffolding Children's Learning

unanticipated events occur, the teacher capitalizes on them to scaffold children's understanding as well as to emphasize her expectation that children contribute to and reap the benefits of an interactive learning situation (Minick 1989).

Cobb, Wood, Yackel, and their collaborators designed a second-grade inquiry math program to deepen children's mathematical understanding and then evaluated it by carefully observing classroom events and measuring gains in knowledge. The program emphasized two interwoven levels of conversation: "doing and talking about mathematics"

and "talking about talking about math" (Cobb, Wood, & Yackel 1993).

At the beginning of the school year, the teacher was explicit and directive in her requests that children engage in dialogue surrounding mathematical activities. She deliberately promoted classroom conditions vital to joint inquiry: listening to one another's ideas, expressing one's own thoughts clearly, cooperating with one another in problem solving, persisting at challenging problems, and attempting to achieve consensus about an answer. These instructions were part of "talking about talking about math." They were intended

with the linguistic experiences of certain low-income, ethnic-minority children, who (unlike their middle-class, ethnic-majority counterparts) have had little prior exposure to recitation-like interaction in their homes (see Chapter 2, p. 15–17).

Teachers-in-training for responsive questioning reported thinking to themselves in ways quite different than they had before. The greatest change involved inner statements directed at carefully attending to children's utterances. Because responsive questioning requires teachers to build on children's contributions, they had to concentrate on what children were trying to say, not just on whether they were right or wrong. Incomplete answers became opportunities to provide assistance, not cues to look for another child who could give the expected answer. Here is one teacher's report of how responsive questioning led to her revised view of children:

I used to be very dependent on the teacher's manual for comprehension questions. [Now] I just listen to what they're saying and from where they're coming. Sometimes, you know, it's really amazing [how they won't have the experiential background you

expect], so [I say], "Just forget the story and let's discuss this." Some days [I think], "Oh my, I thought they knew this." I have to rethink on the spot what I'm going to ask them . . . . It's a lot of changing. (Gallimore, Dalton, & Tharp 1986, 25)

In responsive questioning, the E–T–R combination provides an overall framework for teacher–child interchanges. Exactly what teachers do stems from their reflections on what type of follow-up question might aid children's learning. Unlike recitation, teachers cannot depend on purely automatic processes—scripts or repeated sets of specific acts—to support children's learning in the ZPD. Instead, they must tailor each new question to the immediate conditions. Consequently, teachers are likely to find themselves immersed in a constant inner dialogue through which they reflect on the meaning of children's utterances to choose a course of action that permits children to extend their knowledge and skills. As a result, the experience of teaching becomes more serendipitous and cognitively demanding—and also more experimental, stimulating, and gratifying.

to stimulate classroom norms that convey the view that mathematics is an interactive as well as individual constructive activity. When children were "doing and talking about math," the teacher was far less directive. Instead, the instructional approach was one in which opportunities were provided for children to build mathematical knowledge in collaboration with others—through attempts to resolve opposing points of view, explain a mathematical idea or solution, and create agreed-on ways of coordinating mathematical activities with those of others (Cobb et al. 1991).

Designers of the approach emphasize that their sociocultural perspective to teaching math should be distinguished from the Piagetian view that social interaction is no more than a catalyst for individual cognitive change. Instead, teachers and children form a social organization in which they mutually construct shared mathematical knowledge, itself the product of prior sociocultural negotiations. The process enables children to grasp the meaning and usefulness of mathematical practices and to develop the view that mathematics is a community endeavor, not an adult-imposed system or a private problem-solving activity. Like the Vygotsky-based interventions we have already considered, the teacher's role in implementing an inquiry mathematics curriculum is multifaceted, complex, and demanding. It includes

highlighting conflicts between alternative interpretations or solutions, helping students develop productive small-group cooperative relationships, facilitating mathematical dialogue between students, implicitly legitimizing selected aspects of contributions to a discussion in light of their potential fruitfulness for further mathematical constructions, redescribing students' explanations in more sophisticated terms that are nonetheless comprehensible to stu-

dents, and guiding the development of [shared] representational systems. (Cobb et al. 1991, 7)

To illustrate, let's look at several examples of teacher–child discourse. In the first, a child displays his difficulty in switching away from the answer-centered curriculum he had become accustomed to in first grade, in which children had to use a teacher-sanctioned solution method, were not encouraged to articulate their own understandings, and frequently experienced public evaluations of the worth of their responses. In this excerpt, the teacher assists the child in revising previously acquired social norms and in moving toward the inquiry approach:

(The teacher and children have been discussing the word problem, "How many runners altogether? There are six runners on each team. There are two teams in the race.")

Teacher: Jack, what answer-solution did you come up with? *(The teacher called on Jack with the expectation that he would explain his way of thinking.)*

Jack: Fourteen.

Teacher *(Accepting Jack's answer without evaluation and restating her question):* Fourteen. How did you get that answer?

Jack: Because 6 plus 6 is 12. Two runners on two teams . . . . *(Jack stops talking, puts his hands to the side of his face, and looks down at the floor. Then he looks at the teacher and then at his partner, Ann. He turns and faces the front of the room with his back to the teacher and mumbles inaudibly.)*

Teacher: Would you say that again? I didn't quite get the whole thing. You had—say it again please.

Jack *(Softly, still facing the front of the room):* It's six runners on each team.

Teacher: Right.

Jack *(Turns to look at the teacher):* I made a mistake. It's wrong. It should be twelve. *(He turns and faces the front of the room.)*

Teacher (*At this point, initiating a new conversation in which she and the children "talk about talking about mathematics"*): Oh, okay. Is it okay to make a mistake?

Andrew: Yes.

Teacher: Is it okay to make a mistake, Jack?

Jack: Yes.

Teacher: You bet it is. As long as you're in my class it is okay to make a mistake. Because I make them all the time, and we learn from our mistakes—a lot. Jack already figured out, "Ooops, I didn't have the right answer the first time" (*Jack turns and looks at the teacher and smiles*), but he kept working at it and he got it.

(Adapted from Cobb, Wood, & Yackel 1993, 98–99)

This example illustrates how a teacher strategically combined the two levels of discourse that form the basis of the inquiry math program. In this incident, joint negotiation of mathematical meanings ("doing and talking about mathematics") was disrupted by Jack's embarrassment at having made a mistake and his erroneous assumption that the teacher had evaluated his response. At first, the teacher tried to handle the situation subtly, by restating her initial request. When this did not work, she introduced the second form of discourse ("talking about talking about mathematics"), becoming more directive as she explicitly granted children the right to make errors and justified the importance of being able "to say what they really thought mathematically" (Cobb, Wood, & Yackel 1993, 99). Eventually, the value of attaining understanding through conjecturing, debating, and justifying paths to problem solution (rather than merely seeking answers expected by the teacher) was accepted by the class. Children emerged with a revised interpretation of the terms *understand*, *explain*, and *justify*, permitting "talking

> *In a Vygotsky-based mathematics curriculum, construction of mathematical knowledge is not an adult-imposed system or a private problem-solving activity but a community endeavor of teachers and children together.*

about talking about mathematics" to recede in favor of animated conversation about the subject matter at hand.

Because children had not previously been expected to collaborate in small groups at school, teachers of inquiry math often had to guide and monitor the children's attempts to engage in genuine mathematical communication. Consider the following interactive sequence as Karen and Craig worked on the problems

$47 + 19 = $ __,

$48 + 18 = $ __, and

$49 + 17 = $ __:

Karen (*Holding up her thumb, starting to count*): Forty-eight, forty . . . . That's just the same. (*Karen excitedly points to 47 + 19 = 66 on the activity sheet, but Craig ignores and continues to write his answer to the previous problem. The teacher then takes his turn in the dialogue and asks Karen, "What is just the same?"*)

Karen: If you take 1 from the 19 and put it with the 7 (*She hesitates and looks at the teacher, while Craig leans forward to look closely at the problem*), and [it] makes 48 and that makes just the same [as 48 plus 18].

Teacher: Do you see that, Craig? Do you see what she is trying to say? (*The teacher initiates a sequence involving "talking about talking about mathematics," in which she reminds Craig of his obligation to listen and try to understand Karen's explanation. Then she returns to "talking about mathematics."*)

Negotiating Attitudes and Feelings about Learning through Teacher–Child Discourse

Supporting children in their attempts to explain their ideas to others, define their own questions, and overcome their fears of risk taking often entails more than just assisting them in using literate modes of thinking and communicating. How fully children participate in classroom interaction and the way they approach new tasks often depends on their self-image as a learner. Consequently, to promote effective discourse in the child's ZPD, teachers must negotiate not only new literate meanings but also attitudes and feelings about learning itself.

Fear of making mistakes prevents many children from tackling challenging tasks. Sometimes, to benefit from an activity, they must be prompted into making a start. Here is how one teacher sensitively helped two third-grade boys get started on a task in which they had to select a topic for investigation:

(Brian and Kim are having trouble coming up with a project to pursue, a difficult task for any researcher. The teacher remembers that Brian is interested in maps, so she sends the two boys off to get the globe. When she joins them again, they have been exploring the globe for some time.)

Teacher: OK, I want to talk to you two. Now you've spent a lot of time looking at the globe, haven't you? You both look very interested in maps. I wonder if you could try and draw a map as part of your project. Would that interest you?

(Brian and Kim look dubious.)

Brian: Too hard.

Teacher: For you? Well how about—

Brian: Tracing.

Teacher: Tracing? Pretty small; that's the only trouble, isn't it? Would you feel brave enough to try to draw one to make it larger? You could just use a— a scrap of paper and try it out. Do a rough copy to see how it works. You never know it might work . . . . Want to try a rough copy?

Brian *(Still somewhat reluctant):* I don't know.

Teacher: Well, who's going to know if you don't know? How about you, Kim? Do you want to try?

Kim: *(Inaudible)*

Teacher: It's a good idea to try it out. If you want to, go to the cupboard and just take a piece of—you know, the big paper—the newsprint—just for a rough copy? OK? And see how it works out. If you don't try it, you'll never know.

Brian: OK.

(Adapted from Chang-Wells & Wells 1993, 75–76)

In this interactive sequence, the teacher does not resolve the problem by simply telling the children what to do; rather, she builds on their interests. Once a reticent child embarks on a task, the teacher may need to provide extra encouragement to sustain the child's involvement. Careful selection of activities so that they fall within the child's ZPD, adult expressions of confidence that children can master new challenges with effort, warm support as children do so, and messages that stress the importance of improving knowledge and skills rather than working for grades or concrete rewards are effective ways to nurture young children's confidence in themselves as learners and positive attitudes toward school tasks (Dweck 1991; Heyman, Dweck, & Cain 1992; Churchill 1994).

Teacher: Look at the next problem, 48 plus 18 equals. She said it is the same number.

Karen: Ya, because you take 1 from the 19 and add it to the 47 and that makes . . . *(Hesitates).*

Teacher: Forty-eight.

Karen: Forty-eight and 18 . . .

Craig *(Interrupts):* Oh! I know what she's trying to say. Take 1 from here and add it here.

Teacher: Right!

Craig: It's got to be the same answer, or you can add it here and add to here *(Points from 47 to 48 and from 18 to 19).*

Karen: No, take one from . . . *(She points to 19)* and add it here *(Points to 47).*

(Adapted from Cobb, Wood, & Yackel 1993, 103–04)

This episode illustrates the kind of teacher-guided, joint search for pattern and meaning that leads children to engage in more advanced mathematical activity than they would if they worked by themselves. As these second-graders became actively involved in collaborative dialogues, they became increasingly effective in constructing mutual understandings about math (Yackel, Cobb, & Wood 1991).

How effective is the inquiry mathematics program just described in enhancing children's learning and in changing their views of classroom experience? Results of a quantitative evaluation comparing 17 inquiry classrooms projects with nonproject controls revealed that second-graders in project classrooms were substantially ahead of their peers in conceptual understanding of arithmetic (Cobb et al. 1991). In addition, project children were far more likely to indicate that success in math involves understanding, not simply accepting an authority's solutions, preparing neat papers, and being quiet in the classroom (Nicholls et al. 1990). In the process of participating in inquiry learning, children developed a revised appreciation of instruction—not as transmission of knowledge by those who know more to those who know less, or conformity of children to teacher expectations for good behavior, but "as a forum of negotiation, of re-creation of meaning" (Bruner 1986, 123).

Creating a literate classroom community

In this final example of teacher–child discourse from a Vygotskian perspective, the educational innovation extends from a single subject-matter domain to pervade all learning activities, thereby creating a literate classroom community. Again, the sociocultural theme of extended opportunity for discussion and problem solving in the context of shared activities is evident. But here, the teacher serves not just as a skilled moderator of dialogue but also as a designer of a highly literate environment in which all learning activities serve as social contexts in which children experiment with and use oral and written language to make sense and construct meaning.

Moll and Whitmore (1993) observed a third-grade bilingual classroom comprising monolingual and bilingual Mexican and Anglo children whose teacher describes herself as a whole-language enthusiast. Her classroom typifies the more all-encompassing notion of the ZPD mentioned at the beginning of this chapter—as a social system in which children learn through collective, interrelated zones that are mutually and actively created by teachers and children (Moll 1990). Consider the following daily activities, designed to promote children's mastery of literate modes of expression, in both their native and their second language.

As children participate in inquiry learning, they come to see the educational process not as transmission of knowledge or conformity to teacher expectations for good behavior but "as a forum of negotiation, of re-creation of meaning" (Bruner 1986, 123).

Literature study groups. The morning often begins with literature study groups that provide social reading experiences through which children can analyze content, share reactions, and explore questions about books with teachers and peers. Reading materials usually are organized around the work of a particular author. Study groups are formed on the basis of children's interests and choices, in contrast to traditional "reading groups" that are based on current reading "ability." Consequently, the groups permit children to explore literature with readers of varied levels of progress, as well as with readers of one or two languages. As a result, children frequently mediate each other's learning.

In a typical literature study-group dialogue, children contribute different interpretations of the story. Then the teacher summarizes, offers additional possibilities, and asks the children to explain their reactions, deepening their analyses of the text. As the discussion progresses, children are encouraged to use a variety of sources to mediate their understanding—personal experiences, other stories they have read, the text at hand, peers, and the teacher.

Drop everything and read (DEAR). The teacher also arranges for daily individual reading experiences, which she calls "drop everything and read (DEAR)," to complement social reading groups. DEAR involves an extended period of silent reading (15 to 30 minutes), in which children focus on any materials that interest them—books, newspapers, magazines, writing by class members, comics, and other written works. The teacher joins in the activity by selecting readings of her own, thereby conveying through modeling that reading is among the most pleasurable and enriching of learning activities.

The writing workshop. Literature study groups and DEAR are followed by a writing workshop, in which children collaborate on a wide variety of written products that they sometimes illustrate and publish for the rest of the class. Spelling, punctuation, style, and penmanship lessons are integrated into these real-world, meaningful writing experiences. Children select topics and language of expression, and they can be seen collaborating on stories, letters, and other written forms as the teacher supports their efforts. Sometimes the interests of a few children in mastering new formats for writing spread to other class members, so the teacher stops and provides everyone with a short lesson about the skill. In one instance, she taught the whole class about the use of quotation marks, since many children were attempting to integrate conversations into their stories. All of children's written work is retained to track their progress and explorations of new possibilities.

Thematic units. Afternoons in the classroom are organized around a unit with thematic content, selected for intensive study. At the beginning of the year, the whole class meets with the teacher to brainstorm about topics. Then similar suggestions are grouped together (e.g., "sharks and whales" with "ocean"), and children vote for their 10 most favorite. Thus, unlike traditional classroom experiences, in which tasks are preselected and initiated by the teacher, in this classroom there is considerably more leeway for children to voice their ideas and preferences. Although the teacher has in mind some general goals to be met in a unit that extends over several weeks, children play a significant role in selecting and organizing the tasks to achieve these goals. Thematic units are based on the assumption that children can become active inquirers in the classroom only by being allowed to choose and explore alternatives. These opportunities, guided by teachers' expertise, are important for sparking the interest and curiosity necessary to energize learning.

Thematic units integrate all subject-matter areas and include large-group, small-group, and individual activities. Each unit eventually culminates in a product or demonstration of the class's learning. For example, a theme about the human body led to a newspaper about health, published by the class, that was distributed throughout the school. A Native American unit resulted in a book that included all children as co-authors, as well as a detailed bibliography of additional sources of information about Native Americans. At the same time, thematic units stress learning processes, not just products. Teachers assist children in mastering procedures for tapping research sources. Children, in turn, become responsible for raising research-able questions and keeping records of reference materials. The written reports children create must follow the culturally defined conventions of the genre they have selected. Often their products are entered into the school library, granting children the privilege of providing their community with real, researched, and referenced information.

Sharing control between teachers and children, relying on tasks with authenticity in the real world, engaging in discourse to promote learning, and using children's unique abilities and personal and cultural values (including their bilingualism) as resources permeate all activities in this classroom. Adult-directed lessons in which children are relegated to passive recipients of external input are virtually nonexistent. Moll and Whitmore

(1993) sum up the variety of roles the teacher assumes as she engages in dialogues with children that advance their learning. The teacher serves as

• *a guide and supporter,* who helps children organize their questions and ideas, translate them into manageable activities, and take risks in tackling new tasks within their ZPD, thereby ensuring that each child experiences academic success.

• *an active participant in learning,* who explores, experiments, and collaborates with children.

• *a facilitator,* who consciously plans the environment and the curriculum and selects materials that foster children's purposeful uses of language and learning strategies.

• *an evaluator,* who monitors children's individual and collective development, calling on this information to create and reformulate learning experiences to fit children's continuously changing needs.

Table 6.1 lists a series of general principles that can serve as a guide for teachers attempting to fill these diverse roles. In the words of two Vygotskian educators,

Teachers who use a Vygotskian framework become risk takers and problem solvers in their own instructional practice. They thereby create that margin of excellence in their teaching that, for their children, [serves as a model of higher-order thinking and as] a gateway to empowered performance . . . . (Jones & Thornton 1993, 27)

Child–child discourse: Cooperative learning

Recall from Chapter 2 that Vygotsky's original definition of the ZPD indicates that assisted performance can occur "under adult guidance or in collaboration with more capable peers" ([1930–1935]

Table 6.1. Vygotsky-Based Principles to Guide Teacher–Child Discourse

- Be sensitive to the knowledge, abilities, interests, attitudes, and cultural values and practices that children bring to learning situations.

- Arrange center-based activities that promote interactive problem solving.

- Promote and accept different solutions and strategies.

- Encourage children to tackle tasks within their zones of proximal development—that challenge and stretch their current skills.

- Offer many opportunities for modeling and engaging in higher-order thinking.

- Enrich communication: explain to children the purposes of classroom activities and experiences, and have children explain and justify their thinking.

- Use ongoing assessments of children's zones of proximal development to plan and monitor instruction.

Adapted from Jones & Thornton 1993, 27.

1978, 86). In Vygotsky-based classrooms, children spend a great deal of time engaged in cultural activities with agemates, who are important sources of other-regulation and scaffolding.

In Chapter 2 we noted that Piaget ([1923] 1926, [1932] 1965), too, regarded peers as contributing to cognitive growth but in a different way than did Vygotsky. According to Piaget, interaction with other children provides opportunities for clashing viewpoints, which induce cognitive conflict. Through arguments and disagreements with agemates, children repeatedly see that others hold opinions different from their own. As a result, they start to accommodate, or reorganize their cognitive structures, to fit discrepant information (Tudge & Rogoff 1987). An important component of Piaget's theory is that children benefit more from interaction with same-age peers than from interaction with older children and adults. He asserted that the opposing viewpoints that prompt children to no-

tice inadequacies in their thinking are most likely to be experienced with peers. In Piaget's view, children are not capable of truly harmonious, cooperative interaction with agemates until they overcome their egocentrism—at the concrete operational stage.

Vygotsky, on the other hand, saw cognitive development as resulting from *collaboration* with peers ([1930–1935] 1978, [1934] 1962). According to Vygotsky, peer conflict could contribute to heightened understanding, but only insofar as interacting partners resolve their disagreement and move toward a joint view of the situation. Furthermore, Vygotsky did not identify a starting age at which peer collaboration is possible; instead, he believed that new cognitive capacities could be constructed from child–child interaction at all ages. Vygotsky emphasized the importance of mixed-age groupings of children, which grant each child access to more knowledgeable companions and permit each child to serve as an expert

> *The capacity of young children to collaborate, like other abilities in childhood, is a developmental attainment that must be cultivated by adults.*

resource for others. Finally, peers can lead one another's development forward as long as the help that one child provides is within the other child's ZPD.

Factors that promote effective peer interaction

Early research on the effects of peer interaction on cognitive development emerged largely from the Piagetian tradition (Murray 1972, 1982; Doise, Mugny, & Perret-Clermont 1975, 1976; Perret-Clermont 1980). These studies, which used classic Piagetian tasks such as conservation, found that after pairing "nonconservers" with "conservers," the previously nonconserving child often displayed more mature reasoning. However, although the cognitive growth seen in the less-competent child was assumed to result from cognitive conflict, what actually transpired between the two children was never systematically measured. When investigators began to observe, with the aid of audio- and videotapes, the complex dynamics of peer collaboration, two important findings emerged: (1) while working together on tasks, children rarely showed evidence of social or cognitive conflict in the form of arguments, disagreements, and standoffs; and (2) the occurrence of cognitive growth depended on a combination of factors: instructions to children, modifications in the task to make it appropriate for child participants, and the quality of peer interaction (Forman & Cazden

1985; Tudge 1989, 1990; Forman & McPhail 1993).

Children serve as effective scaffolders of one another under certain conditions. Specifically, peer interaction stimulates cognitive development when children reach intersubjectivity—that is, when they work toward common goals by merging perspectives and engaging in truly cooperative problem solving. Conflict and disagreement do not seem to be as critical in fostering development as the extent to which peers resolve differences of opinion and share responsibility (Light & Glachan 1985; Forman 1987; Tudge & Rogoff 1987; Nastasi, Clements, & Battista 1990; Tudge 1992). When cooperation and sharing of ideas do not occur, then cognitive gains are not typically observed (Rubtsov 1981; Azmitia & Perlmutter 1989; Gauvain & Rogoff 1989; Tudge 1989).

As we noted in Chapter 3, preschool children are not as adept as are school-age children at cooperating with peers, communicating their ideas, and coming to joint solutions during problem solving (Azmitia & Perlmutter 1989; Gauvain & Rogoff 1989). This does not mean that successful peer collaboration is not possible during the preschool years. Recall that preschoolers are advanced in their capacity to work toward shared goals during make-believe play, and eventually they apply these skills to nonplay contexts. A few studies report effective collaboration and cognitive gains from peer interaction during problem solving among preschoolers (Cooper 1980; Azmitia 1988; Brownell 1990; Tudge 1992).

The capacity of young children to collaborate, like other abilities in childhood, is a developmental attainment that must be cultivated by adults. Just as preschool teachers play a critical role in providing scaffolded experiences to promote children's cognitive development and self-regulation, they also need to serve as scaffolders of children's social interaction and social problem-solving skills. In Chapter 3 we discussed ways in which teachers can promote cooperative, harmonious peer relations—by acquiring detailed knowledge of each child's social skills and by intervening in conflicts in such a way that children are encouraged to take over responsibility for establishing intersubjectivity and shared goals within the group (File 1993).

Should children be offered extrinsic rewards for cooperative learning?

One influential approach to maximizing the effectiveness of peer collaboration focuses on motivational and behavioral contingencies designed to ensure cooperation among children in classrooms. According to Slavin (1983, 1987), cognitive gains from peer interaction depend on how teachers set up rewards and contingencies for collaborative activity; teachers must provide children clear incentives to work together. Slavin recommends holding individuals accountable for their contribution to the group and providing group rewards for joint products as the most effective ways to produce learning. Under these conditions, children will strive for group harmony, rapport, and productivity by socially reinforcing one another.

Other researchers, however, criticize the notion of offering external rewards for peer collaboration, emphasizing that joint peer activity supported by interactions that result in heightened understanding is pleasurable and interesting enough to serve as its own reward

(Damon & Phelps 1989). For example, Hatano and Inagaki (1987) point out that using external rewards to foster collaboration leads group members to focus narrowly on the end product of the group effort (the correct answer and the reward) rather than on how and why certain problem-solving procedures result in correct answers. In contrast, discussions and peer partnerships that produce genuine insights are intrinsically satisfying experiences that lead children to want to continue working cooperatively in the future. Consequently, instead of extrinsic rewards, teachers can provide children with interesting, involving activities that stimulate gratifying social interaction—and children will enthusiastically seek cooperative learning environments in the future.

Mixed-age grouping

Recently, early childhood educators have expressed renewed interest in mixed-age grouping—placing children of different ages in one classroom. Mixed-age grouping is regarded as beneficial for children's social and cognitive development, and Vygotsky's theory has been used to support the practice (Katz, Evangelou, & Hartman 1990; Roopnarine & Bright 1992; Winsler 1993; Berk 1994b). Consistent with Vygotsky's belief that more-competent peers can scaffold less-mature classmates and that cognitive development is best stimulated when children are challenged to do something just beyond their current level of development, some researchers have found that children benefit most from peer collaboration when they are paired with a child who is either slightly older or slightly more competent than they are (Mugny & Doise 1978; Azmitia 1988; Rogoff 1990).

Vygotsky emphasized the importance of mixed-age groupings of children, which grant each child access to more knowledgeable companions and permit each child to serve as an expert resource for others.

In several studies, investigators compared mixed-age and same-age early childhood classrooms in terms of occurrence of social-cognitive play types (solitary, parallel, and cooperative; manipulative, constructive, and dramatic). Overall, findings revealed that preschoolers' play in mixed-age classrooms was more complex than in same-age classrooms (Goldman 1981; Mounts & Roopnarine 1987). This suggests that older children in mixed-age settings often provide activities within younger children's ZPDs that challenge them to master new skills. Recently, Roopnarine and his colleagues (1992) observed indoor free-play activities in two same-age classrooms of 3-year-olds, two same-age classrooms of 4-year-olds, and two mixed-age classrooms of 3- and 4-year-olds. Although, in this investigation, play in mixed-age settings was not more complex than play in same-age classrooms, the two types of learning environments differed in important ways. For example, more goal-directed, constructive play occurred in mixed-age classrooms, whereas more dramatic play occurred in same-age classrooms. Each of these types of play supports children's development. The investigators also found that gender segregation occurred more often in same-age than in mixed-age groups and that age differences in the developmental level of children's play were minimized in mixed-age classrooms. From a Vygotskian perspective, mixed-age environments offer more diverse and socially integrated play experiences in terms of the types of play and the age and gender of children's play partners.

Other evidence reveals that older children in mixed-age classrooms frequently assist and lead younger children in a positive, prosocial way (French et al.

1986; Stright & French 1988; Winsler 1993). This type of assistance has been likened to scaffolding (Katz, Evangelou, & Hartman 1990). It also seems to have a positive impact on the less-mature child's private speech. Azmitia (1992) recorded the self-directed utterances of 40 5-year-old novices who worked on a Lego building task by themselves before and after they had worked with either an expert peer, another novice, or alone. She found that those who had worked with an expert used significantly more private speech posttest than pretest, whereas the private speech of the other two groups did not change. More-competent peers seemed to function as facilitators of verbal self-regulation in less-competent children.

Mixed-age classrooms also have benefits for more expert children. Lougee and Graziano (1986, as reported by Katz, Evangelou, & Hartman 1990) proposed that mixed-age classes improve older children's self-regulatory skills. As they enforce classroom rules and help younger peers, older children are better able to reflect on and regulate their own behavior. Given the crucial role that private speech plays in the development of self-regulation, it is quite possible that self-guiding language mediates these gains. Winsler and Diaz (in press) observed kindergarten children in a mixed-age class interact with classmates, some of whom were one year younger and some of whom were one year older. The researchers found that kindergartners used significantly more private speech when they were working with younger classmates than when they were with same-age children, older children, or a group with a mixture of ages. Although the dynamics of interaction were not examined in this study, the authors informally noted that the extra private speech seen in the kindergartners when they were with younger classmates seemed to result from the challenges of mentoring younger children, which prompted older peers to assume increased responsibility for classroom activities.

The benefits of mixed-age interaction in early childhood programs also depend on the classroom context and the amount of teacher-provided structure. For example, in one study, the prosocial and cognitive benefits of mixed-age peer interaction seemed to be strongest during classroom activities only moderately structured by the teacher (Winsler 1993). A great deal of peer scaffolding and prosocial behavior occurred when the teacher provided several activity settings with goal-directed tasks that kindergartners were asked to do but allowed them to decide which classmates to work with and how to go about reaching the activity goals. In sum, mixed-age classrooms can provide unusually rich social experiences for preschool children. However, the benefits of mixed-age interaction depend on how well teachers organize and support children's classroom activities.

A Vygotskian approach to assessment

In previous sections we saw that Vygotsky's ZPD specifies that collaborative activity on yet-to-be-mastered tasks is central to effective instruction. We also mentioned that the concept of the ZPD has important implications for assessment, especially for children with learning and behavior problems (see Chapter 4). Vygotsky expressed dissat-

isfaction with traditional ability and achievement tests as valid measures of children's "capacity to learn," a view shared by other theorists of his time (e.g., Thorndike 1926; Piaget 1952). He pointed out that two children may attain precisely the same test score, but since this measures nothing more than their existing level of competence, it cannot tell us how to instruct them. More importantly, the two children may differ substantially in the breadth of their ZPDs. For one child the zone may be narrow, indicating that the child does best when provided with assistance on problems not very distant from those that he or she can handle independently. For another child the zone may be wide, suggesting that with social support, he or she can perform at a substantially higher level than while working alone. Thus, the ZPD is crucial for specifying each child's *readiness* to profit from instruction. As Vygotsky explained,

the zone of proximal development defines those functions that have not yet matured but are in the process of maturation, functions that will mature tomorrow but are currently in an embryonic state. These functions could be termed the "buds" or "flowers" of development rather than the "fruits" of development. The actual developmental level [IQ or achievement] characterizes mental development retrospectively, while the zone of proximal development characterizes mental development prospectively. ([1930–1935] 1978, 86–87)

In contrast to *static assessment* procedures, which emphasize previously acquired knowledge in terms of intelligence or achievement scores, *dynamic assessment* involves purposeful teaching within the testing situation. It attempts to distinguish a child's apparent level of development, as might be measured by a standardized test, from the

Whereas static assessment procedures emphasize the child's previously acquired knowledge, dynamic assessment seeks to determine what the child is capable of doing with support and thus typically incorporates purposeful teaching within the testing situation.

Chapter 6—Vygotsky's Theory in Early Childhood Classrooms

137

child's potential level of development—the performance the child is capable of attaining with support. The difference between the two is the child's ZPD. To measure the breadth of the zone, dynamic assessment models use a pretest–intervene–retest procedure. It is based on the assumption that the best way to help a child learn is to explore the teaching strategies to which that child is most responsive (Missiuna & Samuels 1989).

Dynamic assessment has been used for some time in Russia; in recent years, it has gained in popularity in North America (Lidz 1991). As yet, the design of instruments and procedures to support dynamic assessment is still in its early stages, and research directed at validating the method is limited; however, the evidence is growing. Over the past two decades, three research programs have addressed the development of dynamic assessment procedures: those of Milton Budoff (1987a, 1987b); Reuven Feuerstein (1979, 1980); and Ann Brown, Joseph Campione, and Roberta Ferrara (Campione et al. 1984; Ferrara, Brown, & Campione 1986).

In each of these programs, reasoning tasks from traditional intelligence tests are used as pretests. If the child does poorly, then an examiner provides instruction. The teaching offered in dynamic assessment models is diverse. In Budoff's, it is highly scripted and focuses on helping the child analyze a complex task by breaking it down into less-intricate components (Babad & Budoff 1974). In Brown, Campione, and Ferrara's program, teaching involves a series of prompts that are graduated with respect to the explicitness of information they provide. If the child is unable to arrive at a solution to a problem independently, the tester introduces general clues that gradually become more specific until the child can solve the problem and transfer the knowledge gained to similar situations (Brown & Ferrara 1985). Feuerstein's approach was originally applied to children ages 8 to 10 and older, but a downward extension for 5- to 8-year-olds now exists (Mearig 1987). His procedures are the most flexible of the three programs, since they are responsive to individual differences in learning styles and needs. Besides the fact that intervention is not scripted, the model moves away from merely giving task-specific clues. Instead, it emphasizes adult communication of principles and strategies that children can generalize to new situations (Feuerstein et al. 1986). An excellent summary and evaluation of the strengths and limitations of each of these dynamic assessment models can be found in Lidz (1991).

Current evidence on the effectiveness of dynamic assessment confirms that it has considerable value for predicting children's learning potential. Age and ability (as measured by static intelligence tests) are positively related to the breadth of children's ZPDs as determined by dynamic assessment, but far from perfectly so. Indeed, especially for children from low-income and ethnic-minority families, IQ alone dramatically underestimates potential for performing intellectual tasks after adult assistance (Brown & Ferrara 1985; Tzuriel 1989). Instead, children's responsiveness to teaching and their capacity to transfer what they have learned to new tasks adds significantly to the prediction of future performance, and sometimes it is a better predictor than is static ability (Feuerstein 1979; Bryant, Brown, & Campione 1983; Campione et al. 1984; Ferrara, Brown, & Campione 1986; Rand & Kaniel

Scaffolding Children's Learning

1987). Moreover, strategy-oriented teaching that conveys information about general principles involved in problem solution (as opposed to scripted assistance or graduated prompts that focus on momentary correct performance) is most effective in inducing cognitive gains and transfer of learning to new situations (Burns 1985; Keane & Kretschmer 1987; Vye et al. 1987). In sum, for many children there is a large difference between actual and potential development. Those who perform poorly when left to their own devices often do substantially better when given appropriate instructional intervention.

Dynamic assessment presents challenges that are much greater than those faced in traditional assessment. The examiner must be able to hypothesize about and respond adaptively to the child's needs during the testing situation, intervening by scaffolding until the child's performance is significantly improved. The method is often difficult and time consuming, but it is just this aspect of dynamic assessment that offers promise for identifying teaching practices that are likely to be effective with children who present diverse learning difficulties in the classroom. Dynamic assessment reduces the possibility that a child who can profit from instruction will be denied opportunities to learn because of a poor score on a static assessment. And even for children who demonstrate fairly narrow ZPDs, the results of interactive sessions are likely to provide important information about forms of intervention that are likely to improve their progress.

Aside from its applicability to evaluating children's learning potential, dynamic assessment conveys an important message about our understanding of cognitive development. In most research, conclusions about children's cognitive competence are drawn from assessments of their unaided performance. Dynamic assessment tells us that these conclusions would change substantially if children were observed under teaching conditions that are sensitive to their learning needs (Campione et al. 1984).

In sum, Vygotsky-inspired dynamic assessment differs from traditional assessment in that it focuses on process rather than product—identifying the strategies the individual child already uses to master academically relevant tasks and the instructional procedures most likely to help that child learn more effectively. In addition to measuring what the child currently knows, the examiner actively tries to facilitate performance in order to gauge the breadth of the child's ZPD. According to Lidz, dynamic assessment represents not just a procedure but an attitude:

Dynamic assessors are convinced children can learn if sufficient time and effort is expended to discover the means by which they can profit from intervention. Dynamic assessors are also more interested in spending this time to derive ideas for intervention rather than for placement or classification decisions. The focus of dynamic assessment is on the assessor's ability to discover the means of facilitating the learning of the child, not on the child's demonstration of ability to the assessor. (1991, 9)

In addressing how to promote active, efficient, and strategic cognitive processing through communication between expert and novice, dynamic assessment embodies the very essence of Vygotsky's theory. Because it seeks to uncover the nature of the learner and to improve the match between that nature and the knowledge and skills necessary for success in school, dynamic assessment has special value for children

Dynamic assessment focuses on the assessor's discovery of how to facilitate the child's learning rather than on the child's demonstrating ability to the assessor.

whose early experiences did not prepare them adequately to cope with the demands of classroom life.

Restructuring schools to scaffold children's learning

A great strength of the Vygotskian approach is that it forces us to look at education and development from multiple vantage points. Although Vygotsky focused on what goes on between teachers and children in early childhood classrooms, he was well aware that creating optimal learning environments is intimately related to the practices of the school's administration as well as to the values and goals held by the local community. From an educational reform perspective, this means that for a classroom-based intervention to work, it has to be consistent with and supported by similar ideals at the level of the educational institution and surrounding society. In the final section of this chapter, we discuss two projects that have this broader focus: the Kamehameha Elementary Education Program (KEEP) and the Reggio Emilia approach to preschool education. The first was explicitly inspired by Vygotsky's sociocultural theory. Although the second was stimulated by diverse theoretical sources (including Vygotsky), it is highly compatible with Vygotsky's ideas.

The Kamehameha Elementary Education Program (KEEP)

The most extensive and well-known educational reform effort that has been explicitly based on Vygotsky's sociocultural theory is KEEP. It started as an innovative educational system for academically at-risk children of ethnic minorities in Honolulu, Hawaii, and has since expanded to serve thousands of children on several Hawaiian islands, as well as children in Arizona and California. Tharp and Gallimore (Tharp 1982; Tharp & Gallimore 1988; Gallimore & Tharp 1990) have reported excellent results for participating first- to third-graders from low-income minority families in terms of literacy skills and academic achievement. For example, in KEEP schools, such children performed at their expected grade level in reading achievement, much better than children of the same background enrolled in traditional schools.

The overarching theme of KEEP is "assisted performance"—sensitive scaffolding of children's learning by teachers, who assist children in accomplishing goals within their ZPDs. Classrooms with an open design are organized into 10 to 12 "activity settings," defined as "contexts in which collaborative interaction, intersubjectivity, and assisted performance occur" (Tharp & Gallimore 1988, 72). Each setting (for example, the library center, the art center, the listening center, and the game center) encourages the development of a different set of individual and interpersonal skills. Small groups of five to six children systematically rotate through the centers over a week's time. Consequently, activity settings provide multiple opportunities for peers to interact and work collaboratively in a wide range of meaningful academic contexts.

A central activity setting, called "Center One," is the focal environment that all children enter at least once each morning for 20 minutes. Here, teacher–child scaffolding of challenging literacy skills at the outer edge of the child's ZPD takes place. Unlike other activity settings, where small-group membership may differ each time, Center One groupings are consistent. Teachers form the groups with the goal of creating as diverse a mix as possible in terms of child characteristics, except for reading/literacy level, which (to facilitate scaffolding of the group as a whole) is fairly comparable across children. During Center One, the teacher engages children in interaction that has features resembling the curricular innovations described earlier in this chapter—text content selected to relate to children's experiences and instruction that relies heavily on questioning, responding to, and building on children's ideas. Other activity settings either extend the instructional objectives of Center One or offer materials that support additional objectives. Like Center One, they are rich in child–child communication, but they provide the child with greater opportunity to work in that portion of the ZPD closest to her independent competence. Each child's weekly selection of activity centers is individualized to suit his or her learning needs.

An essential aspect of KEEP is its insistence that teaching and learning *at each level* of the school system be based on principles of assisted performance. Just as children require scaffolded support in mastering learning activities in the classroom, teachers teach best when their performance is assisted by members of the educational system. Supervisors, principals, consultants, and other teachers provide relevant activity settings for teachers to further develop their competence in assisting children's learning. According to Tharp and Gallimore (1988), the goal of all educational supervisors, from the chair of the board of education to the superintendent and principal, should be to provide effective scaffolding for the educational practitioners that they supervise, transforming schools into a culture of learning for all involved.

This continuing education for teachers can take place in a variety of activity settings, such as workshops, university courses, retreats, or individual consultation. KEEP emphasizes weekly observation-and-conference sessions and peer coaching. A full-time consultant, or facilitator, observes each teacher in the classroom at least once a week. Then a conference is scheduled, in which the consultant and teacher work together to help the teacher provide more effective assisted performance to children. Ideas are shared and feedback is given, sometimes with the aid of video- or audiotapes of the teacher in the classroom. On the basis of this information, new goals are set. Similar activities take place in peer coaching, with teachers volunteering time to assist other teachers.

In summary, the four main features of KEEP are (1) a view of the teaching/learning process as assisted performance; (2) a high priority placed on literacy skills, which are essential for children to become competent users of their culture's representational system, (3) a strong emphasis on activity settings that promote small-group, collaborative interaction; and (4) the involvement of all members of the educational system in collaborative problem solving with teachers to enhance children's learning.

Reggio Emilia

In Reggio Emilia, a small town in north-central Italy, an extraordinary city-run early childhood program has recently captured the attention of educators worldwide. Capitalizing on the energy of motivated parents who began to build their own preschool using materials left over from the rubble of World War II, founder Loris Malaguzzi created a city-funded system for early childhood education that, by 1993, included 22 preschools for 3- to 6-year-olds and 13 infant/toddler centers for 4- to 36-month-olds. A major reason the program is so unusual is the high degree of community support it has received since its inception more than 30 years ago.

A central focus of the Reggio Emilia approach is social construction of knowledge—an emphasis basic to Vygotsky's view. In addition to Vygotsky, Malaguzzi mentions Piaget, Dewey, Gardner, Ferriére, Bruner, and Bronfenbrenner as important influences on the design of his program (Malaguzzi 1993b). Malaguzzi has skillfully woven contributions from many different theories into a well-run and integrated early childhood program. As Gardner notes,

It is the Reggio community, more so than the philosophy or method, that constitutes Malaguzzi's central achievement. Nowhere else in the world is there such a seamless and symbiotic relationship between a school's progressive philosophy and its practices. (1993, x)

The educational community and curriculum. Reggio Emilia education begins with a view of the child as a competent and complex social being who is motivated by and learns from social interaction and relationships with others (Gandini 1993b; Malaguzzi 1993b). This conviction is manifested in a strong community approach to the education and care of young children. Parents, teachers, administrative staff, and government officials join forces to support the efforts of the school. Parents are involved in program planning, spend time working with teachers and children in classrooms, and organize or assist with special projects for the school. In each classroom, pairs of teachers work as equals. They also routinely interact and collaborate with other teachers, as well as with parents and staff. The school's physical environment is designed to support the formation of relationships. In addition to many areas for children to play in small groups, there are special places for teachers, parents, staff, and community members to meet with one another and with children (Katz 1990; Bredekamp 1993; Gandini 1993a).

A strong spirit of collaboration is especially evident in relationships between teachers and children. Filippini describes the role of the Reggio Emilia teacher as

provoking occasions of discovery through a kind of alert, inspired facilitation and stimulation of children's dialogue, co-action, and co-construction of knowledge. Because intellectual discovery is believed to be an essentially social process, the teacher assists even the youngest children to learn to listen to others, take account of their goals and ideas, and communicate successfully. (Edwards 1993, 154)

Teachers view themselves as partners with children in fostering learning. To accomplish this goal, they work not only with other teachers but also with *pedagogistas,* or educational advisors. These staff members meet with teachers

Reggio Emilia education begins with a view of the child as a competent and complex social being who is motivated by—and learns from—social interaction and relationships with others.

regularly to assist in a variety of ways, including designing new projects, communicating with parents, and discussing ways to learn more about the children. One pedagogista captured the task of the Reggio Emilia teacher with the following metaphor: "We [teachers] must be able to catch the ball that the children throw us, and toss it back to them in a way that makes the children want to continue the game with us, developing, perhaps, other games as we go along" (Filippini 1990, as cited in Edwards 1993, 153).

Children in Reggio Emilia schools stay with the same teachers and classmates for three years. This system grants children extended opportunities to form meaningful relationships and develop complex social skills. It also permits teachers to learn more about the children and, as a result, to scaffold them more effectively. Classrooms are explicitly arranged to promote small-group interaction, the preferred social structure of the schools. As Malaguzzi indicates,

We consider small groups the most favorable type of classroom organization for an education based on relationships. Small-group activities involving two, three, or four children are most desirable, allowing for the most efficient communication. In small groups, complex interactions are more likely to occur, constructive conflicts take place, and self-regulatory accommodations emerge. (1993a, 11)

A central component of Reggio Emilia education is implemented by a staff member called the *atelierista,* who is responsible for maintaining a room or set of rooms called the *atelier*. The atelierista is a full-time specialist, and artist, who works with teachers and children to create, store, and document the activities, projects, and progress of the children and the school. Making visual or symbolic representations of their own activities in a variety of media (including paintings, drawings, photographs, clay, audio- or videotapes, music, and transcriptions of conversations) is a central part of children's day. With the atelierista, children and teachers use the artistic materials, and then the atelierista records, organizes, and stores the prod-

In an emergent curriculum, the particulars of what happens from day to day depend on joint teacher and child decision making during mutual explorations.

ucts. Children are encouraged to represent nearly everything they do and think about, including such difficult concepts as shadows, feelings, growth, time, and motion. Vea Vecchi, an atelierista for one of the Reggio Emilia preprimary schools, reports that the atelier has three crucial purposes:

First, it provides a place for children to become masters of all kinds of techniques, such as painting, drawing, and working in clay—all the symbolic languages. Second, it assists adults in understanding processes of how children learn. It helps teachers understand how children invent autonomous vehicles of expressive freedom, cognitive freedom, symbolic freedom, and paths to communication. . . . The other important function of the atelier is to provide a workshop for documentation . . . —materials to use with the children and families, as well as with teachers in in-service training. (1993, 120–22)

An additional feature of the Reggio Emilia curriculum is extensive use of long-term, multifaceted projects and themes that offer a broad and integrative framework for interaction—sometimes for months at a time (Forman 1993). Teachers, parents, pedagogistas, and atelieristas meet to select a theme or project based on the following characteristics:

• it must allow for both individual child contributions and collective purposes;

• it must have some external structure, in terms of general goals, while allowing children to decide on their own subgoals and rules;

• it should provoke much dialogue and discussion among participants; and

• it should lend itself to a variety of modes of representation.

Reggio Emilia teachers are quick to point out that their curriculum is emergent; the particulars of what happens depend on joint teacher and child decision making during mutual explorations. The box on page 146 displays the outline of an eight-week project based on the theme of long jumping. The list of activities reflects a diverse array of interconnected learning experiences, including exploring the technical aspects of long jumping, promoting and implementing an Olympic sports event, calculating running speeds and measuring distances, engaging in scientific experimentation, and, of course, acquiring and communicating knowledge through reading, writing, speaking, and graphic/visual representation.

A Vygotskian interpretation of Reggio Emilia. The Reggio Emilia system of early childhood education echoes central Vygotskian themes. Its reliance on small-group collaboration is highly compatible with a theory of development and education in which thought processes originate in social interaction. The teacher as a creator of activity settings designed to stimulate dialogue and co-construction of knowledge is reminiscent of the concept of scaffolding. Having children stay with the same teacher and the same set of peers for three years is consistent with Vygotsky's emphasis on history and the importance of understanding the development of children's social interactions and relationships over time. The practice of creating diverse symbolic representations of classroom activities and concepts through artistic and technological means exemplifies Vygotsky's belief in the use and internalization of cultural symbol systems as the major route to higher mental functions. Joint teacher–child decision making, adult and peer scaffolding of children's learning through cooperative projects with integrative themes, and richly equipped settings that foster small-group play are consonant with Vygotsky's ideas about experiences that promote self-regulation. Finally, the Reggio Emilia approach explicitly recognizes that a larger sociocultural level of assistance—supportive relationships of teachers and children with members of the educational system and community—must be present to create ideal conditions for children's development.

Conclusion

An important reason that the KEEP and Reggio Emilia approaches are so successful is that they have a history of massive cultural and community support—a quantity of endorsement, sponsorship, and sustenance that is difficult to find in most parts of the United States,

---

The Long Jump Project in a Reggio Emilia School

1. Looking At and Acting Out Photographs of Olympic Long Jumpers
2. Verbal Outpouring of Initial Knowledge of Long Jump
3. Making an Initial Sketch of Track, Jumpers, and How to Score
4. Drawing the Track Layout: Run-up and Landing Area
5. Experimenting with Running Speed x Jumping Distance
6. Laying out the Track in the Courtyard using White Chalk
7. Debating about Handicap for Girls using Small Replica Objects
8. Designing Six Posters for Rules of the Long Jump
9. Presenting the Rules to Whole Class
10. Designing Training, Clothes, and Diet
11. Making Posters Calling for the Registration of Each Participant
12. Making Posters for Designating Ability Flights
13. Making Posters for Calendar of Completion by Ability Flights
14. Writing a Letter of Invitation to All Children of the School
15. Designing Posters of Citywide Advertising
16. Writing the Rules for Prizes

17. Writing the Closing Speech for After the Competition
18. Making a Poster of Rules for Measuring Three Jumps per Person
19. Learning to Measure Distance
    19.1 One: Using string to record the distance jumped
    19.2 Two: Trying to use the tape measure
    19.3 Three: Correcting the tape measure
    19.4 Four: Transcribing tape measure symbols to paper
    19.5 Five: Comparing tape measure to carpenter's rule
    19.6 Six: Reinventing conventional place value notation
20. Preparing Insignia for Each Jumper to Wear at the Meet
21. Writing Rules for the Referee and Assistants
22. Implementing the Plans: The Day of the Final Competition
    22.1 The run and the long jump
    22.2 Measuring each jump with string
    22.3 Posting the strings on the wall
    22.4 Using the tape to measure the longest strings
    22.5 Awarding the trophies
    22.6 The kisses from the misters and misses

(Forman 1993, 173–74)

at least at the present time. Although the educational system of one culture cannot simply be transplanted to schools in different societal contexts, by providing a discussion of the Vygotskian approach together with existing model programs, we hope that practitioners will take the themes and key features they find most useful and develop and reconstruct them to fit the needs of their early childhood programs and communities.

A common thread in Vygotsky-based educational practices, including those we have described, is the planning of activities that teach culturally meaningful cognitive concepts and skills. At the same time, activities are sensitively tuned to each child's capacity to learn, and they nourish children's natural curiosity, drive to discover, and desire to become competent members of their community.

7

A Vision for
Early Childhood Education

During the final decade of the 20th century, the number of children enrolled in preschool and child care settings in the United States continues to rise in response to steady gains in maternal employment. In addition, a poverty rate that now affects 25% of children younger than age 6 means that more young children are approaching the beginning of compulsory schooling at serious risk for developmental difficulties and school failure and are in need of intensive early intervention (Children's Defense Fund 1995). These circumstances increase the urgency for a coherent national policy on early childhood programs that meets the developmental and educational needs of young children.

Throughout this book, we have addressed the question of what kind of educational philosophy is likely to result in development-enhancing early childhood environments, discussing ideas advanced by Vygotsky more than half a century ago that continue to be relevant to controversies over educative experiences for young children to-

day. Should early childhood programs merely provide a stimulating environment for children to explore at leisure (child-centered programs), or should they strengthen children's knowledge of academics with the goal of preparing them for formal schooling (adult-centered programs)?

The debate between these two positions has been energized by the sharply opposing goals underlying them: fostering independent growth on one hand, and socializing children to ensure that they meet the demands of society on the other. As a result, the dilemma facing early childhood educators has often been phrased in an either/or fashion: they must choose between (1) providing nonintrusive environments and (2) training children in school-related knowledge and proper habits. The major problem in framing curricular choices in this way is that the goals of independent development and school readiness are defined as competing and mutually exclusive.

In this and previous chapters, we have seen that according to Vygotsky, the preschool years witness the dawning of children's capacity to reflect on their own thinking and to plan, guide, and monitor their own behavior. Independent exploration, however, is not the route to self-regulatory capacities. Instead, these develop through finely tuned, sensitive instruction—through dialogues between children and their teachers surrounding challenging tasks.

Research indicates that individual differences in self-regulatory capacities are clearly related to variations in quality of adult–child interaction. Highly controlling, traditional classrooms in which teachers grant children little leeway for self-direction are successful in attaining the short-term goal of slightly higher achievement-test scores. Yet in terms of fostering autonomous learning, interest, involvement, and creative thinking, they are disadvantaged relative to more-open settings, in which teachers assume a flexible authority role, share decision making with children, and offer guidance and support in response to individual needs (Horwitz 1979; Thomas & Berk 1981; Hedges, Giaconia, & Gage 1981; Walberg 1986). Alternatively, excessively permissive environments do not provide sufficient structure and challenge to foster children's capacity for self-regulation. When carried to an extreme, child-oriented settings are in danger of generating distractible, impulsive, non–self-controlled behavior (Kohlberg & Mayer 1972; Berk & Lewis 1977).

The findings of several decades of research on childrearing practices are consistent with these generalizations. Parents who use an authoritative style (warmth and sensitivity combined with reasonable demands for mature behavior) have children who are self-confident and effective in their mastery of new tasks, do well in school, and are socially and morally mature. In contrast, children of authoritarian parents (who make excessive demands and are rejecting and punitive when children fail to meet these demands) tend to be anxious, withdrawn, and unhappy and to react with hostility when frustrated. And permissive parenting (the style of parents who avoid making demands of any kind) is associated with children who lack impulse control, displaying rebellious, disobedient, and nonachieving behavior (Baumrind 1967, 1971; Denham, Renwick, & Holt 1991; Buzzelli 1993; Berk & Spuhl 1995).

Neither academic nor child-centered environments are well suited to promote the development of conscious thought and self-regulation in young children. Traditional, academically oriented programs emphasize external control. Consequently, at best they foster rigid self-control (compliance to external commands) rather than a flexible capacity to monitor one's own thinking and adapt it to changing circumstances (Diaz, Neal, & Amaya-Williams 1990). The opposite extreme—child-centered programs—is unlikely to provide the scaffolding experiences that promote the development of self-regulation: collaboration between a child and another person more competent in the skills, tools, and technologies of the child's culture who guides and supports, relinquishing responsibility to the child in accord with his or her capacity to take over the regulating role.

The Vygotskian approach offers a resolution to the debate over early childhood education, since it advocates responsiveness to children's current capacities yet aims to move development forward. By fostering teaching and learning within the zone of proximal development, Vygotsky-based education simultaneously considers where children are and what they are capable of becoming, thereby strengthening young children's readiness for formal schooling and continued learning once they enter the primary grades. In the Vygotskian view, readiness for schooling does not mean a narrow head start in academic knowledge. Instead, it means enhancement of higher mental functions—voluntary attention, logical memory, problem solving, imagination, abstraction, and others—in short, all the ingredients that contribute to the human capacity to engage in deliberate, reflective activity.

The following key themes sum up the Vygotskian approach to early childhood education:

Teachers and children as jointly contributing to development. The role of the teacher includes both designing an educative environment and collaborating with children by scaffolding their efforts to master new skills. From this perspective, Vygotsky-based teaching is *activity centered,* since it emphasizes creating opportunities for children to engage in culturally meaningful activities with the guidance of teachers and peers.

Educational goals that challenge children to reach new levels of competence. The broad objective of early childhood education is to sustain children's progress through the ZPD. Teachers do so by (a) helping children select developmentally appropriate joint and individual activities; (b) modifying the difficulty of tasks to an appropriate level of challenge by adjusting the activity, the degree of adult assistance, or both; and (c) setting expectations for classroom behavior that are consistent with children's emerging cognitive and social capacities. The assumption of

Vygotsky-based education—that adults can and should establish goals for children that lead to ever-higher levels of competence—is based on the notion that the psychological developments of early childhood are so important that they cannot be left to chance. At the same time, for children to move through the ZPD successfully, the goals established and activities offered must be sensitively tuned to each child's momentary developmental progress.

Play as a vital, self-regulatory activity of early childhood. A Vygotskian educational environment does not mean that children's entire day should consist of activities based on teacher-identified goals. As we saw in Chapter 3, Vygotsky granted play a central role in development. Through make-believe, children create and extend their own ZPDs, acquiring self-regulatory and socially cooperative capacities by setting goals, regulating their behavior in pursuit of those goals, and subordinating actions to rules rather than impulse. Vygotsky regarded play as the supreme educative activity of the preschool years.

Dynamic assessment. According to Vygotsky, assessments of children should uncover not just what they can do independently but what they can acquire with the assistance of a more knowledgeable partner. The breadth of the ZPD—the child's potential to learn—must be identified so that learning activities can be planned that lead development forward, resulting in the acquisition of new capacities that the child is currently ready to master.

Focus on language and social interaction. Because of its crucial role in transforming cognitive development

The role of the teacher includes both designing an educative environment and collaborating with children by scaffolding their efforts to master new skills.

and its importance for effective communication and participation in cultural activities, language and literacy development should receive the utmost attention in early childhood programs. Providing children with frequent, rich, and diverse opportunities to develop and use language and literacy skills grants them the psychological and cultural tools to gain control over their own behavior and become competent, contributing members of their society.

Different activities foster different mental capacities. According to Vygotsky, higher mental functions originate in the activities and social dialogues in which children participate. This means that variations in activities and social interactions result in important individual and group differences among children, causing them to acquire certain skills as opposed to others. Vygotsky's approach emphasizes that to understand and nurture children's competencies, teachers must take into account each child's history and cultural background. Children develop best when they are granted access to activities that promote continuity in the learning process and that build on their real-life experiences. Furthermore, Vygotsky's theory underscores that teachers' daily decisions—which activities to encourage and how to collaborate with children—have major consequences for the formation of young children's minds.

* * *

At the larger institutional and societal level, Vygotsky's perspective, and the educational models it has inspired, present us with the following challenges:

• investing more in early childhood education, the most vital period for the development of the child's intellect;

• arranging conditions that foster real community and parent involvement—critical sources of the consensus needed to design schools as communities of learners;

• combating isolation of teachers in self-contained classrooms in favor of teams of educators who work together to reach common goals, share skills, and learn from each other; and

• relinquishing rigid organizational structures and prescribed curricula that assume children automatically learn from what teachers do, in favor of flexible, interactive approaches that respond to and extend children's interests, abilities, and skills.

It is our hope that these challenges will galvanize American educators to seek more effective ways to scaffold young children's learning.

References

Abikoff, H. 1991. Cognitive training in ADHD children: Less to it than meets the eye. *Journal of Learning Disabilities* 24: 205–09.

Alberts-Corush, J., P. Firestone, & J.T. Goodman. 1986. Attention and impulsivity characteristics of the biological and adoptive parents of hyperactive and normal control children. *American Journal of Orthopsychiatry* 56: 413–23.

American Psychiatric Association. 1994. *Diagnostic and statistical manual of mental disorders.* 4th ed. Washington, DC: Author.

Anderson, R.C. 1984. Some reflections on the acquisition of knowledge. *Educational Researcher* 13 (9): 5–10.

Azmitia, M. 1988. Peer interaction and problem solving: When are two heads better than one? *Child Development* 59: 87–96.

Azmitia, M. 1992. Expertise, private speech, and the development of self-regulation. In *Private speech: From social interaction to self-regulation*, eds. R.M. Diaz & L.E. Berk, 101–22. Hillsdale, NJ: Erlbaum.

Azmitia, M., & M. Perlmutter. 1989. Social influences on children's cognition: State of the art and future directions. In *Advances in child development and behavior.* Vol. 22, ed. H.W. Reese, 90–135. New York: Academic.

Babad, E.Y., & M. Budoff. 1974. Sensitivity and validity of learning potential measurement in three levels of ability. *Journal of Educational Psychology* 66: 439–47.

Baillargeon, R. 1987. Object permanence in 3.5- and 4.5-month-old infants. *Developmental Psychology* 23: 655–64.

Baillargeon, R., & J. De Vos. 1991. Object permanence in young infants: Further evidence. *Child Development* 62: 1227–46.

Barkley, R.A. 1989. Attention-deficit hyperactivity disorder. In *Treatment of childhood disorders,* eds. E.J. Mash & R.A. Barkley, 39–72. New York: Guilford.

Barkley, R.A. 1990. *Attention deficit hyperactivity disorder: A handbook for diagnosis and treatment.* 2nd ed. New York: Guilford.

Barkley, R.A. 1994. *Best practices in school-based assessment and treatment of ADHD.* Invited address, annual convention of the National Association of School Psychologists, March, Seattle, Washington.

Barkley, R.A., C.E. Cunningham, & J. Karlsson. 1983. The speech of hyperactive children and their mothers: Comparisons with normal children and stimulant drug effects. *Journal of Learning Disabilities* 16: 105–10.

Barkley, R.A., M. Fischer, C. Edelbrock, & L. Smallish. 1991. The adolescent outcome of hyperactive children diagnosed by research criteria: III. Mother–child interactions, family conflicts and maternal psychopathology. *Journal of Child Psychology and Psychiatry* 32: 233–55.

Baumrind, D. 1966. Effects of authoritative parental control on child behavior. *Child Development* 37: 887–907.

Baumrind, D. 1967. Child care practices anteceding three patterns of preschool behavior. *Genetic Psychology Monographs* 75: 43–88.

Baumrind, D. 1971. Current patterns of parental authority. *Developmental Psychology Monograph* 4 (No. 1, Pt. 2).

Beaudichon, J. 1973. Nature and instrumental function of private speech in problem solving situations. *Merrill-Palmer Quarterly* 19: 117–35.

Behrend, D.A., K.S. Rosengren, & M. Perlmutter. 1989. A new look at children's private speech: The effects of age, task difficulty, and parent presence. *International Journal of Behavioral Development* 12: 305–20.

Behrend, D.A., K.S. Rosengren, & M. Perlmutter. 1992. The relation between private speech and parental interactive style. In *Private speech: From social interaction to self-regulation,* eds. R.M. Diaz & L.E. Berk, 85–100. Hillsdale, NJ: Erlbaum.

Beilin, H. 1978. Inducing conservation through training. In *Psychology of the twentieth century.* Vol. 7, ed. G. Steiner, 260–89. Munich: Kindler.

Berk, L.E. 1986. Relationship of elementary school children's private speech to behavioral accompaniment to task, attention, and task performance. *Developmental Psychology* 22: 671–80.

Berk, L.E. 1992. Children's private speech: An overview of theory and the status of research. In *Private speech: From social interaction to self-regulation,* eds. R.M. Diaz & L.E. Berk, 17–53. Hillsdale, NJ: Erlbaum.

Berk, L.E. 1993. *Infants, children, and adolescents.* Boston: Allyn & Bacon.

Berk, L.E. 1994a. *Child development.* 3rd ed. Boston: Allyn & Bacon.

Berk, L.E. 1994b. Vygotsky's theory: The importance of make-believe play. *Young Children* 50 (1): 30–39.

Berk, L.E. 1994c. Why children talk to themselves. *Scientific American* 271 (5): 78–83.

Berk, L.E., & R.A. Garvin. 1984. Development of private speech among low-income Appalachian children. *Developmental Psychology* 20: 271–86.

Berk, L.E., & S. Landau. 1993. Private speech of learning disabled and normally achieving children in classroom academic and laboratory contexts. *Child Development* 64: 556–71.

Berk, L.E., & N. Lewis. 1977. Sex role and social behavior in four school environments. *Elementary School Journal* 77: 205–17.

Berk, L.E., & M.K. Potts. 1991. Development and functional significance of private speech among attention-deficit hyperactivity disordered and normal boys. *Journal of Abnormal Child Psychology* 19: 357–77.

Berk, L.E., & S.T. Spuhl. 1995. Maternal interaction, private speech, and task performance in preschool children. *Early Childhood Research Quarterly* 10: 145–69.

Biederman, J., S.V. Faraone, K. Keenan, D. Knee, & M.T. Tsuang. 1990. Family-genetic and psychosocial risk factors in DSM III attention deficit disorder. *Journal of the American Academy of Child and Adolescent Psychiatry* 29: 526–33.

Bivens, J.A., & L.E. Berk. 1990. A longitudinal study of the development of elementary school children's private speech. *Merrill-Palmer Quarterly* 36: 443–63.

Blanck, G. 1990. Vygotsky: The man and his cause. In *Vygotsky and education: Instructional implications and applications of sociohistorical psychology,* ed. L.C. Moll, 31–58. New York: Cambridge University Press.

Bloom, L., L. Hood, & P. Lightbown. 1974. Imitation in language development: If, when and why. *Cognitive Psychology* 6: 380–420.

Bornstein, M.H., & M.E. Lamb. 1992. *Development in infancy: An introduction.* 3rd ed. New York: McGraw-Hill.

Bredekamp, S. 1993. Reflections on Reggio Emilia. *Young Children* 49 (1): 13–17.

Bretherton, I., B. O'Connell, C. Shore, & E. Bates. 1984. The effect of contextual variation on symbolic play: Development from 20 to 28 months. In *Symbolic play and the development of social understanding,* ed. I. Bretherton, 271–98. New York: Academic.

Brinich, P.M. 1980. Childhood deafness and maternal control. *Journal of Communication Disorders* 13: 75–81.

Brown, A.L., & R.A. Ferrara. 1985. Diagnosing zones of proximal development. In *Culture, communication, and cognition: Vygotskian perspectives,* ed. J. Wertsch, 273–305. New York: Cambridge University Press.

Brown, J.S., A. Collins, & P. Duguid. 1989. Situated cognition and the culture of learning. *Educational Researcher* 18 (4): 32–42.

Brownell, C.A. 1990. Peer social skills in toddlers: Competencies and constraints illustrated by same-age and mixed-age interaction. *Child Development* 61: 838–48.

Bruner, J.S. 1964. The course of cognitive growth. *American Psychologist* 19: 1–15.

Bruner, J.S. 1983. *Child's talk: Learning to use language.* New York: Norton.

Bruner, J.S. 1984. Vygotsky's zone of proximal development: The hidden agenda. In *Children's learning in the zone of proximal development,* eds. B. Rogoff & J.V. Wertsch, 93–97. San Francisco: Jossey-Bass.

Bruner, J.S. 1986. *Actual minds, possible worlds.* Cambridge, MA: Harvard University Press.

Bruner, J.S., R. Olver, & P. Greenfield. 1966. *Studies in cognitive growth.* New York: Wiley.

Bryant, N.R., A.L. Brown, & J.C. Campione. 1983. Preschool children's learning and transfer of matrices problems: Potential for improvement. Paper presented at the biennial meeting of the Society for Research in Child Development, April, Detroit.

Budoff, M. 1987a. Measures for assessing learning potential. In *Dynamic assessment: An interactional approach to evaluating learning potential,* ed. C.S. Lidz, 173–95. New York: Guilford.

Budoff, M. 1987b. The validity of learning potential assessment. In *Dynamic assessment: An interactional approach to evaluating learning potential,* ed. C.S. Lidz, 52–81. New York: Guilford.

Burns, M.S. 1985. Comparison of "graduated prompt" and "mediational" dynamic assessment and static assessment with young children. Ph.D. diss., Vanderbilt University, Nashville.

Burns, S.M., & C.J. Brainerd. 1979. Effects of constructive and dramatic play on perspective taking in very young children. *Developmental Psychology* 15: 512–21.

Buzzelli, C.A. 1993. Morality in context: A sociocultural approach to enhancing young children's moral development. *Child & Youth Care Forum* 22: 375–86.

Caissie, R., & E.B. Cole. 1993. Mothers and hearing-impaired children: Directiveness reconsidered. *The Volta Review* 95 (1): 49–59.

Camp, B.W., G.E. Blom, F. Hebert, & W.J. van Doorninck. 1977. "Think aloud": A program for developing self-control in young aggressive boys. *Journal of Abnormal Child Psychology* 7: 169–77.

Campbell, S.B. 1973. Cognitive styles in reflective, impulsive, and hyperactive boys and their mothers. *Perceptual and Motor Skills* 36: 747–52.

Campbell, S.B. 1975. Mother-child interaction: A comparison of hyperactive, learning disabled, and normal boys. *American Journal of Orthopsychiatry* 45: 51–57.

Campbell, S.B. 1985. Hyperactivity in preschoolers: Correlates and prognostic implications. *Clinical Psychology Review* 5: 405–28.

Campbell, S.B. 1990. *Behavioral problems in pre-school children: Clinical and developmental is-sues.* New York: Guilford.

Campbell, S.B., & L.J. Ewing. 1990. Hard-to-manage preschoolers: Adjustment at age nine and predictors of continuing symptoms. *Journal of Child Psychology and Psychiatry* 31: 871–89.

Campbell, S.B., M.W. Endman, & G. Bernfeld. 1977. Three year follow-up of hyperactive pre-schoolers into elementary school. *Journal of Child Psychology and Psychiatry* 18: 239–49.

Campbell, S.B., L.J. Ewing, A.M. Breaux, & E.K. Szumowski. 1986. Parent-identified behavior problem toddlers: Follow-up at school entry. *Journal of Child Psychology and Psychiatry* 27: 473–88.

Campbell, S.B., E.W. Pierce, C.L. March, L.J. Ewing, & E.K. Szumowski. 1994. Hard-to-manage preschool boys: Symptomatic behavior across contexts and time. *Child Development* 65: 836–51.

Campione, J.C., A.L. Brown, R.A. Ferrara, & N.R. Bryant. 1984. The zone of proximal develop-ment: Implications for individual differences and learning. In *New directions for child develop-ment,* eds. B. Rogoff & J.V. Wertsch. No. 23, 77–92. San Francisco: Jossey-Bass.

Carson, J., V. Burks, & R.D. Parke. 1993. Parent–child physical play: Determinants and conse-quences. In *Parent–child play: Descriptions and implications,* ed. K. MacDonald, 197–220. New York: State University of New York Press.

Case, R. 1992. *The mind's staircase.* Hillsdale, NJ: Erlbaum.

Ceci, S.J. 1990. *On intelligence . . . More or less.* Englewood Cliffs, NJ: Prentice Hall.

Ceci, S.J. 1991. How much does schooling influ-ence general intelligence and its cognitive com-ponents? A reassessment of the evidence. *Devel-opmental Psychology* 27: 703–22.

Chang-Wells, G.L.M., & G. Wells. 1993. Dynamics of discourse: Literacy and the construction of knowledge. In *Contexts for learning,* eds. E.A. Forman, N. Minick, & C.A. Stone, 58–90. New York: Oxford University Press.

Chess, S., & P. Fernandez. 1980. Do deaf children have a typical personality? *Journal of the Ameri-can Academy of Child and Adolescent Psychiatry* 19: 654–64.

Children's Defense Fund. 1995. *The state of America's children: Yearbook 1995.* Washing-ton, DC: Author.

Churchill, J. 1994. Relation of parental nurturance and restrictiveness to learned helplessness in pre-school children. Paper presented at the biennial meeting of the Society for Research in Child Development, 30 March–2 April, Indianapolis.

Cobb, P. 1994. Where is the mind? Constructivist and sociocultural perspectives on mathematical development. *Educational Researcher* 23 (7): 13–20.

Cobb, P., T. Wood, & E. Yackel. 1993. Discourse, mathematical thinking, and classroom practice. In *Contexts for learning,* eds. E.A. Forman, N. Minick, & C.A. Stone, 91–119. New York: Ox-ford University Press.

Cobb, P., T. Wood, E. Yackel, J. Nicholls, G. Wheatley, B. Trigatti, & M. Perlwitz. 1991. Assessment of a problem-centered second-grade mathematics project. *Journal for Re-search in Mathematics Education* 22: 3–29.

Cole, M. 1990. Cognitive development and formal schooling: The evidence from cross-cultural re-search. In *Vygotsky and education,* ed. L.C. Moll, 89–110. New York: Cambridge University Press.

Connolly, J.A., & A.B. Doyle. 1984. Relations of social fantasy play to social competence in pre-schoolers. *Developmental Psychology* 20: 797–806.

Connolly, J.A., A.B. Doyle, & E. Reznick. 1988. Social pretend play and social interaction in pre-schoolers. *Journal of Applied Developmental Psychology* 9: 301–13.

Cooper, C.R. 1980. Development of collabora-tive problem-solving among preschool chil-dren. *Developmental Psychology* 16: 433–40.

Copeland, A.P. 1979. Types of private speech pro-duced by hyperactive and nonhyperactive boys. *Journal of Abnormal Child Psychology* 7: 169–77.

Corrigan, R. 1987. A developmental sequence of actor-object pretend play in young children. *Merrill-Palmer Quarterly* 33: 87–106.

Corsaro, W. 1983. Script recognition, articulation and expansion in children's role play. *Discourse Processes* 6: 1–19.

Cunningham, C.E., & R.A. Barkley. 1979. The interactions of normal and hyperactive children with their mothers in free play and structured tasks. *Child Development* 50: 217–24.

Damon, W., & E. Phelps. 1989. Critical distinctions among three approaches to peer education. *Inter-national Journal of Educational Research* 5: 331–43.

Danforth, J.S., R.A. Barkley, & T.F. Stokes. 1991. Observations of parent-child interactions with hyperactive children: Research and clinical ap-plications. *Clinical Psychology Review* 11: 703–27.

Dansky, J.L. 1980. Make-believe: A mediator of the relationship between play and associative flu-ency. *Child Development* 51: 576–79.

Davydov, V.V. 1995. The influence of L.S. Vygotsky on education theory, research, and practice. *Edu-cational Researcher* 24 (3): 12–21.

de Villiers, P.A., & J.G. de Villiers. 1992. Language development. In *Developmental psychology: An advanced textbook,* eds. M.H. Bornstein & M.E. Lamb. 3rd ed., 337–418. Hillsdale, NJ: Erlbaum.

Denham, S.A., S.M. Renwick, & R.W. Holt. 1991. Working and playing together: Prediction of preschool social–emotional competence from mother–child interaction. *Child Development* 62: 242–49.

Deutsch, F., & A.H. Stein. 1972. The effects of personal responsibility and task interruption on the private speech of preschoolers. *Human Development* 15: 310–24.

Dias, M.G., & P.L. Harris. 1988. The effect of make-believe play on deductive reasoning. *British Journal of Developmental Psychology* 6: 207–21.

Dias, M.G., & P.L. Harris. 1990. The influence of the imagination on reasoning by young children. *British Journal of Developmental Psychology* 8: 305–18.

Diaz, R.M. 1990. The social origins of self-regulation: A Vygotskian perspective. Paper presented at the annual meeting of the American Educational Research Association, April, Boston.

Diaz, R.M., & L.E. Berk, eds. 1992. *Private speech: From social interaction to self-regulation.* Hillsdale, NJ: Erlbaum.

Diaz, R.M., & L.E. Berk. 1995. A Vygotskian critique of self-instructional training. *Development and Psychopathology* 7: 369–92.

Diaz, R.M., C.J. Neal, & M. Amaya-Williams. 1990. The social origins of self-regulation. In *Vygotsky and education: Instructional implications and applications of sociohistorical psychology,* ed. L.C. Moll, 127–54. New York: Cambridge University Press.

Diaz, R.M., C.J. Neal, & A. Vachio. 1991. Maternal teaching in the zone of proximal development: A comparison of low- and high-risk dyads. *Merrill-Palmer Quarterly* 37: 83–108.

Diaz, R.M., A. Winsler, & I. Montero. 1994. The role of private speech in the transition from collaborative to independent task performance. Stanford University, Stanford, California. Typescript.

Diaz, R.M., A. Winsler, D.J. Atencio, & K. Harbers. 1992. Mediation of self-regulation through the use of private speech. *International Journal of Cognitive Education and Mediated Learning* 2: 1–13.

Dickie, J. 1973. Private speech: The effect of presence of others, task and interpersonal variables. Ph.D. diss. Abstract in *Dissertation Abstracts International* 34: 1292B. (University Microfilms No. 73–20, 329)

DiLalla, L.F., & M.W. Watson. 1988. Differentiation of fantasy and reality: Preschoolers' reactions to interruptions in their play. *Developmental Psychology* 24: 286–91.

Dirks, J. 1982. The effect of a commercial game on children's block design scores on the WISC–R test. *Intelligence* 6: 109–23.

Doise, W., G. Mugny, & A.N. Perret-Clermont. 1975. Social interaction and the development of cognitive operations. *European Journal of Social Psychology* 5: 367–83.

Doise, W., G. Mugny, & A.N. Perret-Clermont. 1976. Social interaction and cognitive development. *European Journal of Social Psychology* 6: 245–47.

Dornbusch, S.M., P.L. Ritter, P.H. Leiderman, D.F. Roberts, & M.J. Fraleigh. 1987. The relation of parenting style to adolescent school performance. *Child Development* 58: 1244–57.

Douglas, V.I. 1983. Attention and cognitive problems. In *Developmental neuropsychiatry.* New York: Guilford.

Douglas, V.I. 1988. Cognitive deficits in children with attention deficit disorder with hyperactivity. In *Attention deficit disorder: Criteria, cognition, intervention,* eds. L. Bloomingdale & J. Sergeant, 65–81. New York: Pergamon.

Duckworth, E. 1964. In *Piaget rediscovered,* eds. R. Ripple & O. Rockcastle. Ithaca, NY: Cornell University Press.

Dunham, P., & R. Dunham. 1992. Lexical development during middle infancy: A mutually driven infant–caregiver process. *Developmental Psychology* 28: 414–20.

Dunn, J., & N. Dale. 1984. I a daddy: 2-year-olds' collaboration in joint pretend with sibling and with mother. In *Symbolic play,* ed. I. Bretherton, 131–58. New York: Academic.

Dunn, J., & C. Wooding. 1977. Play in the home and its implications for learning. In *Biology of play,* eds. B. Tizard & D. Harvey, 45–58. London: Heinemann.

Dush, D.M., M.L. Hirt, & H.E. Schroeder. 1989. Self-statement modification in the treatment of child behavior disorders: A meta-analysis. *Psychological Bulletin* 106: 97–106.

Dweck, C.S. 1991. Self-theories and goals: Their role in motivation, personality and development. In *Nebraska Symposia on Motivation.* Vol. 36, ed. R. Dienstbier, 199–235. Lincoln: University of Nebraska Press.

Edwards, C. 1993. Partner, nurturer, and guide: The roles of the Reggio teacher in action. In *The hundred languages of children: The Reggio Emilia approach to early childhood education,* eds. C. Edwards, L. Gandini, & G. Forman, 151–69. Norwood, NJ: Ablex.

Edwards, C., L. Gandini, & G. Forman, eds. 1993. *The hundred languages of children: The Reggio Emilia approach to early childhood education.* Norwood, NJ: Ablex.

Edwards, P.A. 1989. Supporting lower SES mothers' attempts to provide scaffolding for book reading. In *Risk makers, risk takers, risk breakers,* eds. J. Allen & J.M. Mason, 222–50. Portsmouth, NH: Heinemann.

Elbers, E., R. Maier, T. Hoekstra, & M. Hoogsteder. 1992. Internalization and adult–child interaction. *Learning and Instruction* 2: 101–18.

El'konin, D. 1966. Symbolics and its functions in the play of children. *Soviet Education* 8: 35–41.

El'konin, D. 1978. *Psikhologia igri* (The psychology of play). Moscow: Izdatel'stvo Pedagogika.

Erikson, E.H. 1950. *Childhood and society.* New York: Norton.

Ervin-Tripp, S. 1991. Play in language development. In *Play and the social context of development in early care and education,* eds. B. Scales, M. Almy, A. Nicolopoulou, & S. Ervin-Tripp, 84–97. New York: Teachers College Press.

Fahrmeier, E.D. 1978. The development of concrete operations among the Hausa. *Journal of Cross-Cultural Psychology* 9: 23–44.

Farver, J.M. 1993. Cultural differences in scaffolding pretend play: A comparison of American and Mexican mother-child and sibling-child pairs. In *Parent-child play: Descriptions and implications,* ed. K. MacDonald, 349–66. Albany, NY: State University of New York Press.

Feigenbaum, P. 1992. Development of the syntactic and discourse structures of private speech. In *Private speech: From social interaction to self regulation,* eds. R.M. Diaz & L.E. Berk, 181–98. Hillsdale, NJ: Erlbaum.

Fein, G. 1981. Pretend play: An integrative review. *Child Development* 52: 1095–118.

Ferrara, R.A., A.L. Brown, & J.C. Campione. 1986. Children's learning and transfer of inductive reasoning rules: Studies of proximal development. *Child Development* 57: 1087–99.

Feuerstein, R. 1979. *Dynamic assessment of retarded performers: The learning potential assessment device: Theory, instruments, and techniques.* Baltimore: University Park Press.

Feuerstein, R. 1980. *Instrumental enrichment.* Baltimore: University Park Press.

Feuerstein, R., H.C. Haywood, Y. Rand, M.B. Hoffman, & M.R. Jensen. 1986. *Learning potential assessment device manual.* Jerusalem: Wadasah—W120, Canada Research Institute.

Fiese, B. 1990. Playful relationships: A contextual analysis of mother–toddler interaction and symbolic play. *Child Development* 61: 1648–56.

File, N. 1993. The teacher as guide of children's competence with peers. *Child & Youth Care Forum* 22: 351–60.

Fischer, K.W., & S.L. Pipp. 1984. Processes of cognitive development: Optimal level and skill acquisition. In *Mechanisms of cognitive development,* ed. R.J. Sternberg, 45–80. New York: Freeman.

Flavell, J.H., F.L. Green, & E.R. Flavell. 1987. Development of knowledge about the appearance–reality distinction. *Monographs of the Society for Research in Child Development* 51 (1, Serial No. 212).

Fleer, M. 1992. Identifying teacher–child interaction which scaffolds scientific thinking in young children. *Science Education* 76: 373–97.

Forman, E.A. 1987. Learning through peer interaction: A Vygotskian perspective. *Genetic Epistemologist* 15: 6–15.

Forman, G. 1993. Multiple symbolization in the long jump project. In *The hundred languages of children: The Reggio Emilia approach to early childhood education,* eds. C. Edwards, L. Gandini, & G. Forman, 171–88. Norwood, NJ: Ablex.

Forman, E.A., & C.B. Cazden. 1985. Exploring Vygotskian perspectives in education: The cognitive value of peer interaction. In *Culture, communication, and cognition: Vygotskian perspectives,* ed. J.V. Wertsch, 323–47. New York: Cambridge University Press.

Forman, E.A., & J. McPhail. 1993. Vygotskian perspective on children's collaborative problem-solving activities. In *Contexts for learning,* eds. E.A. Forman, N. Minick, & C.A. Stone, 213–29. New York: Oxford University Press.

Frankel, K.A., & J.E. Bates. 1990. Mother-toddler problem solving: Antecedents in attachment, home behavior, and temperament. *Child Development* 61: 810–19.

Frauenglass, M.H., & R.M. Diaz. 1985. Self-regulatory functions of children's private speech: A critical analysis of recent challenges to Vygotsky's theory. *Developmental Psychology* 21: 357–64.

French, D.C., G.A. Waas, A.L. Stright, & L.A. Baker. 1986. Leadership asymmetries in mixed-age children's groups. *Child Development* 57: 1277–83.

Freyberg, J. 1973. Increasing the imaginative play of urban disadvantaged children through systematic training. In *The child's world of make-believe,* ed. J. Singer, 129–54. New York: Academic.

Gallimore, R., & R. Tharp. 1990. Teaching mind in society: Teaching, schooling, and literate discourse. In *Vygotsky and education: Instructional implications and applications of sociohistorical psychology,* ed. L.C. Moll, 175–205. New York: Cambridge University Press.

Gallimore, R., S. Dalton, & R.G. Tharp. 1986. Self-regulation and interactive teaching: The effects of teaching conditions on teachers' cognitive activity. *Elementary School Journal* 86: 613–31.

Gandini, L. 1993a. Educational and caring spaces. In *The hundred languages of children: The Reggio Emilia approach to early childhood education,* eds. C. Edwards, L. Gandini, & G. Forman, 135–49. Norwood, NJ: Ablex.

Gandini, L. 1993b. Fundamentals of the Reggio Emilia approach to early childhood education. *Young Children* 49 (1): 4–8.

Gardner, H. 1993. Foreword: Complementary perspectives on Reggio Emilia. In *The hundred languages of children: The Reggio Emilia approach* to early childhood education, eds. C. Edwards, L. Gandini, & G. Forman, ix–xiii. Norwood, NJ: Ablex.

Garvey, C. 1974. Requests and responses in children's speech. *Journal of Child Language* 2: 41–60.

Garvey, C. 1990. *Play.* Cambridge, MA: Harvard University Press.

Garvey, C., & T. Kramer. 1989. The language of social pretend play. *Developmental Review* 9: 364–82.

Gaskill, M.N., & R.M. Diaz. 1991. The relation between private speech and cognitive performance. *Infancia y Aprendizaje* 53: 45–58.

Gauvain, M., & B. Rogoff. 1989. Collaborative problem solving and children's planning skills. *Developmental Psychology* 25: 139–51.

Geary, D.C., K.F. Widaman, T.D. Little, & P. Cormier. 1987. Cognitive addition: Comparison of learning disabled and academically normal elementary school children. *Cognitive Development* 2: 249–69.

Gillingham, K.M., & Berk, L.E. 1995. The role of private speech in the development of young children's focused attention during play. Paper presented at the biennial meeting of the Society for Research in Child Development, March, Indianapolis.

Glassman, M. 1994. All things being equal: The two roads of Piaget and Vygotsky. *Developmental Review* 14: 186–214.

Goldman, J. 1981. Social participation of preschool children in same- versus mixed-age groups. *Child Development* 52: 644–50.

Golinkoff, R.M. 1983. The preverbal negotiation of failed messages: Insights into the transition period. In *The transition of prelinguistic to linguistic communication,* ed. R.M. Golinkoff, 57–78. Hillsdale, NJ: Erlbaum.

Göncü, A. 1993. Development of intersubjectivity in the dyadic play of preschoolers. *Early Childhood Research Quarterly* 8: 99–116.

Gonzalez, M.M. 1994. Parental distancing strategies: Processes and outcomes in a longitudinal perspective. Paper presented at the biennial meeting of the International Society for the Study of Behavioral Development, June, Amsterdam, The Netherlands.

Goodlad, J.I. 1984. *A place called school.* New York: McGraw-Hill.

Goodman, K. 1986. *What's whole in whole language?* Portsmouth, NH: Heinemann.

Goudena, P.P. 1987. The social nature of private speech of preschoolers during problem solving. *International Journal of Behavioral Development* 10: 187–206.

Goudena, P.P. 1992. The problem of abbreviation and internalization of private speech. In *Private speech: From social interaction to self-regula-tion,* eds. R.M. Diaz & L.E. Berk, 215–24. Hillsdale, NJ: Erlbaum.

Goudena, P.P. 1994. Vygotsky's concept of internalization: Its strengths and its weaknesses. Paper presented at the biennial meeting of the International Society for the Study of Behavioral Development, June, Amsterdam, The Netherlands.

Gralinski, J.H., & C.B. Kopp. 1993. Everyday rules for behavior: Mothers' requests to young children. *Developmental Psychology* 29: 573–84.

Haight, W.L., & P.J. Miller. 1993. *Pretending at home: Early development in a sociocultural context.* Albany, NY: State University of New York Press.

Halford, G.S. 1993. *Children's understanding: The development of mental models.* Hillsdale, NJ: Erlbaum.

Harris, R.I. 1978. Impulse control in deaf children: Research and clinical issues. In *Deaf children: Developmental perspectives,* ed. L.S. Liben, 137–56. New York: Academic.

Hatano, G. 1993. Time to merge Vygotskian and constructivist conceptions of knowledge acquisition. In *Contexts for learning,* eds. E.A. Forman, N. Minick, & C.A. Stone, 153–66. New York: Oxford University Press.

Hatano, G., & K. Inagaki. 1987. A theory of motivation for comprehension and its application to mathematics instruction. In *The monitoring of school mathematics: Background papers.* Vol. 2, *Implications from psychology; outcomes of instruction* (Program Report 87-2), eds. T.A. Romberg & D.M. Stewart, 27–46. Madison: Wisconsin Center for Educational Research.

Heath, S.B. 1983. *Ways with words: Language, life, and work in communities and classrooms.* Cambridge, England: Cambridge University Press.

Heath, S.B. 1989. Oral and literate traditions among Black Americans living in poverty. *American Psychologist* 44: 367–73.

Hedges, L.V., R.M. Giaconia, & N.L. Gage. 1981. *Meta-analysis of the effects of open and traditional instruction.* Stanford, CA: Stanford University, Program on Teaching Effectiveness.

Heyman, G.D., C.S. Dweck, & K.M. Cain. 1992. Young children's vulnerability to self-blame and helplessness: Relationship to beliefs about goodness. *Child Development* 63: 401–15.

Hinshaw, S.P., & D. Erhardt. 1991. Attention-deficit hyperactivity disorder. In *Child and adolescent therapy: Cognitive-behavioral procedures,* ed. P.C. Kendall, 98–128. New York: Guilford.

Horwitz, R.A. 1979. Psychological effects of the open classroom. *Review of Educational Research* 49: 71–86.

Howes, C., & D. Clemente. 1994. Adult socialization of children's play in child care. In *Children's play in day care settings,* ed. H. Goelman, 20–36. Albany: State University of New York Press.

Hughes, J.N. 1988. *Cognitive behavior therapy with children in schools.* New York: Pergamon.

Jacob, R.B., K.D. O'Leary, & C. Rosenblad. 1978. Formal and informal classroom settings: Effects on hyperactivity. *Journal of Abnormal Child Psychology* 6: 47–59.

Jamieson, J.R. 1994. Teaching as transaction: Vygotskian perspectives on deafness and mother–child interaction. *Exceptional Children* 60: 434–49.

Jamieson, J.R., & E.D. Pedersen. In press. Deafness and mother–child interaction: Scaffolded instruction and the learning of problem-solving skills. *Early Development and Parenting.*

Jones, E., & J. Nimmo. 1994. *Emergent curriculum.* Washington, DC: NAEYC.

Jones, G.A., & C.A. Thornton. 1993. Vygotsky revisited: Nurturing young children's understanding of number. *Focus on Learning Problems in Mathematics* 15: (2–3) 18–28.

Katz, L. 1990. Impressions of Reggio Emilia preschools. *Young Children* 45 (6): 11–12.

Katz, L.G., D. Evangelou, & J.A. Hartman. 1990. *The case for mixed-age grouping in early education.* Washington, DC: NAEYC.

Kavanaugh, R.D., S. Whittington, & M.J. Cerbone. 1983. Mothers' use of fantasy in speech to young children. *Journal of Child Language* 10: 45–55.

Kaye, K., & J. Marcus. 1981. Infant imitation: The sensory-motor agenda. *Developmental Psychology* 17: 258–65.

Keane, K.J., & R.E. Kretschmer. 1987. Effect of mediated learning intervention on cognitive task performance with a deaf population. *Journal of Educational Psychology* 79: 49–53.

Kendall, P.C., & L. Braswell. 1985. *Cognitive-behavioral therapy for impulsive children.* New York: Guilford.

Kinsman, C.A., & L.E. Berk. 1979. Joining the block and housekeeping areas: Changes in play and social behavior. *Young Children* 35 (1): 66–75.

Knox, J.E., & C.B. Stevens. 1993. Vygotsky and Soviet Russian defectology: An introduction. In *The collected works of L.S. Vygotsky.* Vol. 2, *The fundamentals of defectology,* eds. R.W. Rieber & A.S. Carton. New York: Plenum.

Kohlberg, L., & R. Mayer. 1972. Development as the aim of education. *Harvard Educational Review* 42: 449–96.

Kohlberg, L., J. Yaeger, & E. Hjertholm. 1968. Private speech: Four studies and a review of theories. *Child Development* 39: 691–736.

Kozulin, A. 1990. *Vygotsky's psychology: A biography of ideas.* Cambridge, MA: Harvard University Press.

Kuczaj, S.A. 1983. *Crib speech and language play.* New York: Springer-Verlag.

Kuczaj, S.A. 1985. Language play. *Early Child Development & Care* 19: 53–67.

Landau, S., & C. McAninch. 1993. Research in review. Young children with attention deficits. *Young Children* 48 (4): 49–58.

Landau, S., & L. Moore. 1991. Social skills deficits in children with attention-deficit hyperactivity disorder. *School Psychology Review* 20: 235–51.

Lave, J. 1988. *Cognition in practice: Mind, mathematics, and culture in everyday life.* New York: Cambridge University Press.

Lave, J., & E. Wenger. 1991. *Situated learning: Legitimate peripheral participation.* New York: Cambridge University Press.

Lawrence, J.A., & J. Valsiner. 1993. Conceptual roots of internalization: From transmission to transformation. *Human Development* 36: 150–67.

Lederberg, A.R., & C.E. Mobley. 1990. The effect of hearing impairment on the quality of attachment and mother–toddler interaction. *Child Development* 61: 1596–604.

Leont'ev, A.N. 1959. *Problemy razvitiya psikhiki* (Problems in the development of mind). Moscow: Moscow University Press.

Leont'ev, A.N. 1978. *Activity, consciousness, and personality.* Englewood Cliffs, NJ: Prentice Hall.

Leont'ev, A.N. 1981. The problem of activity in psychology. In *The concept of activity in Soviet psychology,* ed. J.V. Wertsch, 37–71. Armonk, NY: Sharpe.

Levenstein, P. 1988. *Messages from home.* Columbus, OH: Ohio State University.

Levenstein, P., & J. O'Hara. 1993. The necessary lightness of mother–child play. In *Parent–child play,* ed. K. MacDonald, 221–37. New York: State University of New York Press.

Levy, E. 1989. Monologue as development of the text-forming function of language. In *Narratives from the crib,* ed. K. Nelson, 123–70. Cambridge, MA: Harvard University Press.

Lidz, C.S. 1991. *Practitioner's guide to dynamic assessment.* New York: Guilford.

Light, P., & A. Perret-Clermont. 1989. Social context effects in learning and testing. In *Cognition and social worlds,* eds. A.R.H. Gellatly, D. Rogers, & J. Sloboda, 99–112. Oxford: Clarendon.

Light, P.H., & M. Glachan. 1985. Facilitation of individual problem solving through peer interaction. *Educational Psychology* 5: 217–25.

Lougee, M.D.R., & W.G. Graziano. 1986. Children's relationships with non-agemate peers. University of Georgia, Athens, GA. Duplicated.

Lucariello, J. 1987. Spinning fantasy: Themes, structure, and the knowledge base. *Child Development* 58: 434–42.

Luria, A.R. 1976. *Cognitive development: Its cultural and social foundations.* Cambridge, MA: Harvard University Press.

Luria, A.R. 1982. *Language and cognition.* New York: Wiley.

Lyytinen, P., H. Rasku-Puttonen, A.M. Poikkeus, M.L. Laakso, & T. Ahonen. 1994. Mother-child teaching strategies and learning disabilities. *Journal of Learning Disabilities* 27: 186–92.

Malaguzzi, L. 1993a. For an education based on relationships. Trans. L. Gandini. *Young Children* 49 (1): 9–12.

Malaguzzi, L. 1993b. History, ideas, and basic philosophy. In *The hundred languages of children: The Reggio Emilia approach to early childhood education,* eds. C. Edwards, L. Gandini, & G. Forman, 41–89. Norwood, NJ: Ablex.

Manning, B.H., & C.S. White. 1990. Task-relevant private speech as a function of age and sociability. *Psychology in the Schools* 27: 365–72.

Mash, E.J., & C. Johnston. 1982. A comparison of the mother-child interactions of younger and older hyperactive and normal children. *Child Development* 53: 1371–81.

McCarthy, E.M. 1992. Anatomy of a teaching interaction: The components of teaching in the ZPD. Paper presented at the annual meeting of the American Educational Research Association, April, San Francisco, California.

McCune, L. 1993. The development of play as the development of consciousness. In *New directions for child development,* No. 59, eds. M.H. Bornstein & A. O'Reilly, 67–79. San Francisco: Jossey-Bass.

McDonald, K., & R. Parke. 1986. Parent–child physical play: The effects of sex and age of children and parents. *Sex Roles* 15: 367–78.

McGee, L.M., & D.J. Richgels. 1990. *Literacy's beginnings: Supporting young readers and writers.* Boston: Allyn & Bacon.

McLoyd, V.C. 1983. The effects of the structure of play objects on the pretend play of low-income preschool children. *Child Development* 54: 626–35.

McLoyd, V.C., D. Warren, & A.C. Thomas. 1984. Anticipatory and fantastic role enactment in preschool triads. *Developmental Psychology* 20: 807–14.

Meadow, K.P. 1980. *Deafness and child development.* Berkeley, CA: University of California Press.

Meadow, K.P., M.T. Greenberg, C. Erting, & H. Carmichael. 1981. Interactions of deaf mothers and deaf preschool children: Comparisons with three other groups of deaf and hearing dyads. *American Annals of the Deaf* 126: 454–68.

Meadow-Orlans, K.P. 1993. Interactions of deaf and hearing mothers with their hearing and deaf infants at 12 and 18 months. Paper presented at the biennial meeting of the Society for Research in Child Development, New Orleans, Louisiana.

Mearig, J.S. 1987. Assessing the learning potential of kindergarten and primary-age children. In *Dynamic assessment: An interactional approach to evaluating learning potential,* ed. C.S. Lidz, 237–67. New York: Guilford.

Meichenbaum, D.H., & J. Goodman. 1971. Training impulsive children to talk to themselves: A means of developing self-control. *Journal of Personality and Social Psychology* 34: 942–50.

Meltzoff, A., & A. Gopnik. 1993. The role of imitation in understanding persons and developing a theory of mind. In *Understanding other minds,* eds. S. Baron-Cohen & H. Tager-Flusberg, 335–66. Oxford: Oxford University Press.

Miller, P., & C. Garvey. 1984. Mother–baby role play: Its origins in social support. In *Symbolic play,* ed. I. Bretherton, 101–30. New York: Academic.

Miller-Jones, D. 1989. Culture and testing. *American Psychologist* 44: 360–66.

Minick, N. 1989. Mind and activity in Vygotsky's work: An expanded frame of reference. *Cultural Dynamics* 2: 162–87.

Missiuna, C., & M. Samuels. 1989. Dynamic assessment: Review and critique. *Special Services in the Schools* 5 (1/2): 1–22.

Moll, L.C. 1990. Introduction. In *Vygotsky and education,* L.C. Moll, 1–30. New York: Cambridge University Press.

Moll, L.C., & J.B. Greenberg. 1990. Creating zones of possibilities: Combining social contexts for instruction. In *Vygotsky and education,* ed. L.C. Moll, 319–48. New York: Cambridge University Press.

Moll, L.C., & K.F. Whitmore. 1993. Vygotsky in classroom practice: Moving from individual transmission to social transaction. In *Contexts for learning,* eds. E.A. Forman, N. Minick, & C.A. Stone, 19–42. New York: Oxford University Press.

Mounts, N.S., & J.L. Roopnarine. 1987. Social-cognitive play patterns in same-age and mixed-age preschool classrooms. *American Educational Research Journal* 24: 463–76.

Mugny, G., & W. Doise. 1978. Socio-cognitive conflict and structure of individual and collective performance. *European Journal of Social Psychology* 8: 181–92.

Murray, F.B. 1972. Acquisition of conservation through social interaction. *Developmental Psychology* 6: 1–6.

Murray, F.B. 1982. Teaching through social conflict. *Contemporary Educational Psychology* 7: 257–71.

Murray, J.D. 1979. Spontaneous private speech and performance on a delayed match-to-sample task. *Journal of Experimental Child Psychology* 27: 286–302.

Nastasi, B.K., D.H. Clements, & M.T. Battista. 1990. Social–cognitive interactions, motivation, and cognitive growth in Logo programming and CAI problem-solving environments. *Journal of Educational Psychology* 82: 1–9.

National Association for the Education of Young Children. 1991. *Accreditation criteria & procedures.* Rev. ed. Washington, DC: NAEYC.

Nelson, K. 1973. Structure and strategy in learning to talk. *Monographs for the Society for Research in Child Development* 38 (1–2, Serial No. 149).

Nelson, K., ed. 1989. *Narratives from the crib.* Cambridge, MA: Harvard University Press.

Neuman, S.B., & K. Roskos. 1991. Peers as literacy informants: A description of young children's literacy conversations in play. *Early Childhood Research Quarterly* 6: 233–48.

Newman, F., & L. Holzman. 1993. *Lev Vygotsky: Revolutionary scientist.* New York: Routledge.

Newman, L.S. 1990. Intentional versus unintentional memory in young children: Remembering versus playing. *Journal of Experimental Child Psychology* 50: 243–58.

Newson, J., & E. Newson. 1975. Intersubjectivity and the transmission of culture: On the social origins of symbolic functioning. *Bulletin of the British Psychological Society* 28: 437–46.

Nicholls, J., P. Cobb, T. Wood, E. Yackel, & M. Patashnick. 1990. Dimensions of success in mathematics: Individual and classroom differences. *Journal for Research in Mathematics Education* 21: 109–22.

Nicolopoulou, A. 1991. Play, cognitive development, and the social world. In *Play and the social context of development in early care and education,* eds. B. Scales, M. Almy, A. Nicolopoulou, & S. Ervin-Tripp, 129–42. New York: Teachers College Press.

Nicolopoulou, A. 1993. Play, cognitive development, and the social world: Piaget, Vygotsky, and beyond. *Human Development* 36: 1–23.

Oakes, J. 1986. Tracking, inequality, and the rhetoric of school reform: Why schools don't change. *Journal of Education* 168 (1): 60–80.

O'Connell, B., & I. Bretherton. 1984. Toddlers' play alone and with mother: The role of maternal guidance. In *Symbolic play,* ed. I. Bretherton, 337–68. New York: Academic.

O'Connor, M., T. Foch, T. Sherry, & R. Plomin. 1980. A twin study of specific behavioral problems of socialization as viewed by parents. *Journal of Abnormal Child Psychology* 8: 189–99.

Okagaki, L., & R.J. Sternberg. 1993. Parental beliefs and children's school performance. *Child Development* 64: 36–56.

Olszewski, P. 1987. Individual differences in preschool children's production of verbal fantasy play. *Merrill-Palmer Quarterly* 33: 69–86.

O'Reilly, A.W., & M.H. Bornstein. 1993. Caregiver–child interaction in play. In *New directions for child development* (No. 59), eds. M.H. Bornstein & A.W. O'Reilly, 55–66. San Francisco: Jossey-Bass.

Pacifici, C., & D.J. Bearison. 1991. Development of children's self-regulations in idealized and mother–child interactions. *Cognitive Development* 6: 261–77.

Packer, M.J. 1993. Away from internalization. In *Contexts for learning,* eds. E.A. Forman, N. Minick, & C.A. Stone, 254–65. New York: Oxford University Press.

Palincsar, A.S., & A.L. Brown. 1984. Reciprocal teaching of comprehension-fostering and monitoring activities. *Cognition and Instruction* 1: 117–75.

Palincsar, A.S., & A.L. Brown. 1989. Classroom dialogues to promote self-regulated comprehension. In *Advances in research on teaching.* Vol. 1, ed. J. Brophy, 35–72. Greenwich, CT: JAI.

Palincsar, A.S., & L. Klenk. 1992. Fostering literacy learning in supportive contexts. *Journal of Learning Disabilities* 25: 211–25.

Palincsar, A.S., A.L. Brown, & J.C. Campione. 1993. In *Contexts for learning,* eds. E.A. Forman, N. Minick, & C.A. Stone, 43–57. New York: Oxford University Press.

Palkes, H., M. Stewart, & B. Kahana. 1968. Porteus maze performance of hyperactive boys after training in self-directed verbal commands. *Child Development* 39: 817–26.

Parten, M. 1932. Social participation among preschool children. *Journal of Abnormal and Social Psychology* 2: 243–69.

Pelham, W.E., Jr. 1987. What do we know about the use and effects of CNS stimulants in the treatment of ADD? In *The young hyperactive child: Answers to questions about diagnosis, prognosis and treatment,* ed. J. Loney, 99–110. New York: Haworth.

Pelham, W.E., Jr. 1992. Children's summer day treatment program: 1992 program manual. Unpublished manuscript, University of Pittsburgh School of Medicine, Western Psychiatric Institute and Clinic, Pittsburgh, Pennsylvania.

Pelham, W.E., Jr. 1993. Pharmacotherapy for children with attention-deficit hyperactivity disorder. *School Psychology Review* 22: 199–227.

Pellegrini, A.D. 1981. The development of preschoolers' private speech. *Journal of Pragmatics* 5: 445–58.

Pellegrini, A.D., & L. Galda. 1982. The effects of thematic-fantasy play training on the development of children's story comprehension. *American Educational Research Journal* 19: 443–52.

Pellegrini, A.D., & M. Horvat. 1995. A developmental contextualist critique of attention deficit hyperactivity disorder. *Educational Researcher* 24 (1): 13–19.

Pepler, D.J., & H.S. Ross 1981. The effect of play on convergent and divergent problem solving. *Child Development* 52: 1202–10.

Pepperberg, I.M., K.J. Brese, & B.J. Harris. 1991. Solitary sound play during acquisition of English vocalizations by an African Grey parrot (Psittacus erithacus): Possible parallels with children's monologue speech. *Applied Psycholinguistics* 12: 151–78.

Perlmutter, M., S.D. Behrend, F. Kuo, & A. Muller. 1989. Social influences on children's problem solving. *Developmental Psychology* 25: 744–54.

Perner, J., S.R. Leekam, & H. Wimmer. 1986. The insincerity of conservation questions: Children's growing insensitivity to experimenters' epistemic intentions. University of Sussex. Duplicated.

Perret-Clermont, A.N. 1980. *Social interaction and cognitive development in children.* London: Academic.

Perret-Clermont, A.N., J-F. Perret, & N. Bell. 1991. The social construction of meaning and cognitive activity in elementary school children. In *Perspectives on socially shared cognition,* eds. L.B. Resnick, J.M. Levine, & S.D. Teasley, 41–62. Washington, DC: American Psychological Association.

Piaget, J. [1923] 1926. *The language and thought of the child.* New York: Harcourt, Brace & World.

Piaget, J. [1926] 1930. *The child's conception of the world.* New York: Harcourt, Brace & World.

Piaget, J. [1932] 1965. *The moral judgment of the child.* New York: Free Press.

Piaget, J. [1945] 1951. *Play, dreams, and imitation in childhood.* New York: Norton.

Piaget, J. 1950. *The psychology of intelligence.* New York: International Universities Press.

Piaget, J. 1952. Jean Piaget (autobiographical sketch). In *A history of psychology in autobiography,* eds. E.G. Boring, H.S. Langfeld, H. Werner, & R.M. Yerkes, 237–56. Worcester, MA: Clark University Press.

Piaget, J. [1962] 1979. Comments on Vygotsky's critical remarks. *Archives of Psychology* 47: 237–49.

Piaget, J. 1985. *The equilibration of cognitive structures: The central problem of intellectual development.* Chicago: University of Chicago Press.

Podrouzek, W., & D. Furrow 1988. Preschoolers' use of eye contact while speaking: The influence of sex, age, and conversational partner. *Journal of Psycholinguistic Research* 17: 89–93.

Pratt, M.W., D. Green, J. MacVicar, & M. Bountrogianni. 1992. The mathematical parent: Parental scaffolding, parent style, and learning outcomes in long-division mathematics homework. *Journal of Applied Developmental Psychology* 13: 17–34.

Pratt, M.W., P. Kerig, P.A. Cowan, & C.P. Cowan. 1988. Mothers and fathers teaching 3-year-olds: Authoritative parents and adult scaffolding of young children's learning. *Developmental Psychology* 24: 832–39.

Radziszewska, B., & B. Rogoff. 1988. Influence of adult and peer collaboration on the development of children's planning skills. *Developmental Psychology* 24: 840–48.

Rand, Y., & S. Kaniel. 1987. Group administration of the LPAD. In *Dynamic assessment: An inter-actional approach to evaluating learning potential,* ed. C.S. Lidz, 196–214. New York: Guilford.

Ratner, N., & J.S. Bruner. 1978. Social exchange and the acquisition of language. *Journal of Child Language* 5: 391–402.

Resnick, L.B. 1991. Shared cognition: Thinking as social practice. In *Perspectives on socially shared cognition,* eds. L.B. Resnick, J.M. Levine, & S.D. Teasley, 1–20. Washington, DC: American Psychological Association.

Roberts, R.N. 1979. Private speech in academic problem solving: A naturalistic perspective. In *The development of self-regulation through private speech,* ed. G. Zivin, 295–323. New York: Wiley.

Roberts, R.N., & M.L. Barnes. 1992. "Let momma show you how": Maternal–child interactions and their effects on children's cognitive performance. *Journal of Applied Developmental Psychology* 13: 363–76.

Rogoff, B. 1990. *Apprenticeship in thinking: Cognitive development in social context.* New York: Oxford University Press.

Rogoff, B., & K.J. Waddell. 1982. Memory for information organized in a scene by children from two cultures. *Child Development* 53: 1224–28.

Rogoff, B., J. Mistry, A. Göncü, & C. Mosier. 1993. Guided participation in cultural activity by toddlers and caregivers. *Monographs of the Society for Research in Child Development* 58 (8, Serial No. 236).

Rogoff, B., C. Mosier, J. Mistry, & A. Göncü. 1993. Toddlers' guided participation with their caregivers in cultural activity. In *Contexts for learning,* eds. E.A. Forman, N. Minick, & C.A. Stone, 230–53. New York: Oxford University Press.

Roopnarine, J.L., & J. Bright. 1992. The social-individual model: Mixed-age socialization. In *Approaches to early childhood education,* eds. J. Roopnarine & J. Johnson. 2nd ed., 223–42. Columbus, OH: Macmillan.

Roopnarine, J.L., M. Ahmeduzzaman, S. Donnely, P. Gill, A. Mennis, L. Arky, K. Dingler, M. McLaughlin, & E. Talukder. 1992. Social-cognitive play behaviors and playmate preferences in same-age and mixed-age classrooms over a 6-month period. *American Educational Research Journal* 29: 757–76.

Rubin, K.H. 1979. Impact of the natural setting on private speech. In *The development of self-regulation through private speech,* ed. G. Zivin, 265–94. New York: Wiley.

Rubin, K.H. 1982. The private speech of preschoolers who vary with regard to sociability. Paper presented at the annual meeting of the American Educational Research Association, April, New York.

Rubin, K.H., & L. Dyck. 1980. Preschoolers' private speech in a play setting. *Merrill-Palmer Quarterly* 26: 219–29.

Rubin, K.H., G.G. Fein, & B. Vandenberg. 1983. Play. In *Handbook of child psychology*. Vol. 4, *Socialization, personality, and social development*, ed. E.M. Hetherington, 693–744. New York: Wiley.

Rubtsov, V.V. 1981. The role of cooperation in the development of intelligence. *Soviet Psychology* 19: 41–62.

Sachs, J. 1980. The role of adult–child play in language development. In *New directions for child development* (No. 9), ed. K.H. Rubin, 33–48. San Francisco: Jossey-Bass.

Saltz, E., & J. Brodie. 1982. Pretend-play training in childhood: A review and critique. *Contributions to Human Development* 6: 97–113.

Saltz, E., & J. Johnson. 1974. Training for thematic fantasy play in culturally disadvantaged children: Preliminary results. *Journal of Educational Psychology* 66: 623–30.

Saltz, E., D. Dixon, & J. Johnson. 1977. Training disadvantaged preschoolers on various fantasy activities: Effects on cognitive functioning and impulse control. *Child Development* 48: 367–80.

Schlesinger, H.S., & K.P. Meadow. 1972. *Sound and sign: Childhood deafness and mental health*. Berkeley, CA: University of California Press.

Schunk, D.H., & B.J. Zimmerman, eds. 1994. *Self-regulation of learning and performance: Issues and educational applications*. Hillsdale, NJ: Erlbaum.

Scribner, S., & M. Cole. 1981. *Psychology of literacy*. Cambridge, MA: Cambridge University Press.

Siegal, M., L.J. Waters, & L.S. Dinwiddy. 1988. Misleading children: Causal attributions for inconsistency under repeated questioning. *Journal of Experimental Child Psychology* 45: 438–56.

Siegler, R.S. 1981. Developmental sequences within and between concepts. *Monographs for the Society for Research in Child Development* 46 (2, Serial No. 189).

Sigel, I. 1982. The relationship between parental distancing strategies and the child's cognitive behavior. In *Families as learning environments for children*, eds. L. Laosa & I. Sigel, 47–86. New York: Plenum.

Sigel, I.E., A.V. McGillicuddy-DeLisi, & J. Johnson. 1980. *Parental distancing, beliefs, and children's representational competence within the family context*. Princeton, NJ: Educational Testing Service.

Silvern, S.B., J.B. Taylor, P.A. Williamson, E. Surbeck, & M.F. Kelley. 1986. Young children's story recall as a product of play, story familiarity, and adult intervention. *Merrill-Palmer Quarterly* 32: 73–86.

Singer, D.G., & J. Singer. 1990. *The house of make-believe*. Cambridge, MA: Harvard University Press.

Slade, A. 1987. A longitudinal study of maternal involvement and symbolic play during the toddler period. *Child Development* 58: 367–75.

Slavin, R.E. 1983. *Cooperative learning*. New York: Longman.

Slavin, R.E. 1987. Developmental and motivational perspectives on cooperative learning: A reconciliation. *Child Development* 58: 1161–67.

Smolucha, F. 1991. The origins of object substitutions in social pretend play. Ph.D. diss., University of Chicago.

Smolucha, F. 1992a. The relevance of Vygotsky's theory of creative imagination for contemporary research on play. *Creativity Research Journal* 5: 69–76.

Smolucha, F. 1992b. Social origins of private speech in pretend play. In *Private speech: From social interaction to self-regulation*, eds. R.M. Diaz & L.E. Berk, 123–41. Hillsdale, NJ: Erlbaum.

Spencer, P.E., & M.K. Gutfreund. 1990. Directiveness in mother–infant interactions. In *Educational and developmental aspects of deafness*, eds. D.F. Moores & K.P. Meadow-Orlans, 350–65. Washington, DC: Gallaudet University Press.

Steinberg, L., J. Elmen, & N. Mounts. 1989. Authoritative parenting, psychosocial maturity, and academic success among adolescents. *Child Development* 60: 1424–36.

Stone, C.A. 1993. What is missing in the metaphor of scaffolding? In *Contexts for learning*, eds. E.A. Forman, N. Minick, & C.A. Stone, 169–83. New York: Oxford University Press.

Stright, A.L., & D.C. French. 1988. Leadership in mixed-age children's groups. *International Journal of Behavioral Development* 11: 507–15.

Sutton-Smith, B. 1974. *How to play with your children (and when not to)*. New York: Hawthorne.

Sutton-Smith, B. 1986. *Toys as culture*. New York: Gardner.

Tallmadge, J., & R.A. Barkley. 1983. The interactions of hyperactive and normal boys with their fathers and mothers. *Journal of Abnormal Child Psychology* 11: 565–80.

Tamis-LeMonda, C.S., & M.H. Bornstein. 1989. Habituation and maternal encouragement of attention in infancy as predictors of toddler language, play and representational competence. *Child Development* 60: 738–51.

Tamis-LeMonda, C.S., & M.H. Bornstein. 1991. Individual variation, correspondence, stability, and change in mother and toddler play. *Infant Behavior and Development* 14: 143–62.

Tamis-LeMonda, C.S., & M.H. Bornstein. 1993. Play and its relations to other mental functions in the child. In *New directions for child development* (No. 59), eds. M.H. Bornstein & A. O'Reilly, 17–27. San Francisco: Jossey-Bass.

Tharp, R.G. 1982. The effective instruction of comprehension: Results and description of the Kamehameha Early Education Program. *Reading Research Quarterly* 17: 503–27.

Tharp, R.G., & R. Gallimore. 1988. *Rousing minds to life.* New York: Cambridge University Press.

Thomas, N.G., & L.E. Berk. 1981. Effects of school environments on the development of young children's creativity. *Child Development* 52: 1152–62.

Thompson, R.A. 1990. On emotion and self-regulation. In *Nebraska Symposium on Motivation.* Vol. 36, ed. R.A. Thompson, 383–483. Lincoln: University of Nebraska Press.

Thorndike, E.L. 1926. *The measurement of intelligence.* New York: Teachers College Press.

Tomasello, M. 1990. The role of joint attentional processes in early language development. *Language Sciences* 10: 68–88.

Trevarthen, C. 1989. Origins and directions for the concept of infant intersubjectivity. *SRCD (Society for Research in Child Development) Newsletter,* Autumn, 1–4.

Tudge, J.R.H. 1989. When collaboration leads to regression: Some negative consequences of sociocognitive conflict. *European Journal of Social Psychology* 19: 123–38.

Tudge, J.R.H. 1990. Vygotsky, the zone of proximal development, and peer collaboration: Implications for classroom practice. In *Vygotsky and education: Instructional implications and applications of sociohistorical psychology,* ed. L.C. Moll, 155–72. New York: Cambridge University Press.

Tudge, J.R.H. 1992. Processes and consequences of peer collaboration: A Vygotskian analysis. *Child Development* 63: 1364–79.

Tudge, J.R.H., & B. Rogoff. 1987. Peer influences on cognitive development: Piagetian and Vygotskian perspectives. In *Interaction in human development,* eds. M.H. Bornstein & J.S. Bruner, 17–40. Hillsdale, NJ: Erlbaum.

Tudge, J.R.H., & P.A. Winterhoff. 1993. Vygotsky, Piaget, and Bandura: Perspectives on the relations between the social world and cognitive development. *Human Development* 36: 61–81.

Tulviste, P. 1991. *The cultural-historical development of verbal thinking.* Commack, NY: Nova Science Publishers.

Tzuriel, D. 1989. Inferential thinking modifiability in young socially disadvantaged and advantaged children. *International Journal of Dynamic Assessment and Instruction* 1: 65–80.

Valsiner, J. 1988. *Developmental psychology in the Soviet Union.* Sussex, Great Britain: Harvester.

van der Veer, R., & J. Valsiner. 1991. *Understanding Vygotsky: A quest for synthesis.* Cambridge, MA: Blackwell.

Vecchi, V. 1993. The role of the atelierista. In *The hundred languages of children: The Reggio Emilia approach to early childhood education,* eds. C. Edwards, L. Gandini, & G. Forman, 119–27. Norwood, NJ: Ablex.

Vye, N.J., M.S. Burns, V.R. Delclos, & J.D. Bransford. 1987. A comprehensive approach to assessing intellectually handicapped children. In *Dynamic assessment: An interactional approach to evaluating learning potential,* ed. C.S. Lidz, 327–59. New York: Guilford.

Vygotsky, L.S. [1916] 1986. Tragedija o Gamlete, prince Datskom, U. Shekspira (The tragedy of Hamlet, Prince of Denmark, by Shakespeare). In *Psikhologija iskusstva* (The psychology of art), L.S. Vygotsky, 336–491. Moscow: Iskusstvo.

Vygotsky, L.S. [1925] 1979. Consciousness as a problem in the psychology of behavior. *Soviet Psychology* 17 (4): 3–35.

Vygotsky, L.S. 1925. Principles of social education for deaf and dumb children in Russia. In *International Conference on the Education of the Deaf,* 227–37. London: William H. Taylor & Sons.

Vygotsky, L.S. [1925] 1986. *Psikhologija iskusstva* (The psychology of art). Moscow: Iskusstvo.

Vygotsky, L.S. [1925] 1971. *The psychology of art.* Cambridge, MA: MIT Press.

Vygotsky, L.S. 1926. *Pedagogicheskaja psikhologija* (Pedagogical psychology). Moscow: Rabotnik Prosveshchenija.

Vygotsky, L.S. 1929. The problem of the cultural development of the child. *Journal of Genetic Psychology* 36: 415–34.

Vygotsky, L.S. [1930] 1990. Imagination and creativity in childhood. *Soviet Psychology* 28: 84–96. (Original work presented as a lecture.)

Vygotsky, L.S. [1930] 1981. The instrumental method in psychology. In *The concept of activity in Soviet psychology,* ed. J.V. Wertsch, 134–43. Armonk, NY: Sharpe.

Vygotsky, L.S. [1930–1935] 1978. *Mind in society: The development of higher mental processes,* eds. & trans. M. Cole, V. John-Steiner, S. Scribner, & E. Souberman. Cambridge, MA: Harvard University Press.

Vygotsky, L.S. 1931. Kollektiv kak faktor razvitija defektivnogo rebenka (The collective as a factor in the development of the abnormal child). *Voprosy Defektologii* 1–2: 8–17.

Vygotsky, L.S. [1931] 1960. *Razvitie vysshikh psikhicheskikh funktsii* (The development of higher mental functions). Moscow: Izdatel'stvo Akademii Pedagogicheskikh Nauk RSFSR.

Vygotsky, L.S. [1933] 1966. Play and its role in the mental development of the child. *Soviet Psychology* 12 (6): 62–76.

Vygotsky, L.S. 1934. *Myshlenie i rech: Psikhologicheskie issledovaniya* (Thinking and speech: Psychological investigations). Moscow-Leningrad: Gosudarstvennoe Izdatel'stvo.

Vygotsky, L.S. [1934] 1987. Thinking and speech. In *The collected works of L.S. Vygotsky.* Vol.

1., *Problems of general psychology,* eds. R. Rieber & A.S. Carton, trans. N. Minick, 37–285. New York: Plenum.

Vygotsky, L.S. [1934] 1962. *Thought and language,* eds. & trans. E. Hanfmann & G. Vakar. Cambridge, MA: MIT Press.

Vygotsky, L.S. [1934] 1986. *Thought and language,* trans. A. Kozulin. Cambridge, MA: MIT Press.

Vygotsky, L.S. 1956. *Selected psychological investigations.* Moscow: Izdstel'sto Akademii Pedagog-icheskikh Nauk SSSR.

Vygotsky, L.S. [1960] 1981. The genesis of higher mental functions. In *The concept of activity in Soviet psychology,* ed. J.V. Wertsch, 144–88. Armonk, NY: Sharpe.

Vygotsky, L.S. 1972. Problema vozrastnoj periodizacii detskogo razvitija (The problem of stage periodization in child development). *Voprosy Psikhologii* 2: 114–23.

Vygotsky, L.S. 1982a. *Sobranie sochinenji.* Tom 1, *Voprosy teorii i istorii psikhologii* (Collected works. Vol. 1, Questions in the theory and history of psychology). Moscow: Pedagogika.

Vygotsky, L.S. 1982b. *Sobranie sochinenji.* Tom 2, *Problemy obshchej psikhologii* (Collected works. Vol. 2, Problems of general psychology). Moscow: Pedagogika.

Vygotsky, L.S. 1983a. *Sobranie sochinenji.* Tom 3, *Problemy razvitija psikhiki* (Collected works. Vol. 3, Problems in the development of mind). Moscow: Pedagogika.

Vygotsky, L.S. 1983b. *Sobranie sochinenji.* Tom 5, *Osnovy defektologii* (Collected works. Vol. 5, Foundations of defectology). Moscow: Pedagogika.

Vygotsky, L.S. 1984a. *Sobranie sochinenji.* Tom 4, *Detskaja psikhologija* (Collected works. Vol. 4, Child psychology). Moscow: Pedagogika.

Vygotsky, L.S. 1984b. *Sobranie sochinenji.* Tom 6, *Nauchnoe nasledstvo* (Collected works. Vol. 6, Scientific legacy). Moscow: Pedagogika.

Vygotsky, L.S. 1993. *The collected works of L.S. Vygotsky.* Vol. 2, *The fundamentals of defectology,* eds. R.W. Rieber & A.S. Carton, trans. J.E. Knox & C.B. Stevens. New York: Plenum.

Vygotsky, L.S., & A.R. Luria. [1930] 1993. *Studies on the history of behavior: Ape, primitive, and child,* eds. & trans. V.I. Golod & J.E. Knox. Hillsdale, NJ: Erlbaum.

Walberg, H.J. 1986. Synthesis of research on teaching. In *Handbook of research on teaching,* ed. M.C. Wittrock. 3rd ed., 214–29. New York: Macmillan.

Warren, A.R., & C.S. Tate. 1992. Egocentrism in children's telephone conversations. In *Private speech: From social interaction to self-regulation,* eds. R.M. Diaz & L.E. Berk, 245–64. Hillsdale, NJ: Erlbaum.

Watson, D.J. 1989. Defining and describing whole language. *Elementary School Journal* 90: 129–41.

Wedell-Monning, J., & J. Lumley. 1980. Child deafness and mother–child interaction. *Child Development* 51: 766–74.

Weir, R. 1962. *Language in the crib.* The Hague: Mouton.

Weiss, G., & L.T. Hechtman. 1993. *Hyperactive children grown up.* 2nd ed. New York: Guilford.

Wertsch, J.V., ed. 1985a. *Culture, communication, and cognition: Vygotskian perspectives.* New York: Cambridge University Press.

Wertsch, J.V. 1985b. *Vygotsky and the social formation of mind.* Cambridge, MA: Harvard University Press.

Wertsch, J.V. 1991a. A sociocultural approach to socially shared cognition. In *Perspectives on socially shared cognition,* eds. L.B. Resnick, J.M. Levine, & S.D. Teasley, 85–100. Washington, DC: American Psychological Association.

Wertsch, J.V. 1991b. *Voices of the mind.* New York: Harvard University Press.

Wertsch, J.V., & B. Rogoff. 1984. Editors' notes. In *Children's learning in the "zone of proximal development",* eds. B. Rogoff & J.V. Wertsch, 1–6. San Francisco: Jossey-Bass.

White, R.W. 1959. Motivation reconsidered: The concept of competence. *Psychological Review* 66: 297–333.

Whiting, B., & C.P. Edwards. 1988. *Children of different worlds.* Cambridge, MA: Harvard University Press.

Winsler, A. 1993. The social interactions and task activities of young children in mixed-age and same-age classrooms: An observational study. Paper presented at the biennial meeting of the Society for Research in Child Development, March, New Orleans, Louisiana. ERIC, ED 356 074.

Winsler, A. 1994. The social origins and self-regulatory quality of private speech in hyperactive and normal children. Ph.D. diss., Stanford University, Stanford, CA.

Winsler, A., & R.M. Diaz. In press. Private speech in the classroom: The effects of activity type, presence of others, classroom context, and mixed-age grouping. *International Journal of Behavioral Development.*

Wong, B.Y.L. 1985. Issues in cognitive-behavioral interventions in academic skill areas. *Journal of Abnormal Child Psychology* 13: 425–41.

Wood, D.J. 1980. Teaching the young child: Some relationships between social interaction, language, and thought. In *The social foundations of language and thought,* ed. R. Olson, 280–96. New York: Norton.

Wood, D.J. 1989. Social interaction as tutoring. In *Interaction in human development,* eds. M.H. Bornstein & J.S. Bruner, 59–80. Hillsdale, NJ: Erlbaum.

Wood, D.J., & D. Middleton. 1975. A study of assisted problem solving. *British Journal of Psychology* 66: 181–91.

Wood, D.J., J. Bruner, & G. Ross. 1976. The role of tutoring in problem solving. *Journal of Child Psychology and Psychiatry* 17: 89–100.

Woolley, J.D., & H.M. Wellman. 1990. Young children's understanding of realities, non-realities, and appearances. *Child Development* 61: 946–61.

Yackel, E., P. Cobb, & T. Wood. 1991. Small group interactions as a source of learning opportunities in second grade mathematics. *Journal for Research in Mathematics Education* 22: 390–408.

Zentall, S.S. 1988. Production deficiencies in elicited language but not in the spontaneous verbalizations of hyperactive children. *Journal of Abnormal Child Psychology* 16: 657–73.

Zentall, S.S., D.E. Gohs, & B. Culatta. 1983. Language and activity of hyperactive and comparison children during listening tasks. *Exceptional Children* 50: 255–66.

Zimmerman, B.J., & D.H. Schunk, eds. 1989. *Self-regulated learning and academic achievement: Theory, research, and practice.* New York: Springer-Verlag.

Zivin, G. 1972. Functions of private speech during problem-solving in preschool children. Ph. D. diss. Abstract in *Dissertation Abstracts International* 33 (2-B): 1834. (University Microfilms No. 72–26, 224)

Zukow, P.G. 1986. The relationship between interaction with the caregiver and the emergence of play activities during the one-word period. *British Journal of Developmental Psychology* 4: 223–34.

Zukow, P.G. 1989. Siblings as effective socializing agents: Evidence from central Mexico. In *Sibling interaction across cultures,* ed. P.G. Zukow, 79–105. New York: Springer-Verlag.

Resources

Vygotsky's Life and Contributions

Blanck, G. 1990. Vygotsky: The man and his cause. In *Vygotsky and education,* ed. L.C. Moll, 31–58. Cambridge, MA: Cambridge University Press.

Wertsch, J.V. 1985. *Vygotsky and the social formation of mind.* Cambridge, MA: Harvard University Press.

Wertsch, J.V., & P. Tulviste. 1992. L.S. Vygotsky and contemporary developmental psychology. *Developmental Psychology* 28: 548–57.

Language and Thought

Berk, L.E. 1992. Private speech: An overview of theory and the status of research. In *Private speech: From social interaction to self-regulation,* eds. R.M. Diaz & L.E. Berk, 17–53. Hillsdale, NJ: Erlbaum.

Berk, L.E. 1985. Research in review. Why children talk to themselves. *Young Children* 40 (5): 46–52.

Berk, L.E. 1994. Why children talk to themselves. *Scientific American* 271 (5): 78–83.

Genishi, C. 1988. Research in review. Children's language: Learning words from experience. *Young Children* 44 (1): 16–23.

Goffin, S.G., & C.Q. Tull. 1985. Problem solving: Encouraging active learning. *Young Children* 40 (3): 28–32.

Hatch, J.A. 1992. Improving language instruction in the primary grades: Strategies for teacher-controlled change. *Young Children* 47 (6): 54–59.

Rogoff, B. 1990. *Apprenticeship in thinking: Cognitive development in social context.* New York: Oxford University Press.

Play

Berk, L.E. 1994. Research in review. Vygotsky's theory: The importance of make-believe play. *Young Children* 50 (1): 30–39.

Cartwright, S. 1988. Play can be the building blocks of learning. *Young Children* 43 (5): 44–47.

Christie, J.F., & F. Wardle. 1992. How much time is needed for play? *Young Children* 47 (3): 28–32.

Dyson, A.H. 1990. Research in review. Symbol makers, symbol weavers: How children link play, pictures, and print. *Young Children* 45 (2): 50–57.

File, N. 1993. The teacher as guide of children's competence with peers. *Child & Youth Care Forum* 22: 351–60.

Gowen, J.W. 1995. Research in review. The early development of symbolic play. *Young Children* 50 (3): 75–84.

Hirsch, E.S., ed. 1984. *The block book.* Rev. ed. Washington, DC: NAEYC.

Nourot, P.M., & J.L. Van Hoorn. 1991. Research in review. Symbolic play in preschool and primary settings. *Young Children* 46 (6): 40–50.

Rogers, D.L., & D.D. Ross. 1986. Encouraging positive social interaction among young children. *Young Children* 41 (3): 12–17.

Rogers, C.S., & J.K. Sawyers. 1988. *Play in the lives of children.* Washington, DC: NAEYC.

Sawyers, J.K., & C.S. Rogers. 1988. *Helping young children develop through play: A practical guide for parents, caregivers, and teachers.* Washington, DC: NAEYC.

Steward, E.P. 1995. *Beginning writers in the zone of proximal development.* Hillsdale, NJ: Erlbaurm.

Wittmer, D.S., & A.S. Honig. 1994. Encouraging positive social development in young children. *Young Children* 49 (5): 4–12.

Children with Learning and Behavior Problems

Chandler, P.A. 1994. *A place for me: Including children with special needs in early care and education settings.* Washington, DC: NAEYC.

Diaz, R.M., & L.E. Berk. 1995. A Vygotskian critique of self-instructional training. *Development and Psychopathology* 7: 369–92.

Landau, S., & C. McAninch. 1993. Research in review. Young children with attention deficits. *Young Children* 48 (4): 49–58.

Wolery, M., & J.S. Wilbers, eds. 1994. *Including children with special needs in early childhood programs.* Washington, DC: NAEYC.

Educational Applications

Bredekamp, S., ed. 1987. *Developmentally appropriate practice in early childhood programs serving children from birth through age 8.* Exp. ed. Washington, DC: NAEYC.

Clements, N.E., & E.W. Warncke. 1994. Helping literacy emerge at school for less-advantaged children. *Young Children* 49 (3): 22–26.

DeVries, R., & L. Kohlberg. 1987. *Constructivist early education: Overview and comparison with other programs.* Washington, DC: NAEYC.

Edwards, C., L. Gandini, & G. Forman, eds. 1993. *The hundred languages of children: The Reggio Emilia approach to early childhood education.* Norwood, NJ: Ablex.

Forman, E.A., N. Minick, & C.A. Stone. 1993. *Contexts for learning: Sociocultural dynamics in children's development.* New York: Oxford University Press.

Forman, G.E., & D.S. Kuschner. 1983. *The child's construction of knowledge: Piaget for teaching children.* Washington, DC: NAEYC.

Jones, E., & J. Nimmo. 1994. *Emergent curriculum.* Washington, DC: NAEYC.

Klein, A. 1991. All about ants: Discovery learning in the primary grades. *Young Children* 46 (5): 23–27.

Mills, H., & J.A. Clyde. 1991. Children's success as readers and writers: It's the teacher's beliefs that make the difference. *Young Children* 46 (2): 54–59.

Moll, L.C., ed. 1990. *Vygotsky and education.* Cambridge, MA: Cambridge University Press.

Rivkin, M., ed. 1992. Science is a way of life. *Young Children* 47 (4): 4–8.

Strickland, D.S., & L.M. Morrow, eds. 1989. *Emerging literacy: Young children learn to read and write.* Washington, DC: NAEYC.

Tharp, R.G., & R. Gallimore. 1988. *Rousing minds to life: Teaching, learning, and schooling in social context.* Cambridge, MA: Cambridge University Press.

Tudge, J., & D. Caruso. 1988. Cooperative problem solving in the classroom: Enhancing young children's cognitive development. *Young Children* 44 (1): 46–49.

Willert, M.K., & C. Kamii. 1985. Reading in kindergarten: Direct vs. indirect teaching. *Young Children* 40 (4): 3–9.

Wright, J.L., & Shade, D.D. 1994. *Young children: Active learners in a technological age.* Washington, DC: NAEYC.

Glossary

attention-deficit hyperactivity disorder (ADHD). A disorder involving inattentiveness, impulsivity, and excessive motor activity. These self-regulatory deficits often lead to academic failure and social problems.

authoritarian style. A childrearing style that is high in structure and expectations but low in warmth and responsiveness. Conformity and obedience are valued over open communication with the child. Associated with anxious, withdrawn, and unhappy child behavior and hostility in the face of frustration. Distinguished from *authoritative* and *permissive styles.*

authoritative style. A childrearing style characterized by appropriate structure and expectations combined with warmth and responsiveness—a democratic approach that encourages child independence within limits negotiated between parent and child. Associated with cognitive and social competence and positive emotional adjustment in children. Distinguished from *authoritarian* and *permissive styles.*

concrete operational stage. Piaget's third stage of development, during which thought becomes logical, flexible, and organized in its application to concrete information; however, the capacity for abstract thinking is not yet present. Spans the years from 7 to 11.

cooperative learning. A learning environment structured into groups of peers who work toward a common goal.

crib speech. An early form of private speech that toddlers engage in, typically before they go to sleep and after they wake up.

cultural line of development. Vygotsky's term for developmental changes that result from interacting with other members of the individual's culture. The cultural line merges with, and eventually transforms, the *natural line of development,* resulting in the construction of higher mental processes.

defectology. Transliteration of *defektologii,* the Russian term for the scientific study of children with disabilities, or abnormal child development.

development. All physical and psychological changes in the individual that occur over time. Theorists disagree on whether these changes are largely due to biological maturation, learning, or both.

distancing strategies. Styles of adult communication that vary in the extent to which they encourage children to distance themselves from immediate stimuli and approach a task at a conceptual level. High-level distancing strategies foster awareness of relations not perceptually present in the situation, encourage children to use language to mediate their behavior, and therefore promote effective problem solving.

dynamic assessment. An approach to assessment based on Vygotsky's theory that involves purposeful teaching within the testing situation, permitting measurement of what the child is capable of attaining with social support (the child's zone of proximal development).

effectance motivation. According to White, children's sense of being able to master the environment and their joy at this mastery. Together, these two aspects of motivation promote competence.

egocentric speech. The name given by Piaget to children's speech not directly addressed to others or not expressed in ways that can easily be understood by a listener.

egocentrism. In Piaget's theory, the inability to take the perspective of others or to understand that others' viewpoints differ from one's own.

guided participation. Active involvement by children in culturally structured activities with the guidance, support, and challenge of companions who transmit a diverse array of knowledge and skills.

inaudible muttering. Partially internalized private speech that consists of either overt, whispered utterances too faint to be understood by a listener or silent movements of the lips in the form of words.

inner speech. Silent, inner verbal thought.

internalization. The process by which communication with signs between people is transferred to the individual, psychological plane of functioning. As a result, signs become self-communicative.

intersubjectivity. The process whereby two participants who begin a task with different understandings arrive at a shared understanding. Creates a common ground for communication as each partner adjusts to the perspective of the other.

Kamehameha Early Education Program (KEEP). An innovative educational program for academically at-risk elementary school children based on Vygotsky's theory that has as its overarching theme "assisted performance." Assumes that just as children require scaffolded support, teachers teach best when their performance is assisted by members of the educational system.

learning. New understandings and responses that result from observation, instruction, or other experiences.

mediation. The use of language, or another cultural sign or tool, to intercede between a stimulus–response association. For example, in natural memory, one stimulus is merely associated with another stimulus. In higher-order, mediated memory, a culturally constructed sign, such as a knot tied around a finger, is used to assist recall. Similarly, a child's behavior is unmediated when he or she reacts impulsively to stimuli. In contrast, a child's behavior is mediated when he or she uses the cultural tool of language to reflect on stimuli and deliberately plan and implement a response.

microgenesis. The development of competence at a single task or activity by a child or adult. Distinguished from *ontogenesis* and *phylogenesis*.

natural line of development. Vygotsky's term for developmental changes governed by genetic and biological factors. Distinguished from *cultural line of development*.

ontogenesis. The development of the individual through childhood and adulthood. Distinguished from *microgenesis* and *phylogenesis*.

permissive style. A childrearing style that is low in structure and expectations but high in warmth and responsiveness. An overly tolerant approach to parenting, resulting in excessive freedom for the child. Associated with lack of impulse control— rebellious, disobedient, and nonachieving child behavior. Distinguished from *authoritarian* and *authoritative* styles.

phylogenesis. The development of the human species through evolution. Distinguished from *microgenesis* and *ontogenesis*.

preoperational stage. Piaget's second stage of development, in which rapid development of representation takes place; however, thought is not yet logical. Spans the years from 2 to 7.

private speech. Overt speech addressed to the self, generally for the purpose of regulating one's own behavior.

reciprocal teaching. A method of teaching based on Vygotsky's theory, in which a teacher and two to four children form a collaborative learning group. Dialogues occur that create a zone of proximal development, in which reading comprehension and subject-matter knowledge are likely to improve.

Reggio Emilia. A small town in north-central Italy that developed a system of early childhood education that draws on a variety of educational philosophies and developmental theories, including Vygotsky's. Offers a strong community approach to the education and care of young children, in which parents, teachers, administrative staff, and government officials collaborate to provide environments that foster social interaction, the formation of relationships, and symbolic representation of learning activities. The term *Reggio Emilia* is used to refer to the approach.

scaffolding. A changing quality of support over a teaching session, in which a more skilled partner adjusts the assistance he or she provides to fit the child's current level of performance. More support is offered when a task is new; less is provided as the child's competence increases, thereby fostering the child's autonomy and independent mastery.

scientific concepts. Concepts mastered through instruction. Once these concepts are acquired, children are consciously aware of what they know and can articulate their understanding with verbal definitions.

self-instructional training. A cognitive-behavioral intervention that teaches impulsive, non–self-controlled, and inattentive children to talk to themselves through modeling and direct instruction. Has not been effective in reducing impulsivity and improving task accuracy.

self-regulation. The process of planning, guiding, and monitoring one's own attention and behavior.

sign. A symbolic tool (such as a word or an image) used to influence the thinking and behavior of another person or the self.

spontaneous concepts. Concepts mastered in the course of everyday life. Acquisition is not conscious or deliberate but rather occurs with little or no awareness by the child that he or she is thinking conceptually.

zone of proximal development (ZPD). The distance between what an individual can accomplish during independent problem solving and what he or she can accomplish with the help of an adult or more competent member of the culture. The hypothetical, dynamic region where learning and development take place.

Author Index

A

Abikoff, H.   91
Alberts-Corush, J.   92
Amaya-Williams, M.   7, 27, 30, 37, 7, 92, 150
American Psychiatric Association   88
Anderson, R.C.   116
Azmitia, M.   20, 48, 132, 133, 135

B

Babad, E.Y.   138
Baillargeon, R.   13, 154
Barkley, R.A.   89, 90, 92, 93, 94, 96
Barnes, M.L.   30, 32, 33
Bates, J.E.   23
Battista, M.T.   20, 132
Baumrind, D.   33, 150
Bearison, D.J.   33
Beaudichon, J.   44
Behrend, D.A.   44, 45, 48
Beilin, H.   19
Bell, N.   18
Berk, L.E.   7, 27, 35, 37, 38, 39, 42, 44, 46, 48, 49, 71, 73, 76, 77, 81, 91, 92, 94, 95, 96, 133, 150
Bernfeld, G.   93
Biederman, J.   92
Binet, A.   26
Bivens, J.A.   38, 46, 48
Blanck, G.   1, 3
Bloom, L.   104
Bornstein, M.H.   13, 23, 55, 66, 155, 156, 161, 162, 164, 165, 166,
Brainerd, C.J.   58
Braswell, L.   91
Bredekamp, S.   142
Brese, K.J.   42
Bretherton, I.   55, 66, 68, 70
Bright, J.   133

Brinich, P.M.   87
Brodie, J.   58
Bronte, C.   65
Brown, A.L.   138
Brown, J.S.   6, 27, 118, 121, 122, 138
Brownell, C.A.   132
Bruner, J.S.   20, 26, 27, 63, 72, 108, 127
Bryant. N.R.   138
Budoff, M.   138
Burks, V.   63
Burns, M.S.   139
Burns, S.M.   58
Buzzelli, C.A.   150

C

Cain, K.M.   126
Caissie, R.   89
Camp, B.W.   91
Campbell, S.B.   90, 92, 93, 94
Campione, J.C.   121, 122, 138, 139
Carson, J.   63
Case, R.   21
Cazden, C.B.   132
Ceci, S.J.   18
Cerbone, M.J.   64
Chang-Wells, G.L.M.   113, 126
Chess, S.   88
Children's Defense Fund 149
Churchill, J.   126
Clemente, D.   74
Clements, D.H.   20, 132
Cobb, P.   109, 123, 124, 125, 127
Cole, E.B.   89
Cole, M.   4, 6
Collins, A.   27
Connolly, J.A.   58
Cooper, C.R.   132
Copeland, A.P.   94
Corrigan, R.   55

Corsaro, W.   73
Culatta, B.   94
Cunningham, C.E.   92

D

Dale, N.   64, 78
Dalton, S.   116, 123
Damon, W.   133
Danforth, J.S.   92
Dansky, J.L.   58
Davydov, V.V.   94
de Villiers, J.G.   13
de Villiers, P.A.   13
De Vos, J.   13
Denham, S.A.   150
Deutsche, F.   44
Dias, M.G.   59
Diaz, R.M.   7, 27, 30, 32, 37, 38, 44, 45, 48, 49, 91, 92, 94, 135, 150
Dickie, J.   94
DiLalla, L.F.   61
Dinwiddy, L.S.   14
Dirks, J.   18
Dixon, D.   59
Doise, W.   132, 133
Dornbusch, S.M.   33
Douglas, V.I.   90
Doyle, A.B.   58
Duckworth, E.   99
Duguid, P.   27
Dunham, P.   23
Dunham, R.   23
Dunn, J.   64, 66, 78
Dush, D.M.   91
Dweck, C.S.   126
Dyck, L.   42

E

Edwards, C.   16, 78, 113, 142, 143
Edwards, P.A.

Subject Index

Q–R

speech, parental. *See* intervention, adult
spontaneous (naturally acquired) concepts
     100–101, 106
     definition of 171
     distinction from scientific concepts, in Piaget's
          vs. Vygotsky's theories 102
symbolism
     as a feature of play 53

T–V

task competence, as a level of human development. *See* microgenesis
task difficulty and private speech 44
tasks, structuring. *See* zone of proximal development: keeping the child in
text. *See* literacy
Teacher's College (Gomel), Vygotsky's time
     teaching at 2
"tool of the mind" 22, 23, 113. *See also* sign
     language as pre-eminent 21
troika, and origin of sociocultural theory 3
Ukrainian Psychoneurological Academy
Vygotsky
     biographical information 1–4, 6–7
     published works 6, 7–9, 35
          dissemination in the U.S. 7
          Stalin's ban on 7
          topics 9
          translation into English 7, 8–9
Vygotsky's theory 100–102, 104–108, 111
     application in schools 140–147
     dissemination of, impediments to 6–7
     early childhood classrooms, application in
          113–147
          activities, features of 147
          classroom as community of learners, emphasis
               on 115
          teachers, role of 114
     education, sociocultural approach to 115
     main ideas 5
          assisted discovery 108
          child, role of 26, 108
          cross-cultural variation 5

development
     four levels of 4
     sociocultural approach to 1, 4
     two lines of (cultural and social) 5; 170, 171
          (definitions)
developmental (genetic) method 5
education, role of 26
environment, role of 108, 109
"expert" partners 108
imitation, role of 104
instruction, role of 104, 106, 109
     comparison with discovery learning and didactic teaching 108
language, importance of 99–100
mixed-age grouping, importance of 131–132
play, importance of 51–79, 114
potential development, level of 104
scaffolding 108
scientific vs. spontaneous concepts 106
social side of development, emphasis on 109
teacher, role of 104
written expression, emphasis on 114
zone of proximal development 10, 104, 108,
     115–116
other major perspectives, comparison with 99–
     111

W–Z

Wechsler Intelligence Scale for Children–Revised
     17–18
whispering. *See* private speech
whole-language movement 114–115
zone of executive functioning 30
zone of proximal development (ZPD) 5, 48, 65, 70,
     104, 108, 115–116, 127, 131, 136–138, 150–151
     breadth of, in determining readiness to learn 136,
          138, 151
     and children with special needs 84, 136
     definition of 24, 171
     keeping the child in, as a component of scaffolding 29, 33, 45, 106
     play and creation of 56
     private speech and 46, 52, 56
     sociodramatic play 73

Information about NAEYC

NAEYC is ...

... a membership-supported organization of people committed to fostering the growth and development of children from birth through age 8. Membership is open to all who share a desire to serve and act on behalf of the needs and rights of young children.

NAEYC provides ...

... educational services and resources to adults who work with and for children, including

- *Young Children, the* journal for early childhood educators
- **Books, posters, brochures,** and **videos** to expand your knowledge and commitment to young children, with topics including infants, curriculum, research, discipline, teacher education, and parent involvement
- An **Annual Conference** that brings people from all over the country to share their expertise and advocate on behalf of children and families
- **Week of the Young Child** celebrations sponsored by NAEYC Affiliate Groups across the nation to call public attention to the needs and rights of children and families
- **Insurance plans** for individuals and programs
- **Public affairs information** for knowledgeable advocacy efforts at all levels of government and through the media
- The **National Academy of Early Childhood Programs,** a voluntary accreditation system for high-quality programs for children
- The **National Institute for Early Childhood Professional Development,** providing resources and services to improve professional preparation and development of early childhood educators
- **Young Children International** to promote international communication and information exchanges

For free information about membership, publications, or other NAEYC services, contact

National Association for the Education of Young Children
1509 16th Street, NW
Washington, DC 20036-1426

202-232-8777 or 800-424-2460